Dear Russell

May this ... do you continue

to he an ...

peaceab...

Peace

Andy

A FAITH EMBRACING ALL CREATURES

The Peaceable Kingdom Series

The Peaceable Kingdom Series is a multivolume series that seeks to challenge the pervasive violence assumed necessary in relation to humans, nonhumans, and the larger environment. By calling on the work of ministers, activists, and scholars, we hope to provide an accessible resource that will help Christians reflect on becoming a more faithful and peaceable people. The series editors are Andy Alexis-Baker and Tripp York.

Volumes include:

VOLUME I: *A Faith Not Worth Fighting For:*
Addressing Commonly Asked Questions about Christian Nonviolence
Edited by Tripp York and Justin Bronson Barringer

VOLUME II: *A Faith Embracing All Creatures:*
Addressing Commonly Asked Questions about Christian Care for Animals
Edited by Tripp York and Andy Alexis-Baker

VOLUME III: *A Faith Encompassing All of Creation: Addressing Commonly*
Asked Questions about Christian Care for the Environment
Edited by Andy Alexis-Baker and Tripp York (Forthcoming, 2013)

For study guides and further resources see
http://www.peaceablekingdomseries.com

A FAITH EMBRACING
ALL CREATURES

Addressing Commonly Asked Questions
about Christian Care for Animals

EDITED BY
Tripp York
and Andy Alexis-Baker

FOREWORD BY
Marc Bekoff

AFTERWORD BY
Brian McLaren

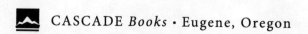 CASCADE *Books* • Eugene, Oregon

A FAITH EMBRACING ALL CREATURES
Addressing Commonly Asked Questions about Christian Care for Animals

The Peaceable Kingdom Series 2

Cascade Books
An Imprint of Wipf and Stock Publishers
199 W. 8th Ave., Suite 3
Eugene, OR 97401

www.wipfandstock.com

ISBN 13: 978-1-61097-701-2

Cataloging-in-Publication data:

A faith embracing all creatures : addressing commonly asked questions about Christian care for animals / edited by Tripp York and Andy Alexis-Baker ; foreword by Marc Bekoff ; afterword by Brian McLaren.

xviii + 194 p. ; 23 cm. —Includes bibliographical references.

The Peaceable Kingdom Series 2

ISBN 13: 978-1-61097-701-2

1. Animals—Religious aspects—Christianity. 2. Animal welfare—Religious aspects—Christianity. I. York, Tripp. II. Alexis-Baker, Andy. III. Bekoff, Marc. IV. McLaren, Brian. V. Title. II. Series.

BT746 .F35 2012

Manufactured in the U.S.A.

Contents

Contributors

Carol J. Adams is an independent scholar whose focus is on interrelated oppressions and whose books include *The Sexual Politics of Meat* (1990, 2010), *Prayers for Animals* (2004), and *The Inner Art of Vegetarianism* (2000). Her website is www.caroljadams.com.

Andy Alexis-Baker is a PhD candidate in systematic theology and theological ethics at Marquette University. He is coeditor with Theodore J. Koontz of John Howard Yoder's *Christian Attitudes to War, Peace, and Revolution* (2009) as well as coeditor with Gayle Gerber Koontz of Yoder's forthcoming *Theology of Missions* (2013).

Nekeisha Alexis-Baker is an occasional writer and speaker. Her recent publications include "Freedom of Voice: Non-Voting and the Political Imagination," in *Electing Not to Vote* (2008), and "The Church as Resistance to Racism and Nation: A Christian, Anarchist Perspective," in *Religious Anarchism: New Perspectives* (2009).

Judith Barad is Professor of Philosophy and Women's Studies at Indiana State University. She is the author of three books: *Consent: The Means to an Active Faith according to St. Thomas Aquinas* (1992), *Aquinas on the Nature and Treatment of Animals* (1995), and *The Ethics of Star Trek* (2000).

Marc Bekoff is a former Professor of Ecology and Evolutionary Biology at the University of Colorado, Boulder. His books include *The Emotional Lives of Animals* (2007), *Animals Matter: A Biologist Explains Why We Should Treat Animals with Compassion and Respect* (2007), and *The Animal Manifesto* (2010).

John Berkman is the author of "Towards a Thomistic Theology of Animality," in *Creaturely Theology*, "The Consumption of Animals and the Catholic Tradition," in *Food for Thought* (2004), "Prophetically Pro-Life: John Paul II's Gospel of Life and Evangelical Concern for Animals" (1999), and "The Chief End of All Flesh" (with Stanley Hauerwas, 1992).

Malinda Elizabeth Berry is currently a member of the teaching faculty at Bethany Theological Seminary in Richmond, Indiana, and is director of the MA program.

Stephen R. L. Clark, formerly Professor of Philosophy at the University of Liverpool (1984–2009), is now retired from paid employment. His books include *The Moral Status of Animals* (1977), *Biology and Christian Ethics* (2000), and *Philosophical Futures* (2011).

David Clough is Senior Lecturer in Theology at the University of Chester. He coauthored with Brian Stiltner *Faith and Force: A Christian Debate about War* (2007) as well as coedited with Celia Deane-Drummond *Creaturely Theology: On God, Humans and Other Animals* (2009), and is the author of *On Animals* (2012).

Laura Hobgood-Oster is Professor of Religion and Environmental Studies and holder of the Paden Chair at Southwestern University. Her most recent publications are *The Friends We Keep: Unleashing Christianity's Compassion for Animals* (2010) and *Holy Dogs and Asses: Animals in the Christian Tradition* (2008).

Michelle Loyd-Paige is Professor of Sociology and the Dean for Multicultural Affairs at Calvin College. She is ordained and serves on the ministerial staff at her home church.

Brian McLaren is an author, speaker, activist, and public theologian. He is the author of numerous books, including *Everything Must Change* (2007) and *A New Kind of Christianity* (2010).

Danielle Nussberger is Assistant Professor of Theology at Marquette University. Her publications include "John Henry Newman's Art of Communicating Christian Faith" in the *Newman Studies Journal*.

Anika Spalde and **Pelle Strindlund** live in a Gandhian community in Mjölby, Sweden. They have published several books on animal ethics, nonviolence, and Christian spirituality, among them *Every Creature a Word of God: Compassion for Animals as Christian Spirituality* (2008).

Stephen H. Webb is Professor of Religion and Philosophy at Wabash College. He is the author of eleven books including *On God and Dogs* (1998) and *Good Eating* (2001). He cofounded the Christian Vegetarian Association (www.all-creatures.org/cva).

Tripp York teaches in the Religious Studies Department at Virginia Wesleyan College in Norfolk, VA. He is the author and editor of numerous books including *Third Way Allegiance*, *Living on Hope While Living in Babylon*, and *The Devil Wears Nada*.

Foreword: Expanding Our Compassion Footprint

Once we realize the common bonds of compassion we share with other animals, we can more easily hear their persistent plea to treat them better or leave them alone. This is their manifesto, as I call it in a recent book. To do what they are asking of us would be an easy and commonsense decision. It is a matter of making different choices about *who* (not what) we eat and buy, how we educate, entertain, and amuse ourselves, and how we conduct research. But it is also a matter of how we see ourselves. Are we above all other creatures? Or do we share intimate connections, each of us being exceptional in unique ways?

Throughout my years as a field biologist and ethologist, I have spent thousands of hours studying and learning a great deal about animal virtues and passions. The most crucial lesson has been the importance of recognizing the deep bonds we share with other creatures and how much their feelings and lives matter to them—and must matter to us. Far too often this isn't the case. Knowing that animals have beliefs and feelings carries with it an enormous responsibility to love and look out for the well-being of the other beings with whom we share the planet. This requires a degree of empathy with other animals' interests. It requires seeing the world as they see it, taking into account their thoughts and feelings and what they want and need from us. It is taking this other point of view that really matters. It requires us to practice what I call "deep ethology."

Yet, too often in science and religion, we act as if our human worldview is all that exists. Respect for the dignity of other animals' lives is rare, and vulgar utilitarianism usually wins the day. The costs and benefits of our actions are weighed carefully from a human standpoint with no consideration of the nonhuman view. Yet, that great Christian maxim to do unto others as you would have them do to you calls us to look at things from another standpoint. Why should we not look at things from the perspective of nonhuman animals? They are rational, sentient creatures who care as much about their lives as we do our own.

I hope this book, with its indebtedness to both religious and scientific resources, can help Christians see Christianity anew and help all of us expand our compassion footprint. Reading the Bible with new eyes, and reading the Christian tradition with a focus not only on its failures in this area but also on its successes, can only enlarge that compassion to which Jesus called his disciples so long ago—and which many have so imperfectly practiced over the centuries. As we "mind" animals by respecting their individuality, appreciating their viewpoints, and trying to understand their feelings—all while recognizing that they are intelligent creatures in their own right—we begin to see the world as much more awe-inspiring and wonderful than when we center on our own abilities. We live as kin in a magnificent house with many creatures. We must appreciate that other animals allow us into their lives, trusting that we will have their best interests at heart.

Seeing through the eyes of other animals has deep religious significance. This realization challenges the old hierarchies, which situate humans on top of an absolute divide between us and other animals, and places humans in continuity with other animals. Furthermore, it has significant ethical implications for the way we treat other animals as "covenantal partners" (as Tripp York calls it in his essay), with hospitality (as Laura Hobgood-Oster so eloquently argues in her chapter), and with a "dominion" of servanthood rather than domination (as Carol Adams so powerfully articulates in chapter 1). Seeing animals in this way can truly deepen our own spiritual experiences as we search for and seek to live out a peaceable kingdom in our own limited ways.

This collection of essays is a sign of hope for Christianity and for religion in general. It is possible to look again at one's beliefs and to expand one's outlook. After all, when a Gentile woman came to Jesus asking for a blessing, he told her he had come for Israel and not "dogs." She responded by saying that even dogs get scraps from the table when a person is compassionate. Jesus liked that answer, blessed her, and expanded his own view as a result. Why should Christians not do likewise as ethologists knock on the door asking for reconsideration? As I think about the lives of our nonhuman animal friends, I smile. But I also feel a twinge of sadness as I realize that we have created whole areas where life can no longer sustain itself. This planet is the only home we have; and we have it together or not at all.

I have hope that once a book like this one has whetted your appetite, you will feast on the plethora of studies that bring even more in-depth explorations on the many areas that the animal question raises. Our insatiable appetite for knowledge need not destroy but can build up loving lives full of curiosity at this wondrous miracle we call life. We suffer the indignities to which we expose other animals, and heartfelt coexistence will be beneficial to nonhuman and human alike as we move into the future. Our children (and their children) depend on goodwill to all beings. Let's not let them down.

Marc Bekoff
Caparica, Portugal

Introduction

Andy Alexis-Baker

Having grown up in a meat-eating household without the good fortune of vegetarian friends or relatives, I did not have many reasons to think about the animals that I ate on a regular basis. Looking back, the very idea of eating a plant-based diet would have sounded strange to me. And since my family was convinced that a meal without meat is no meal at all, the thought of excluding it from our dinner table would have been laughable. Even after converting to Christianity in my twenties, I still didn't give other animals much thought. Church functions regularly featured some kind of animal body to celebrate a baptism or a holiday, or as a dish at a fun gathering, and foregoing meat was even discouraged sometimes. Once, a minister who had been a vegetarian back in his "wild, experimental youth" asked me if I had tried vegetarianism. Knowing that I leaned toward the "liberal" side of politics, he informed me that he had long outgrown the practice and that Christianity does not support that sort of thing. I suppose I agreed; I don't remember objecting. After all, I had been raised to believe—both in church and elsewhere—that other animals were made for human use.

It was not until I attended a small liberal arts college that I encountered the idea of a vegetarianism rooted in Christian faith. I stumbled upon and became haunted by the idea in an essay written by Stanley Hauerwas and John Berkman (the latter of whom has written for this volume).[1] Already convinced (by Hauerwas no less) that Christians were

1. Hauerwas and Berkman, "Trinitarian Theology of the 'Chief End of All Flesh.'"

called to witness to the peaceable kingdom, I found compelling their argument about living as signs of the coming peaceable kingdom, which has to include others in creation. Still, I couldn't completely erase some of the common biblical questions like those featured in this book.

In my case, these questions took on a new urgency and served, not as a way to uphold my previous assumptions, but as a way to test whether those previous assumptions lined up with the trajectory of the gospel. And they were quickly joined by other questions: If I am to be part of a people who witness to God's creating, reconciling, and redeeming activity, which culminates in the end of all suffering and death, what relationship should I have to nonhuman animals *now*? If wolves, lions, calves, and lambs have a peaceable relationship in the final consummation of all things, how can I continue participating in the intentional killing of other creatures when it is not at all necessary for my survival? How do my choices regarding nonhuman animals affect my witness to God's good purposes? I could no longer assert a biblical position that lined up with my unexamined practices. A certain logic of the gospel, or theological trajectory, utterly gripped my life. I still had biblical questions, but I put them aside and gradually gave up eating anything that had a face on it. I had already claimed a pacifist identity; but now my pacifism became hospitable enough to include nonhuman animals.

Questions for Christian Vegans and Vegetarians

Since I have made the transition from consumer of other animals to vegetarian and then to vegan, I now face biblical and theological questions from others about my decisions: Didn't God tell Noah to eat the animals? Aren't humans more important than animals? Aren't Christian vegetarians and vegans just avoiding the natural cycle of life and death? I quickly found that I had to delve more deeply into the Christian tradition's rich resources to figure out how to begin to respond to such questions. Sometimes the questions feel like accusations that I am being "heretical" by witnessing to God's peaceable kingdom for all creatures, or that I am engaging in some weird experiment that I should not talk about or even exhibit in polite society. Other times, the questions—genuine and heartfelt—come from people seeking to understand. In either case, I needed to know more, so I did what book lovers do: I read lots of books and articles.

In my search for answers, I found a variety of authors who answered one or more of the kinds of questions I was encountering. But I could not find a single source to which to point people who wanted to know more about a biblically and theologically rich Christian vegetarianism. Moreover, some of the answers I read needed a new approach. So I approached various authors I had read or people I know to ask if they'd be willing to share how they answer these questions—or at least how they would answer them once they had finished studying the issues. Along the way, Tripp York joined in to help with all the tasks of editing as well as to share his wisdom from the publishing world. We also came up with a vision for a "peaceable kingdom series" in which this book would be the second entry.

Altogether, the essays move from topics dealing with the Old Testament to the New Testament to reflections on the tradition and theology around animals more broadly. Written from a Christian vegetarian or vegan perspective,[2] these chapters take the Bible, theology, and church history seriously in an effort to increase our literacy around the place of nonhuman animals within our faith. The authors, including philosophers, professors, activists, students, and others, take different approaches in responding to their questions; some individuals take a literal, focused approach to the Bible, while others put multiple texts in conversation with one another or explore broad themes and trajectories. All the contributions enrich the ongoing and growing discussion about the place of nonhuman animals in the Christian life and theology.

---

2. Vegetarians are those who abstain from animal flesh in their diets. Sometimes they also avoid using products that have been tested on animals or wearing clothing made from dead animals. Vegans are distinct from vegetarians in that, in addition to eliminating animal flesh from their diets, they also abstain from dairy and eggs, and more rigorously avoid clothing, medical and other products that use nonhuman animal bodies as test subjects or byproducts. Both groups are concerned with cruelty toward animals and the ways in which they are seen (and used) as machines for human desire rather than as living creatures with their own unique lives worth more than any human can measure. Because of these concerns, vegetarians and vegans often see their practice as a lifestyle choice rather than a simple dietary restriction.

Vegetarian, Vegan, or Omnivore-with-Questions? This Book Is for You

Tripp and I have designed this book to appeal to at least three audiences. People who see their veg-lifestyle as part of their commitment to following Jesus, yet who feel at a loss when explaining their decision in light of Scripture, will find this book a helpful resource for addressing common questions. Meanwhile, those who use nonhuman animal bodies as part of their diets and other lifestyle habits will discover ideas that may challenge preconceived notions about what the Bible does or doesn't say about the status of other animals. Finally, advocates for nonhuman animals who see Christianity and the Bible as a primary instrument for dominating other species will find that the Bible can be a resource for defending nonhuman animals from cruelty and indifference. In an effort to reach people with multiple perspectives, Tripp and I have also been diligent in seeking gender, racial, and national diversity among the contributors. No other book on Christianity and animals has had so many women authoring chapters, with more than half of the essays written by women, three of whom are women of color. Although the book contains no Latino/a or Asian (or other non-Western) perspectives, we see the diversity herein as a small but significant step in a more inclusive conversation about nonhuman animal welfare from a Christian perspective.

An Invitation

When the prophet Nathan went to confront King David about his illegal and immoral activities, he used the example of a poor man and his little lamb to illustrate his message. In Nathan's story, the man raised the lamb, and "it grew up with him and with his children; it used to eat of his meager fare, and drink from his cup, and lie in his bosom, and it was like a daughter to him" (2 Sam 12:2–4). While many people denounce companion animals in modern times as a luxury of modernity and affluence, it is worth noting that this man is *poor*, and that this is an ancient example of human and animal bonds. The man did not place the animal beneath his daughters but treated her as family. When Nathan described how a wealthy person killed the little lamb, King David became outraged. Yet his anger was not merely at the rich exploiting the poor; he was also incensed by the killer's disrespect for the loving relationship between the man and his lamb. David could have said, "Well, lambs are for eating—why should I be bothered about the death of such a creature?" Instead, the king of Israel showed deep compassion and grief.

After reading this book, Tripp and I hope that you—like the poor man and King David—are better able to see other animals with new eyes. This book is neither the beginning nor the end of the discussion. But we hope it will be a significant resource along the way toward expanding what Marc Bekoff has called "our compassion footprint."[3]

3. See Bekoff, *Animal Manifesto: Six Reasons for Expanding Our Compassion Footprint*. Tripp York and I would like to thank Nekeisha Alexis-Baker for her careful reading of this entire manuscript. Her suggestions as well as editing helped us to make the chapters better. Her dedication and love for all creatures is inspiring.

1

What about Dominion in Genesis?

Carol J. Adams

IT IS UNFORTUNATE THAT Christians often choose Genesis 1, a chapter that so poetically describes relationship and goodness, to justify human abuse and exploitation of other animals. Genesis 1 describes God's relationship to the created world in powerful and elegant prose. Yet, when most modern readers reflect on other animals, this beautiful landscape and focus on God and God's relationship with all creatures disappears. Instead, we often narrow our attention to Genesis 1:26 and 28—and, at times, even more narrowly to the word *dominion*.

> Then God said, "Let us make humankind in our image, according to our likeness; and let them have dominion over the fish of the sea, and over the birds of the air, and over the cattle, and over all the wild animals of the earth, and over every creeping thing that creeps upon the earth." So God created humankind in his image, in the image of God he created them; male and female he created them. God blessed them, and God said to them, "Be fruitful and multiply, and fill the earth, and subdue it, and have dominion over the fish of the sea and over the birds of the air and over every living thing that moves upon the earth." (Gen 1:26–28)

With these verses, we find ourselves in the midst of controversy. Ironically, a chapter that evokes images of peace among all becomes the source of heated disagreement. Many are confused by the word *dominion*—what it means and what it allows. As issues of veganism and animal rights gain more cultural legitimacy, the question, "Didn't God give people dominion over animals and doesn't that permit us to [fill in the blank: eat them, wear them, experiment on them, cage them]?" becomes an honest attempt to reconcile the cultural worldview about other animals (they are ours to use) with the biblical mandate by which many wish to live their lives. Isn't dominion over the other animals what God permits? Isn't this the message of these passages? At other times, the question about God granting human beings dominion is asked not out of confusion but out of defensiveness. It is thrown at someone to cut off discussion rather than to open up discussion; it arises from a desire to justify contemporary practices.

This chapter seeks to answer the question by looking at dominion, both the word and its context—not just the context of Genesis 1, though it is a very important context, but also the christological context. Let's start with a different question: What does dominion look like today? Why do we move away from other animals in seeking to establish who we are? Why is our identity so fragile that acts of denial are required to hide our actions? What is being protected—our relationship to Scripture or our relationship to dinner?

It has been said that if kings and queens exercised dominion over their subjects the way human beings do over the other animals, kings and queens would have no subjects. So why is being in God's image often interpreted in view of power, manipulation, and hegemony instead of compassion, mercy, and emptying unconditional love? We often anthropomorphize God as powerful, fierce, and angry (if not belligerent). When we are lording over others, using power—it is then that we are most likely to assert the image of God. Acts of unconditional love, suspensions of judgment, mercy for the weak, and kindness to animals get associated with a wishy-washy picture of who Jesus was, but are rarely discussed regarding God the Creator.

By beginning with beginnings, we are offered the opportunity to reflect not only on the meaning of dominion in the context of Genesis 1, but on what it means to read and heed the biblical story, what it means to live in God's creation, and what it means to follow Jesus.

Genesis 1: A Habitat and Its Inhabitants

Genesis 1 shows us how human and nonhuman animals are the inhabitants of God's created world. There is a movement in Genesis 1. Not just a poetic movement conveyed by the repetition of certain words, or a creative movement from chaos and darkness to order and light, but a movement of intent and relationship. God creates a habitat for inhabitants. The commonality of humans and nonhumans as the inhabitants is emphasized through God's instructions concerning their shared diet, that is, how they will use the habitat.

In Genesis 1:26–28, the word *dominion* appears twice, as we saw above. But day six remains incomplete. Then immediately follows:

> God said, "See, I have given you every plant yielding seed
> that is upon the face of all the earth, and every tree with seed
> in its fruit; you shall have them for food. And to every beast
> of the earth, everything that has the breath of life, I have
> given every green plant for food." And it was so. God saw
> everything that he had made, and indeed, it was very good.
> And there was evening and there was morning, the sixth day.

A vegan diet for all inhabitants culminates all of God's creative activity.

Parallels between Days 1–3 and Days 4–6

Some commentators see a parallel construction between the creation of days 1–3 and days 4–6. During God's creative acts of days 1–3, the creation of light results in the naming of day and night, the creation of the sky gives us sky and water, and the creation of land provides plants yielding seed of every kind. So days 1–3 feature the creation of the habitat: "structure and light, sky and water, land and plants."[1] With days 4–6, God creates the inhabitants of those habitats: heavenly lights, living creatures who fill the waters and fly in the sky, living creatures for the land, and humankind.

1. Bland, "Homiletical Perspective on Genesis 1:1–2, 4a," 29.

Days 1–3: HABITAT		Days 4–6: INHABITANTS	
Day 1:	Let there be Light Named Day/Night	Day 4:	lights in the sky heavenly lights/stars that rule the sky "Rule"
Day 2:	Dome that separates water Named sky	Day 5:	living creatures that inhabit the waters and the sky
Day 3:	dry land	Day 6:	land creatures and human beings Dominion for human beings
	Plant reproduction Their "reproductive powers are included in their creation"[2]		Human reproduction "These livings beings are endowed with the right of self-propagation by a separate act—a benediction."[3]
	plants yielding seed, and fruit trees of every kind on earth that bear fruit with the seed in it.		Your food will be plant yielding seeds and fruit trees

After all this dynamic, creative activity that relates inhabitants to habitat, the word *radah* (translated as "dominion") appears. The word appears twice (Gen 1:26, 28). In 1:28, the inhabitants of the sea, the air, and the land (still in the order of creation) are said to be under the dominion of humankind. One more thing occurs: God tells humankind about the habitat, especially that which was created on day three. The "plants yielding seed, and fruit trees of every kind" (Gen 1:10) created on day three are now presented as food for humankind. The parallels between days 1–3 and days 4–6 culminate here, in God's instructions about what to consume from the created world. "Everything that has the breath of life" (that is, the inhabitants) are "given every green plant for food" (habitat).[4]

2. Skinner, *Genesis*, 28.

3. Ibid.

4. Ibid., 29, 31.

Here in Genesis, God's word is spoken, and all creation flows from it. In Genesis 1, creation and God's presence throughout the earth are linked. Moreover, creation and blessing are linked. Dry land appears out of the water and it is good. Fruit-bearing trees appear and they are good. Heavenly lights appear and they are good. Living creatures of the sea appear and God sees they are good. God blesses them. God creates land creatures and they, too, are good. God creates humankind and blesses them. At the end of the sixth day, "God saw everything that he had made, and indeed, it was very good." Unlike God's acts of blessing other parts of creation, God does not say that humans are good apart from all the other inhabitants and habitats. Instead, "everything" is "very good." That humans get no statement of goodness apart from all other creation highlights the fact that this text means to intimately connect us to all other created beings and everything on the earth.[5] Roberta Kalechofsky, remarking on the repeated statement "it was good," observes that "the depiction of the creation of fish, fowl, and animal in Genesis, is each species with its integrity, and substantiates the view that animals were regarded as integral subjects in their own right. God's delight in these creations, stated with blessing or with simple majesty, 'And it was good,' does not reflect a god who created animal life to be in bondage."[6]

The more the word *dominion* is broken away from its context of Genesis 1, the more likely it is that what one is defending is a broken relationship between humans and the other animals and the world they inhabit. In contemporary culture, the constant reference to the dominion established in Genesis 1 suggests not just a devolution in the meaning of the word *dominion*, but also the loss of the sense of blessing in our beginnings and our relationships. And if God calls humanity good only in their relationship to the land, the sea, the air, and to the other living creatures, then referring to dominion in Genesis to justify human domination of animals also misses a crucial aspect of the biblical story: humanity is intimately bound up in relationship to habitat and other inhabitants, as well as with God. How have so many Christians missed this crucial point?

5. For a discussion of this connection, see Spanner, "Tyrants, Stewards—or Just Kings?" 217–18.

6. Kalechofsky, "Hierarchy, Kinship, and Responsibility," 95.

Whatever dominion humans have been granted over nonhuman animals is constrained not just by Genesis 1:29 and its dictates about food, but by the entire movement of God's creative acts up to this point. Humans and nonhuman animals are not the devourers of each other, but of plants. We could say literally, if you accept 1:26, you have to accept 1:29—they are hooked, they are yoked. As Andrew Linzey states, "Herb-eating dominion is hardly a license for tyranny."[7] There is no commandment to eat animals, and there is no association between dominion and the presumption that humans should eat other animals.

John Skinner, commenting a century ago, notes: "the first stage of the world's history—that state of things which the Creator pronounced very good—is a state of peace and harmony in the animal world."[8] As sacred Scripture, this first chapter of the first book of the Bible shows us a movement: creation and blessing and acknowledging the goodness that exists in sky and land, plants and living creatures.

What Does *Dominion* Mean?

What does the word *dominion* mean when it appears in Genesis 1? How can we know what to say about dominion if we do not know what the word means?

Though it is very difficult to know, exactly, what the word *dominion* meant more than two thousand years ago, scholars have attempted to identify possibilities for what it means within Genesis 1. Though we

---

7. Linzey, "Vegetarianism as a Biblical Ideal," 127. Of course, Genesis does not give humans license to wantonly kill and destroy plant life either. God gives them to us for food. The center point of Eden and the New Jerusalem involves trees (Rev 22:2). Moreover, the cedars of Lebanon, which once stood so tall and beautiful, had in the biblical era been clear-cut so that nothing was left but a barren wasteland. The Scriptures attest to the beauty of these forests (Pss 29:4; 92:12; 104:16; Song 4:5, 8) and lament the clear-cutting that devastated them, which was carried out to build luxury palaces (and with conscripted labor). In place of the forests, the ancient empires sought to set up towering cities, which the prophets denounce (Isa 37:22–24; Ezek 31:3–11; Amos 2:9; Zech 11:1–2). For an accessible treatment of this issue, see Myers, "The Cedar Has Fallen!" 211–22.

8. Skinner, *Genesis*, 34.

cannot know with certainty, the word *dominion* does not seem to carry the harsh tones often associated with it in current debates.

Let's consider the discussions that try to establish what the Hebrew term translated as dominion means. In what follows you may feel like you are slogging through mud, but it is important for us to know what the scholarship about the word is. After all, a lot hangs on the word *dominion*, and we have a responsibility to try to be as informed as possible about its meaning.

James Barr suggests that *radah* was generally used in relation to kings ruling over certain areas. "For instance in 1 Kings v. 4 the verb is used to express Solomon's dominion (expressly a peaceful dominion) over a wide area."[9] Barr argues that dominion carries no idea of exploitation; indeed, "man would lose his 'royal' position in the realm of living things if the animals were to him an object of use or of prey."[10] Yoel Arbeitman, a Semitic language scholar, summarizing the scholarship, identifies these possibilities for the word's meaning:

- "to rule or shepherd in a neutral sense";

- "to lead about";

- "to lead, accompany; master, punish";

- "to be governed/controlled," as in "to tame."[11]

Mary Phil Korsak translates the Hebrew word *radah* as "govern,"[12] and Clare Palmer writes about the issue of dominion in Genesis 1:

> God is understood to be an absentee landlord, who has put humanity in charge of his [*sic*] possessions. . . . Within the framework of this model, God's actions and presence are largely mediated through humans. This is so both in the feudal perception, where God the Master leaves man [*sic*] in charge of his [*sic*] estate, and also in the financial perception, where God, the owner of financial resources, puts them in

9. Barr, "Man and Nature," 22.

10. Ibid., 23.

11. Cited in Kalechofsky, "Hierarchy, Kinship, and Responsibility," 93.

12. Korsak, ". . . et Genetrix: A five-page poem," 27.

the trust of humanity, the investor, to use for him [*sic*] as best it can.[13]

While the above-noted scholars see dominion as a somewhat benevolent force, Gerhard von Rad sees in the word *radah* a much more powerful force: "the expressions for the exercise of this dominion are remarkably strong: *rādā*, 'tread,' 'trample' (e.g., the wine press); similarly *kābaš*, 'stamp.'"[14]

The New Interpreter's Bible suggests a less forceful reading of both words (*radah* and *kabas*).

> A study of the verb *have dominion* . . . reveals that it must be understood in terms of care-giving, even nurturing, not exploitation. As the image of God, human beings should relate to the nonhuman as God relates to them. This idea belongs to the world of the ideal conceptions of royal responsibility (Ezek 34:1–4; Ps 72: 8–14) and centers on the animals.[15]

As for *kabas*, *The New Interpreter's Bible* says,

> The command to "subdue the earth" . . . focuses on the earth, particularly cultivation (see 2:5, 15), a difficult task in those days. While the verb may involve coercive aspects in interhuman relationships (see Num 32:22, 29), no enemies are in view here. More generally, "subduing" involves development in the created order. This process offers to the human being the task of intra-creational development, of bringing the world along to its fullest possible creational potential. Here paradise is not a state of perfection, not a stable state of affairs. Humans live in a highly dynamic situation.[16]

---

13. Palmer, "Stewardship," 74, quoted in Habel, *Readings from the Perspective of Earth*, 50. The use of [*sic*] to correct for the lack of generic language is the choice of the Earth Bible Team, who edited the volume.

14. Von Rad, *Genesis*, 60.

15. *New Interpreter's Bible*, 346.

16. Ibid.

One hundred years ago, the International Critical Commentary passed over the issue of the word *dominion* with little attention; instead, it focused almost exclusively on what the "likeness" of humans and the Creator entails. "The truth is that the image [of God] marks the distinction between man and the animals, and so qualifies him for dominion: the latter is the consequence, not the essence, of the divine image."[17] John Skinner, the author of this commentary, spends more time considering the different forms of plant reproduction than what dominion entails.

Claus Westermann suggests that the use of *radah* ("have dominion, govern") "can be compared with what is said in 1:16 about the sun and the moon, which are to 'govern' the day and night."[18] Westermann is referring to Genesis 1:16–17: "God made the two great lights—the greater light to rule the day and the lesser light to rule the night—and the stars. God set them in the dome of the sky to give light upon the earth, to *rule* over the day and over the night." The common characteristic of dominion in these definitions is its benignity.

No matter which interpretative approach we choose, there is no possible way to read the dominion of Genesis 1:26 and 1:28 as divine authorization for contemporary treatment of nonhuman animals, specifically animals domesticated for human consumption.

In Genesis 1, we know God by what and who God created. Did God actually create a living creature who invokes dominion when separating calf and cow within twenty-four hours so that the cow's milk can be diverted to human beings? A living creature for whom dominion includes caging the baby calves so that their flesh will be white? Who cuts off the beaks of chickens without any painkiller? Who brings into life living creatures who never experience the habitat God created for them, but instead are kept within large, enclosed spaces—pigs with nothing to root, hens with nothing to peck, cows with little to graze upon? Who takes the lives of animals they have named and cared for, and upon dropping the bloody knife, calls their actions humane? Or who chooses a go-between to protect them from using the bloody knife themselves while still accepting the idea that God's creatures are their dinner?

17. Skinner, *Genesis*, 32.

18. Quoted in Barr, "Man and Nature," 23.

What kind of God do we as God's representatives on earth make known through our treatment and killing of animals? If dominion is a good thing and granted by God, why don't we own up to what the dominion we assert for ourselves actually involves?

Jesus Christ: From Confusion to Revelation, from Separation to Love

Perhaps the spiritual state of human beings parallels the creation of the world. At first, there is darkness, confusion. What is our purpose on earth? How do we relate to others? In an opposite action to the creation story of Genesis 1 in which the void is separated into night and day, sky and sea, sea and earth, we go from being separate individuals to recognizing interrelationship. We move from confusion to revelation, from separation to love.

How do we know to think in this way? The biblical writers show us how: Thinking about the relationship between habitat and inhabitants, we are family, with different responsibilities but a shared home, habitat, and a shared diet. God's revelation, described in the beginning of Genesis 1, is fulfilled in Jesus Christ. Jesus offers another way to know God. Reading forward to the Gospels, how does this inform the ways we approach this passage? What is dominion in light of Jesus Christ?

If we see Jesus as the ultimate "image" of God, then how Jesus operates in his earthly ministry, through a kind of "non-power" and attentive care of others, has bearing on how we interpret what it means for us as images of Christ to exercise dominion. Dominion would come to basically mean serving others in such a way as to help them flourish as the creatures they have been created to be. Understood christologically, therefore, dominion cannot be attached to a will-to-power, but is intimately bound up with God's love and God's creation.

So many of the stories about Jesus's ministry show how he foreswears any power or dominion that has been culturally bestowed. Jesus's ministry is not about dominion but unconditional love. Jesus teaches us to welcome the stranger in our midst. Jesus teaches us hospitality. Does this not include sheltering animals as a hen would gather her chicks? In the twenty-first century, does this not require working against factory farms and recognizing that table hospitality extends to not putting animals on the plate? Jesus teaches us nonviolence—to put down the sword. For the twenty-first-century Christian, does this not include our knives and forks when used against the other animals? Jesus's ministry was not based on earthly dominion, as many Christians have understood that word. What matters is the quality of our relationships with each other.

Skinner, the author of a century ago who did not dwell on the meaning of dominion, did note that dominion is not the *essence* of the divine image. Yet, the more dominion becomes the focus of justifications for what humans beings are doing to domesticated animals, the more it is claimed as the essence of those beings created in God's image. Fragmenting the passage from any greater context has drastic consequences for our relationships with other creatures, for relationships between ourselves, and for attaching an essence of raw power not just to human beings but also to God.

David Bland writes:

> God is the creator of the world; but the primary focus is not that God created the world but why God created the world. The reason: God loves humans. God's speciality is loving and caring for creation. . . . Humans are given dominion, not domination; they are caregivers, not exploiters (cf Ps. 72: 8–14). We do unto creation as God has done unto us; we express love and care toward the world.[19]

How is the God of Genesis 1 first described? The first image of God in the Bible is of a brooding female bird. In the beginning, God hovered or brooded over the earth. The earth is God's egg, or chick, over which God is hovering, or brooding. John Wesley's notes to Genesis 1:2 observe that "the Spirit of God was the first Mover; He moved upon the face of the waters. He moved upon the face of the deep, as the hen gathereth her chicken under her wings, and hovers over them, to warm and cherish them, Mt 23:37 as the eagle stirs up her nest, and fluttereth over her young, ('tis the same word that is here used) Deut 32:11."

Before there were humans, the biblical writers tell us, there was the idea of the chicken, or of some fowl who behaves similar to chickens. So,

19. Bland, "Homiletical Perspective on Genesis 1:1–2, 4a," 29, 31.

as I thought about the way that the opening to Genesis was recorded, one thing it seems to say is that before chickens even existed, God had in God's mind the idea of the chicken, the idea of what a chicken's maternal care looked like, and it was good.

Dominion is not our identity, our end, our essence, or our way of life. Following Genesis 1, let's consider that maybe it is now our turn to relate to the world, to the created order, as a hen does her chicks, as God did at creation, and take them—the other animals—under our wing.

2

What about the Covenant with Noah?

Judith Barad

MANY PEOPLE SUPPORT THEIR decision to eat meat based on God's directives found in Genesis. Although we find such a command in the narrative of Noah's Ark, God clearly instructs people to be vegetarian prior to the Great Flood. If we take these accounts literally, why might God's mind have changed? In order to shed light on these seemingly conflicting biblical passages, we need to examine them more closely and then determine the interpretation that makes the most sense. However, we must be careful of rationalizing that the outcome we prefer is the best interpretation. If our desire to know God's will is greater than our desire to eat Big Macs or confirm our ideology, we must maintain an open mind as we study the Genesis passages and speculate about their inconsistencies.

It is common for religious people to oppose vegetarianism because they claim that God put animals on earth for humans to eat. They insist that this is God's sole purpose for creating animals. Is it possible that these believers either have not attentively read Genesis or that they have ignored God's words in the creation narrative? To see whether or not God created animals only to be human food, let us revisit the first chapter of Genesis.

After creating Adam and Eve, God said to them, "See, I have given you every plant yielding seed that is upon the face of all the earth, and every tree with seed in its fruit; you shall have them for food" (Gen 1:29). With these words, God directs humans to eat vegetables and fruits. This instruction indicates that God distinguishes between plants and animals and that God requires humans to treat animals differently than plants. God showed Adam that the moral status of animals is more elevated than that of plants by approving human consumption of plants—and not of animals. It makes sense to treat animals differently because animals suffer, whereas plants do not, lacking the necessary physiological conditions for suffering. The Garden of Eden, devoid of suffering and violence, was a true paradise on earth. This is the way God intended humans to live: in a world full of harmony between human life and animal life, a world in which violence has no place. Examining the new creation, including vegetarian humans, God found it "very good" (Gen 1:31).

When this section of Genesis is pointed out to people, they often respond with resistance. One rationalization that people sometimes give is that God did not explicitly forbid humans to eat the flesh of other animals at this time. However, this fact alone is inconsequential. God did not say that we couldn't eat each other, dirt, stones, metals, and so forth. Our Creator did not provide us with a "do not eat" list, but only told us what we are *allowed* to eat. The idea of a carnivorous diet would not have occurred to Adam and Eve, who knew what God approved of for food and had no experience of eating meat.

Moreover, God did not structure humans to be carnivorous. Unlike natural carnivores, we have nails instead of claws; we perspire through our skin rather than through our tongue; our colons are long and complex; our saliva has digestive enzymes; our front teeth are short and blunted, rather than sharp and long for tearing flesh; and our molars are flattened for grinding, not pointed like a carnivore's molars. Further, unlike natural carnivores, we have a long intestinal tract, which is ten to twelve times our body length, and we have stomach acid twenty times weaker than flesh-eaters. So, not only were we *instructed* to be vegetarians, but God *designed* us to be vegetarian.

Yet if animals were not created for us to eat, what is God's purpose in creating animals? We only need to look at the second creation narrative to find God's answer to this question:

> The Lord God said, "It is not good that the man should be alone; I will make him a helper as his partner." So out of the ground the Lord God formed every animal of the field and every bird of the air, and brought them to the man to see what he would call them; and whatever the man called each living creature, that was its name. (Gen 2:18–19)

One noteworthy point of this passage is that we do not name the animals we eat, for in doing so, they become more personal to us. But even more importantly, in God's own words, animals are created for *partnership* with humans. In other words, animals are meant to be our companions. Since we do not eat our partners or companions, this narrative reinforces God's approval of the vegetarian diet given to us in the first creation narrative.

But if God created animals to be our partners, does this mean that God created animals and humans as equals? Umberto Cassuto (1883–1951), in *From Adam to Noah*, part one of his commentary on Genesis, stated: "You are permitted to make use of the living creatures and their service, you are allowed to exercise power over them so that they may promote your subsistence; but you may not treat the life-force within them contemptuously and slay them in order to eat their flesh; your proper diet shall be vegetable food."[1] Cassuto's observation accords well with the biblical texts. The partnership between humans and animals is an unequal partnership, but a partnership nonetheless. We should treat our partners respectfully, not "contemptuously."

A common objection to the verse that God created animals to be the partner of humans is that after Adam named the animals, and found none to be an ideal partner, God created Eve to be his partner. Cassuto lists seven reasons why this interpretation is unacceptable. For the sake of brevity, let's just look at the first three. First, Cassuto observes, this interpretation does not reflect God's nature as expressed in this section of the Bible. Second, the section says that God's intentions were acted on immediately; and in Cassuto's words, "it would be strange if just in this

---

1. Cassuto, *Commentary on the Book of Genesis*, 1:58. The book was first published in 1944. Cassuto's translator, Israel Abrahams, describes Professor Cassuto in these words: "His almost unrivalled knowledge of ancient Semitic literature, his authoritative understanding of all branches of Biblical inquiry, and his outstanding critical acumen marked him as one of the great Bible exegetes of our age."

particular instance He should have failed to accomplish what He intended." Third, Cassuto writes, "It would be stranger still to declare that God did not understand . . . what man understood, that among the animals there was none fit to become a helper corresponding to him."[2] It would be impossible for Adam to know better than the all-knowing Creator that animals were not appropriate partners. So why did God create Eve after bringing the animals before Adam to be his partner? Cassuto suggests that the section only says that God wanted to produce in Adam a desire for a helper, a soulmate, who would correspond to him exactly.[3] An examination of the text supports Cassuto's conclusion. Moreover, Cassuto's responses preserve both God's omniscience and complete goodness, which are traditional attributes of God. If he is indeed correct, then the fact that God created animals to be the partner of humans still stands, even granting that Eve was created to be Adam's soulmate. Partnerships have different levels of intimacy. But the point remains that one should not eat one's partners, regardless of how close or distant their relationship to us.

As we see, before the flood in Genesis 7, people were vegetarians. Even when Adam and Eve were evicted from Eden, God told Adam to "eat the plants of the field" (Gen 3:18). God continued to express the desire that humans be vegetarian when speaking the following words to Noah before the Great Flood:

> "And of every living thing, of all flesh, you shall bring two of every kind into the ark, to keep them alive with you; they shall be male and female. Of the birds according to their kinds, and of the animals according to their kinds, of every creeping thing of the ground according to its kind, two of every kind shall come in to you, to keep them alive. Also take with you every kind of food that is eaten, and store it up; and it shall serve as food for you and for them." (Gen 6:19–21)

God makes it very clear that the animals Noah brings into the ark must be kept alive and nourished. Note that God makes a clear separation in this passage between animals and food. Animals are to be given food; they are not to *be* food.

2. Ibid., 127–28.
3. Ibid., 128.

However, a major change occurred after the great deluge that covered the earth. God tells Noah,

> "Be fruitful and multiply, and fill the earth. The fear and dread of you shall rest on every animal of the earth, and on every bird of the air, on everything that creeps on the ground, and on all the fish of the sea; into your hand they are delivered. Every moving thing that lives shall be food for you; and just as I gave you the green plants, I give you everything." (Gen 9:1–3)

Note that the last sentence, if taken literally, would include Noah's relatives. Granting that this statement should not be taken literally, why should we take the statements that precede it literally? If we only take the statements about animals literally, and not the statement about "every moving thing that lives," then it is quite possible that we are simply being arbitrary in order to fulfill a habitual craving for meat.

Further, what should we make of an all-good, all-loving God saying that "fear and dread of you shall rest on every animal of the earth" (Gen 9:2)? If this passage means that God is condoning or ordering fear, dread, and violence, then it could present a problem for maintaining God's complete goodness. However, if we interpret this passage as merely descriptive rather than prescriptive, the tension in this passage between God's loving nature and the words spoken dissipates. Our omniscient Lord knows what will happen once humans start eating animals. Norm Phelps writes in *The Dominion of Love*, "How that must have saddened God. . . . God was not commanding that it should be so, but acknowledging that humanity was still so mired in greed and violence that it could not be otherwise."[4]

Another question that this passage raises is why God's mind may have changed about eating animals, given God's directive in the Garden of Eden. Common sense tells us that in the aftermath of a flood of the magnitude described in Genesis, there was no vegetation to eat. In place of the abundant vegetation and fruit that God had originally given humans to eat, there was a barren wasteland. If God wanted humans to survive, they would have had to eat other animals. But, if this is the case, then Noah and his family were given a special dispensation to eat flesh. God does not

4. Phelps, *Dominion of Love*, 95–96.

decree that flesh-eating must be a practice that *all* humans adopt for *all* time. This special dispensation differs greatly from the admonition God issued to Adam about his prescribed diet in Eden. Although it may be that God desires the human species to continue, even going so far as to permit humans to eat other animals in times of environmental catastrophe, God says nothing about eating animals on a daily basis in ordinary times. What is permissible in times of emergency is *not* necessarily permissible in ordinary times. For instance, we accept people eating the flesh of their dead friends when there is nothing else to eat, as in the case of the soccer team stranded in the Andes. But since there is an abundance of food sources in the modern world, there is no necessity to eat any kind of flesh.

Having given Noah and his family a temporary dispensation to eat meat, God then admonishes them, "Only, you shall not eat flesh with its life, that is, its blood" (Gen 9:4). The ancient Hebrews regarded blood as sacred, as the source of life, because a living creature dies when it loses most of its blood. Since we cannot remove all the blood from animal flesh, this verse is not simply telling us to drain the blood before we eat an animal. In fact, whenever a person eats meat, he or she is eating blood. Cassuto comments:

> Apparently the Torah was in principle opposed to the eating of meat. When Noah and his descendants were permitted to eat meat this was a concession conditional on the prohibition of the blood. This prohibition implied respect for the principle of life and an allusion to the fact that . . . all meat should have been prohibited.[5]

The Jerusalem Bible lends support to this view, translating the supposed permission to eat meat as, "Every living and crawling thing shall provide food for you, no less than the foliage of plants." Consider that we can be *provided* with food from animals without killing them; think about ice cream! Examining these two verses together, it follows that we can eat eggs and dairy products, but not meat. If this is the case, then God has not permitted us to eat meat even temporarily in a great emergency!

---

5. Quoted in Schwartz, *Judaism and Vegetarianism*, 5. The direct quote is found in Leibowitz, *Studies in the Book of Genesis*, 77.

Clearly, an examination of the text shows that God displays similar concern and treatment for both human and animal creations. Just as prior to the flood, God tells Noah that animals "must be kept alive and nourished" (Gen 7:3, NAB). Immediately after the flood, God commands both Noah's family and the animals to "be fruitful and multiply" (Gen 9:1). This similar care and treatment is further shown by the covenant God made with both humans and animals following the flood. In fact, God says *six* times in a row that the covenant is not only with Noah and his sons, but also with every animal that was with Noah. (The Hebrew writers often used repetition to emphasize a point.[6]) Upon the first announcement of a covenant, God says, "As for me, I am establishing my covenant with you and your descendants . . . and with every living creature that is with you, the birds, the domestic animals, and every animal of the earth with you, as many as came out of the ark" (Gen 9:9–10). Note that God's covenant mentions only humans and animals—not plants. If God wanted animals to be equal in moral status to edible plants, then why was the covenant with humans and other animals, excluding such plants?

For a likely answer, we need only return to the Eden passage where God prescribes the human diet. Both the edict given in the Garden of Eden and the passages in which God establishes the covenant with humans and other animals suggest that animals must not be devalued to the level of plants, which are necessary for human and animal sustenance. There is a kinship between humans and other sentient beings, a kinship which is made explicit in the covenant. Like humans, most animals have the ability to learn (which requires thinking), a rich emotional life, social ties, and a strong desire to live. The thirteenth-century Jewish commentator Nachmanides observed that this kinship is the reason God created humans to be vegetarian.[7] God continued to recognize this kinship by making the safety of other animals a condition for Noah's surviving the flood.

Proclaiming the covenant the second time, God says, "I establish my covenant with you, that never again shall all flesh be cut off by the waters of a flood, and never again shall there be a flood to destroy the earth" (Gen 9:11). Not only is God once more referring to both humans and animals,

---

6. Hyland, *God's Covenant with Animals*, 22.

7. Schwartz, *Judaism and Vegetarianism*, 1.

but the words are very specific that the flood shall never happen again. God emphasizes the covenant's permanence the fifth time it is connected to both Noah and the animals, saying, "When the bow is in the clouds, I will see it and remember the everlasting covenant between God and every living creature of all flesh that is on the earth" (Gen 9:16).[8] The covenant, God's promise not to inundate the earth with water ever again, is clearly intended to be everlasting, unlike the injunction to eat animals. In that passage, there is nothing to suggest that people should eat meat for all time; there is nothing to suggest that the permission to eat animals is everlasting. Rabbi Isaac Kook (1865–1935) maintained that the permission to eat meat was a "temporary concession." He believed that "a God who is merciful to His creatures would not institute an everlasting law permitting the killing of animals for food." God regarded the permission to slaughter animals for food as a temporary dispensation until a "brighter era" is reached when people would return to vegetarian diets.[9]

Given that God's permission to eat meat was merely temporary, why might people have taken this permission as permanent rather than returning to the diet recommended in the Garden of Eden? After all, a vegetarian diet promotes peace and harmony, while the temporary diet permitted to Noah after the flood involves death and violence. In accord with this observation, the Jerusalem Bible offers the following commentary on Genesis 9: "In the beginning man was blessed and was consecrated lord [steward] of creation; he is now blessed and consecrated anew, but his role is tranquil no longer. In this new age man will be at war with the beasts and with his fellows. The peace of Paradise will not return until the latter days." Being at war "with the beasts" and other humans, we are engaged in violence. We cannot eat animals without consuming the results of violence. Numerous studies have shown that there is a strong connection between violence toward other animals and violence towards people.

8. The three other passages in Genesis 9 where God makes a covenant with humans and animals are: "This is the sign of the covenant that I make between me and you and every living creature that is with you, for all future generations" (9:12); "I will remember my covenant that is between me and you and every living creature of all flesh; and the waters shall never again become a flood to destroy all flesh" (9:15); and "This is the sign of the covenant that I have established between me and all flesh that is on the earth" (9:17).

9. Schwartz, *Judaism and Vegetarianism*, 3.

A study conducted by Northeastern University and the Massachusetts ASCPA found that people who are violent toward animals are *five times* more likely to commit violent crimes against people. And according to psychologist Randall Lockwood, violence toward animals easily escalates to killing people. Explaining this connection, one expert says, "It is a matter of escalation; people who want to victimize start with something they can easily control, then they work their way up. A person who feels powerful . . . while inflicting pain or death must continually sustain that 'high' by committing acts that are more heinous or morbid."[10]

These insights, which highlight the connection between violence toward animals and violence toward people, have been observed by religious writers as well as scientists and animal welfare advocates. Charles Vaclavik, a Quaker, writes that after the flood, "the human herbivore, newly turned to eating meat, found the killing instinct perpetually turned ON. They killed whether hungry or not. They killed when angry, they killed when greedy, they killed when sexually aroused. There was practically no time when the human beast could not find some excuse to kill."[11] Vaclavik notes that in contrast to natural carnivores, whose instinct to kill depends on hunger, humans are unnatural carnivores who kill to fulfill any urge they may have.

The connection between violence toward other animals and violence toward people can also be found as far back as Plato, who twenty-five hundred years ago argued in *The Republic* that meat-eating initiated violence and war. Plato wrote that if we want to construct the ideal state, people must eat a vegetarian diet. He suggested such food as salt, olives, cheese, boiled roots, vegetables, figs, chickpeas, beans, roasted myrtle, and acorns (372d). However, a friend objected that such food is fit only for pigs. Nowadays people would say that Plato is recommending "rabbit" food. In response, Plato insisted that only a sick, unhealthy society will eat meat. First, he observed that if people eat meat, they will become unhealthy. So the society will need more doctors. Then, he said, when people raise animals for food, they require more land for the animals to graze. The desire for more land leads people to forcibly take land away

10. Daugherty, "Animal Abusers May Be Warming Up for More." See also Linzey, *Link between Animal Abuse and Human Violence.*

11. Vaclavik, *Vegetarianism of Jesus Christ*, 69.

from other people, which, in turn, leads to war (373d–e). While Plato was not acquainted with Genesis, he was essentially giving us the same teachings on food. Plato's notion of the diet in the ideal society echoes the diet prescribed in the idyllic Garden.

In conclusion, Genesis tells us that God made humans the stewards of creation. Adam and Eve were trusted stewards for the animals. A steward is undoubtedly accountable for the care he gives to the owner's possessions. By recognizing our stewardship role, we are acknowledging God as the ruler of creation. We cannot justifiably usurp the role of ruler and exploit the rest of creation for our own arbitrary purposes. The role of steward entails limitations and accountability—an accountability that excludes the view that "man is the measure of all things." Humans are answerable to God for their actions. Assuming us to be responsible agents, God casts judgment on us for our failure to live up to our responsibility. This is why God sent the flood to cover the face of the earth.

Christians and many others commonly believe that God has given us free will. It follows that it is our choice to live as God intended us to live in the Garden of Eden, or to choose a lifestyle that involves willful and deliberate violence. As Reverend J. R. Hyland says, "Genesis tells the story of creatures whose natural condition is one of peaceful coexistence with their own species and with all other species. And although all have fallen from a higher state, their innate goodness—their nonviolent nature—remains waiting to be activated."[12] The choice is ours—a diet that yields peace and harmony or one that entails death and violence. We can freely choose to overlook the food choices God gave us in the Garden of Eden, the provisional nature of God's permission to eat animals, and the Covenant between God and all of sentient creation. But why would anyone who attempts to reflect God's love choose war and violence over peace and harmony?

---

12. Hyland, *God's Covenant with Animals*, 16.

3

What about Animal Sacrifice in the Hebrew Scriptures?

Malinda Elizabeth Berry

THE FOCUS QUESTION FOR this chapter—"What about animal sacrifice in the Hebrew Scriptures?"—begins with an assumption that bears spelling out. The assumption is this: because faithful Hebrew communities slaughtered animals as sacrifices to God, killing animals is in line with, or at least not against, God's will for both our spiritual and ecological well-being. Moreover, when we think about offering animal sacrifices to God as an act of obedience, if we refuse to kill a creature to fulfill ritual requirements, then we are choosing disobedience. In other words, the question at hand invites us to ponder larger questions. Can faith-based vegetarians and vegans cite our scriptural tradition as a moral source that is unequivocal about its refusal to willfully kill *any* of God's creatures? If so, how? If not, then what role *does* Scripture play in leading us to our lifestyle choices?

In addition to some extracanonical issues, many of the questions featured in this book fall into the province of biblical theology, the branch of biblical studies that invites readers to pay close and careful attention to the context of the biblical text's original audience. My task here is to outline what biblical theology has to say about the role of animal sacrifice in ancient times and then suggest how these understandings of the biblical world can inform our perspective as Christians who receive the Bible as Scripture even though we live in a very different place and time.[1]

The world of the Hebrew Bible is complex and ancient, which means that to be faithful biblical interpreters, we are often left in a position where we have to hypothesize about the original intention of scriptural passages and discern how we apply that intention to our lives now. In the case of animal sacrifice and religion in the Hebrew Bible, a question we need to ask at the outset is this: When we read the Bible's descriptions of a practice that is foreign to us, how do we avoid using snippets of Scripture to simply make arguments for or against animal sacrifice as the norm for biblical faith? One approach is to unearth information that can provide more context for passages that seem to speak to our questions. We can also use tools from religious studies, sociology, and historical studies to compare and contrast twenty-first-century religious practices with those chronicled in the Bible, written so long ago.[2] In either case, we are talking about hermeneutics—a term that biblical scholars use to describe various ways of interpreting the Bible.

Any time we read the Bible, we interpret each passage using a set of beliefs or concerns that guide our interpretation. These beliefs and concerns form principles that, in turn, form a hermeneutic. Let me use myself as an example. Along with my family, faith community, and personal experience, my commitment to robust theological education and critical thinking are the building blocks of my hermeneutics. I believe that God's

1. There is a long tradition of distinguishing different types of theology from each other based on their function within both the church and the academy. Biblical theology is done by those trained in the biblical languages and exegesis. They study the Bible carefully and help us understand what was happening in the world that provides the immediate context of a particular part of Scripture. Systematic theology, also referred to as constructive theology, is done by those who are familiar with the traditional doctrines of Christian tradition and thus seek to use the Bible as a resource for answering questions that we have today but that the Bible does not always address *directly*. Biblical and systematic/constructive theologians work together to identify the limits and possibilities of what defines Christian faith in the twenty-first century. In this task they often begin with the ancient ideas recorded in Scripture by biblical writers.

2. The proof-texting impulse is a strong one! Here are a few passages from the Old Testament that Christian vegetarians and vegans often cite as evidence that God rejects animal sacrifice and therefore killing nonhuman animals: Isa 1:11; Isa 66:3; Jer 7:21–23; Hos 6:6; and Deut 25:4.

hope for planet Earth is that it will know *shalom,* a deep sense of peace and well-being based on the belief that everything that is part of God's good creation is connected. When I read the Bible, I am always asking, what does this passage tell me about God's hope for *shalom* and humanity's response to that hope? In this way, I am building my hermeneutical framework around this basic belief: from the birth of creation to the end of time, God desires that all of creation be at peace and unafraid.

As Christian readers, we have a responsibility to make informed decisions about the materials we use to construct our hermeneutical frameworks. For this reason, it is important to turn to those trained in a variety of academic disciplines for their expertise and thoughtful scholarship. A foundational approach we can use—especially when we are interested in challenging long-held arguments about what the Bible means and says—comes from the work of Paul Ricouer, a twentieth-century pioneer in the area of hermeneutics and its application to the Bible. Ricouer coined the term "hermeneutics of suspicion," which has become a basic tool for many types of theological reflection. This hermeneutical approach does *not* mean that we are suspicious about the *truth and integrity* of the biblical witness. It means that we imagine ourselves to be detectives *trying to find out as much as we can* about biblical authors' decisions on how to tell a story or chronicle history, while also keeping in mind some of the Bible's broad themes like righteousness, justice, redemption, holiness, and *shalom*.

From a vegetarian/vegan point of view, a hermeneutics of suspicion unearths all kinds of questions about animal sacrifice in the Bible. For me, many questions bubble to the surface when I think about animal sacrifice in relation to my choice for a vegetarian diet: What is the basic religious meaning of sacrifice for the Hebrews, who were God's covenant people and out of whose faith grew both Judaism and Christianity? In the Hebrew communities that span the ages from Abraham to Mary and Joseph, what was the role and function of nonhuman animals in sacrificial rituals? What is the difference in offering vegetation, animals, or even human beings as sacrifices to God? Why is physical sacrifice important to God? What interpretive approach might we develop to help us frame these and other questions so that we might answer them in ways that remain faithful to our Christian beliefs?

In the rest of this essay, I will offer vegetarians, vegans, and omnivores some hermeneutical food for thought to help us respond thoughtfully when we wonder together, "What about animal sacrifice in the Hebrew Scriptures?" My goal is to help all of us see that whether we are vegetarians, vegans, or omnivores, the Bible invites us to reflect on the intricate web of life God has woven on this planet. Regardless of where you or I stand on the theological meaning of our human creatureliness in relation to other creatures, I hope you will agree that turning to Scripture to look for ammunition to convince others we are right and they are wrong flies in the face of the compassion and nonviolence that should ground our exploration of the issues dealt with in this book.

Understanding Sacrifice

Encyclopedia articles on sacrifice contain detailed information about the origins of this widespread and long-practiced religious phenomenon. From theories to examples of sacrifice, scholars have tried for decades to develop consensus about sacrifice to help us make useful generalizations about it. For example, literature on sacrifice identifies three distinct forms: blood offerings, bloodless offerings, and divine offerings. Blood offerings refer to those sacrifices that involve spilling blood by killing a creature, human or nonhuman. Bloodless offerings include things such as herbs, fruits, vegetables, grains, beverages, oils, and other symbols of Earth's fertility. In divine offerings, the deity becomes the offering rather than receiving a sacrifice.

It does not take much intensive research to learn that sacrifice was an important part of religion in the ancient Near Eastern world where Jewish and Christian traditions were born. But how did this come to be so? This is a difficult question to answer, but we can glean some general information from the attitudes and practices of different cultures. From my own research, I have found five interwoven cultural and theological ideas that are important to identify because they impact the way we might interpret biblical references to (animal) sacrifice: the theologies of the ancient Near East; a view of nonhuman animals known as "instrumentalism"; violence in its personal, structural, and predatory forms; relationship expressed through sacrifice; and our view of Jesus's death on the cross as a form of sacrifice.

Sacrifice in the Theologies of the Ancient Near East

As I noted above, Christianity is a "descendant" of Hebrew religion, which felt the competing influences of other religions practiced around it. From the Mediterranean Sea to the Caspian Sea, there were many theologies that based their worldviews on the interactions between a pantheon of deities and humans. While the stories that shaped worship and ethics among the region's peoples were different in particular details, they shared common principles. These commonalities meant it was not unusual for people to incorporate symbols and rituals from other religions into their own. Animal sacrifice was one practice found in so many of the religious cults of the time that scholars do not attempt to determine exactly where the practice originated.

Scholars have, however, examined the patterns of sacrifice among various cultures and religions. Through comparative analysis, we can say that the purpose, or function, of sacrifice from culture to culture is to create a relationship between humans and the spiritual, sacred world of the divine. By establishing this relationship, sacrifice invites expressions of divine power to manifest in our reality in ways that are beneficial to those offering the sacrifice. Indeed, while we may think of the animals and humans offered in these rituals as victims, in the context of sacrificial practice, to be the sacrifice was an honorable and noble thing.

Beginning in about 1200 BCE with the rise of ancient Greece and extending into the fifth century of the common era, the Greco-Roman world dominated the Ancient Near East. It makes sense to look at how the ancient Greek and Roman religious cults practiced animal sacrifice and to compare that view of divinity with the deity Abraham encounters in Genesis. Greco-Romans believed that their sacrifices fed the gods and goddesses. In homes and temples people would, based on a deity's patronage, lay out food (vegetation or carefully prepared and slaughtered domesticated animals) and drink (libations) for the gods and goddesses to eat. If we survey biblical references in Leviticus, Numbers, and even Malachi, what do we find? Writers explaining that the foods and libations on the altar are food for God.[3] In other words, as animal sacrifice became an important part of tending their covenantal relationship, the Hebrew people also theologized their practices, reflecting broader ancient Near Eastern and Greco-Roman beliefs about the human's relationship to the divine.

But the Greeks and Romans did not describe their relationship with deity in terms of covenant. For them, the deities they worshipped and served could be very temperamental. In return for the care they showed to gods and goddesses through sacrificial rites, humans hoped to receive favor and blessing from the deities. On the other hand, if humans neglected the Olympians, they could expect all kinds of calamities as punishment. While we might know some Christians who use this kind of thinking about Yahweh—being obedient or disobedient to God will result in good or bad things happening—there is still a big difference between Greco-Roman beliefs about their deities and the way the Hebrew Bible describes God. Besides the concept of covenant, the Greeks and Romans differed from the Hebrews in that they based their tradition of sacrifice on a radically different creation story. Unlike the book of Genesis, nowhere in the stories about the Titans and Olympians or Romulus and Remus is there thematic emphasis on the relationship between humans and their ecological surroundings that points to vegetarianism as the norm.

One thing we can see is that rites of animal sacrifice were part of life in the ancient Near East and undoubtedly shaped the lives of the people who became Yahweh's covenant people, from Abraham, Sarah, and Hagar all the way to Mary and Joseph. In fact, sacrifice was an important part of how they understood this covenantal relationship. But a second thing that we can see is that within biblical religion there is a theological reason for rejecting animal sacrifice: God's original intention for the community of creatures where there was no killing. There is a real tension between these observations. If God did not originally intend for humans to kill their kindred in Eden, then how did killing later become an acceptable and even expected part of worship? One explanation is this: animal sacrifice

---

3. Wright, "Study of Ritual in the Hebrew Bible." Wright refers readers to Leviticus 11–15, Numbers 19, and Malachi 1, which together explain how the purity laws "are part of the larger metaphor of waiting on God in His 'palace' (the sanctuary)," 131.

made its way into God's community of Israel through outside influences. But that answer alone does not settle the question.

From Equality to Instrumentalism

As I noted above, in the opening chapters of Genesis, Scripture paints a picture of the world as a lush garden teeming with life. God explains to Adam and Eve that the vegetation around them is designed to nourish and sustain human and nonhuman animals alike. But the situation described in Genesis 1–3 changes rather dramatically. By chapter 4, Cain and Abel present sacrifices to Yahweh. Cain's sacrifice, comprised of some kind of vegetable produce, is not acceptable to God in the way that Abel's animal sacrifice is. By chapters 8 and 9, we read that part of God's blessing on Noah's family includes what sounds like a *mixed* blessing, or even a curse: "The fear and dread of you shall rest on every animal of the earth. . . . Every moving thing that lives shall be food for you; and just as I gave you the green plants, I give you everything. Only, you shall not eat flesh with its life, that is, its blood" (Gen 9:2a, 3–4).

The community of creatures has disintegrated. J. W. Rogerson explains: "Taken together, the pre- and post-Flood mandates imply that the world of our experience is not the world as God intended or intends it to be. That original world was one in which . . . there was no predatory violence within nature."[4] In other words, the violence that defines the relationship of humans to other creatures is part of the world's sin, the way we miss the mark and contribute to harm and discord. Rogerson adds that one way we twenty-first-century readers differ from our biblical counterparts is that we have resigned ourselves to violence as a fact of life. "The importance for biblical readers of a violence-free world lay not in the *fact* of its supposed existence, but in the way in which it witnessed to a possible form of existence that was also a radical criticism of the actual world of human existence."[5]

I will return to the theme of violence below. For the moment I want to underscore the vision that Rogerson argues biblical readers imagined and hoped for: a *shalom* community where humans, wolves, sheep, snakes,

4. Rogerson, "What Was the Meaning of Animal Sacrifice?" 12.

5. Ibid., 12–13.

cattle, bears, lions, and all manner of creatures are part of God's reign of justice and righteousness; a community of creatures not identical in their nature, but equal in their worth to one another and to God. The inequity in the community of creatures that God seems to put in place after the flood is discordant with the harmony God orchestrates in Eden. But what is the problem with this inequality?

Consider the common saying, "Those people are acting like animals!" This judgment captures the cultural—and theological—bias that we humans are not animals when we use our reason, but are the same as animals when we do not employ our reason; this logic seems impossible to overcome, becoming even more problematic when race ideologies are brought into the mix.[6] Andrew Linzey and Dan Cohn-Sherbok, in their book *After Noah: Animals and the Liberation of Theology*, explain that regardless of our personal views, all Christians have received an "instrumentalist" view of animals. In this view, animals are part of the ecosystem so that humans can use them as we see fit; they are *instruments* for us to achieve our own desires: for religious ritual, sustenance, labor, clothing, medicinal purposes, companionship, and even entertainment. This tradition holds that nonhuman animals are devoid of reason as well as a rational soul. Without human-like reason or rational souls, animals are destined to be ruled by their instincts, because they cannot develop a "self." Tracing this philosophical viewpoint from sources that include Aristotle (384–322 BCE) and Rabbi Simeon ben Eliezer (of the Tannaim era, 70–200 CE), Linzey and Cohn-Sherbok write, "The logic was inexorable, animals were made for our use and we eat them; we eat them because they were made for our use."[7] Carried forward into Christian theology, instrumentalism was shaped by philosophers and theologians alike, from Augustine

---

6. For examples of such race-based ideologies that are linked to attitudes about nonhuman animals, see polygenism and monogenism theories of human origins. Advocates of polygenism, especially popular in the nineteenth century, argue that the races are so different that it is impossible that all humans have the same origin (i.e., Adam and Eve). The theory creates a hierarchy, arguing that Adam and Eve and thus the Hebrew people were part of the "white," Caucasian race. The "yellow," Mongolian and "black," Ethiopian races were born of catastrophe rather than being part of God's original creative design. Another feature of the polygenism theory was to say that the black race was clearly descended from apes, not the white race.

7. Linzey and Cohn-Sherbok, *After Noah*, 8.

of Hippo to René Descartes, from Thomas Aquinas to John Calvin and Martin Luther. It is not surprising, Linzey and Cohn-Sherbok argue, that even Karl Barth's theology has unwittingly perpetuated instrumentalism by focusing on humans as the most important feature of God's creation.[8]

In sum, while mainstream Christian practice does not include animal sacrifice, the belief in a fundamental inequity between humans and nonhuman animals allowed the biblical references to both animal sacrifice and a difference between human and nonhuman animal blood to become part of Christianity's theological tradition as if this was the only and most faithful view of creation. For this reason, conventional wisdom says, we should not be bothered by the death of animals either in the Bible or in the world we live in today.

Violence: Personal, Structural, and Predatory

Many theologians have described the reality of violence in the world as evidence of sin because the world is in a fallen state. Blood sacrifice involves violence at several levels. First, there is the personal violence committed by the one who kills the sacrifice as well as the personal violence experienced by the sacrificial object (either a human or nonhuman animal). Second, there is the structural violence that becomes institutionalized in the community by blood sacrificial practices when they become the norm. An example of structural violence is the instrumentalist view of nonhuman animals in which violence is woven into the fabric of religious life, making it impossible to have moral integrity without participating in a structure that raises animals to kill them as part of worship. A third level is predatory violence, which is the enmity in God's community of creatures that biblically begins after the Great Flood. Predatory violence is the sense of dread we feel because of a threat that comes from knowing another can or even will kill us. As humans we feel this sense of dread when we see a lion prowling in the savannah. It is also present in a mouse toward an owl, or perhaps even in a pig when a human enters the barn.

From a Christian perspective focused on *shalom,* if violence is a form of sin, then all violence is contrary to God's will, intention, and hope for the community of creatures that inhabit Earth. Richard Alan Young ar-

8. Ibid., 118–19.

gues that the introduction of meat into the human diet and the use of animals in worship is an example of God making a concession to us. "God's commands are designed to inspire us toward divine ideals, whereas God's concessions . . . are designed to deal with us as we are."[9] I am not interested in passing judgment on meat-eating. I am interested in challenging the prejudice faced by people who eat a vegetarian/vegan diet: refusing to eat meat is out of order because God gave us meat to eat, so we should eat it. But God never actually commands us to eat meat. Therefore, a meatless diet is a choice we can make to live into and out of a vision of nonviolence, by consistently and daily making choices that seek to do justice by cherishing the tender web of life on Earth.

Whether people were hunting or raising animals, spilling their blood was part of the equation of these sacrifice rituals. Walter Burkert argues, "Aggression and human violence have marked the progress of our civilization and appear, indeed, to have grown so during its course that they have become a central problem of the present."[10] I agree with Burket's assessment of our situation. Let me return to the question I raised above as to why God allowed animal sacrifice to become part of religious life among the Hebrews. While I think that animal sacrifice made its way into Yahweh's community of Israel through the influence of the broader religious culture, I also think God chose to tolerate the practice as a compromise in deference to human choices. Animal sacrifice has also contributed to the predatory violence—where we are the predators and they are our prey—that continues to distort our relationship to other creatures. Elevating humans above other creatures in this way leads to structural violence.[11]

Scripture also contains stories of human sacrifice. It is difficult to understand how these stories can be called sacred. Both the acts and prospects of violence in them require some kind of explanation other than God's divine command. Whether we are interpreting Abraham and Isaac's journey up Mount Moriah (Gen 22) or Jephthah's tragic and prideful promise that leads to the sacrifice of his own daughter (Judg 11), our

9. Young, *Is God a Vegetarian?*, 56.

10. Burkert, *Homo Necans*, 1.

11. For an excellent analysis of the connection between patriarchal oppression and meat, see Adams, *Sexual Politics of Meat*.

tradition has some explaining to do. Traditionally, we have answered the questions about human sacrifice by noting, in the first case, that God sent Abraham a ram to use in place of his child. In the second case, many agree that Jephthah was a proud fool to have made and kept such a promise because Torah forbids human sacrifice. Micah's word to God's people that all God requires of them is justice, kindness, and humility reinforces the fact that neither animal sacrifice nor human sacrifice is primary for right relationship with God (Mic 6:8).

Sacrifice as Relationship and Communication

As I explained above, various cultures and peoples who practiced animal sacrifice did so to appease and honor deities in highly ritualized fashion. In this way sacrifice was a form of communication between the material world and the spiritual world. Sacrificial rituals developed as they did because they came to reflect the relationship between those performing the ritual, the deity receiving the offering, and the object being sacrificed. From raising the appropriate animals in the appropriate way to preparing, killing, and consuming them, these rituals were complex and involved layer upon layer of meaning. But what kind of relationship among God, humanity, and animals did animal sacrifice foster?

It is not surprising that there are different ways to answer this question. One approach is to see the human-sacrificial animal relationship as analogous to the relationship between God and the covenant community. Jonathan Klawans makes this argument by first acknowledging that "the selective killing of animals for the sake of worshipping God will never sit well with those of us raised in modern nonsacrificing religious traditions." He goes on to argue that the rituals requiring blood, and thus nonhuman animals, were about relationship. "The sacrificial animal must be birthed, protected, fed, and guided—all things that Israel wished for themselves from their God." Sacrifice was not about what the death of a lamb, calf, or dove offered Israel. Sacrifice, he contends, was about the parallel between the provision Israel offered to the animals they prepared for purification sacrificial rituals and the provision they hoped to receive from God.[12]

12. Klawans, "Sacrifice in Ancient Israel," 74. For an excellent introduction to the specific forms and content of sacrifice in the Hebrew Bible, see Rainey, Rothkoff, and

Klawans's conventional interpretation seems to suggest that killing was a regrettable part of sacrificial rituals rather than, as Burkert argues, a display of humanity's capacity for and perpetuation of violence.

Another approach is to explore how biblical writers understood sacrifice in social terms. In his book *The Social Meanings of Sacrifice in the Hebrew Bible,* David Janzen explains that, as a form of ritual, sacrifice was and is a way of communicating social practices that help give a culture or group of people a sense of meaning and identity. So, despite the diversity in practice, another generalization we can make about the various forms of sacrifice is this: throughout the ancient Near Eastern world, from Egypt to Mesopotamia, sacrifice in any setting, including the Hebrew Bible, had many, many layers rather than one, universal meaning.[13] For the religious world of ancient Israel, sacrifice was a communication in worship that established a relationship between God and the community. While sacrificial rituals took formal shape in the life of Israel, the regulations called for its monarchs and priests to be the ones to preside over the rites, acting on behalf of the community.

As biblical religion was emerging, idolatry was a huge problem—that is one thing we have in common with these ancient communities—so one of the basic commands God gave the people was to worship Yahweh alone. Janzen writes, "It is worship of YHWH alone that will save Israel, and it is sacrifice that expresses this worship."[14] Sacrifice had a strict code that applied not only to *how* Israel makes its offerings but *why.* For example, in the Deuteronomistic History that recorded the practices of sacrifice, researchers like Janzen note, "right moral action" must accompany a properly prepared sacrifice; thus God could be sure that the offering was real and sincere.[15]

With this in mind, we can use a hermeneutics of suspicion to ask, in the oft-cited passages in which the prophets decry *blood* sacrifice, are they concerned about something larger than whether animals are used? What if the prophets are decrying a lack of moral action in everyday life that God expects to accompany offerings? If we consider this angle, then we

---

Dan, "Sacrifice," 639–49.

13. Janzen, *Social Meanings of Sacrifice in the Hebrew Bible,* 67.

14. Ibid., 132.

15. Ibid., 161.

can see that *blood* sacrifice is not the only way to nurture relationship and communication with God; moral action also nurtures the relationship.[16]

Jesus and Sacrifice

The tradition of blood sacrifice that runs through the Hebrew Bible also becomes an important interpretive thread in the Gospels and Paul's letters in the Christian Testament as the apostles and early generations of Jesus's followers try to make sense of his crucifixion. What are the implications of viewing Jesus's death purely in sacrificial terms? I answer this question using some of the tools and perspectives offered by feminist and womanist theologies. These perspectives urge us to explore the symbolism of traditional understandings of Jesus's atoning death on the cross. In these traditional perspectives, the theme of necessary violence and killing quickly become justifiable because such actions are redemptive, much like killing animals to perform blood sacrifice.

The metaphor and image of Jesus as the paschal lamb fits with the traditions of both blood and divine sacrifice: Jesus is both the sacrifice and the high priest; he is both the firstborn son of God and the lamb whose blood provides the cover for the Passover; and, as God incarnate, he is the sacrifice to end all atoning sacrifices. When we speak of Jesus Christ as the *Agnus Dei* (lamb of God), God in human flesh becomes a nonhuman animal, metaphorically speaking, so he is a literal human sacrifice and a figurative nonhuman animal sacrifice. It is tempting to answer the question about animal sacrifice in the Hebrew Bible by simply saying, "Sure, Jewish religion used animal sacrifice, but Jesus ends all of that when he sacrifices himself, making his blood atonement for us." But this interpretation glosses over the themes explored in this essay. If we think about Jesus's death as divine blood sacrifice, then it would seem that we must believe that God wanted sacrifice to become part of biblical religion so that we would have the theological system to comprehend God's plan for our redemption.

But as I have argued in this essay, we have biblical and cultural resources to develop an alternative way of affirming the importance of

16. It is important to note that when Jerusalem's Second Temple fell in 70 CE, this brought an end to sacrificial worship.

Jesus's atoning death by recognizing that while the sacrifice paradigm is an important part of Scripture's original context, this paradigm is not the Bible's primary paradigm for understanding salvation. I like to describe this alternative paradigm as a hermeneutics of *shalom*. From a *shalom* perspective, Perry Yoder explains that Jesus's atoning death initiates a process of reconciliation between God and the whole of creation. Reconciliation brings about a transformation because it has both internal and external dimensions. Internally, we receive a new nature that enables us to live as God's children. Externally, social concerns have a priority in informing our worldview. He writes, "We are liberated from the power of sin so that we might all be free, and being free so that we might serve one another."[17]

If we return to the image of Jesus Christ as the paschal lamb, we are also invited to return to the images of the Hebrew Bible that speak of a peaceable kingdom. In both Isaiah 11 and 65, the prophet delivers God's hopeful message of a time when life in the world will be like it was in Eden:

> The wolf shall live with the lamb, the leopard shall lie down with the kid, the calf and the lion and the fatling together, and a little child shall lead them. The cow and the bear shall graze, their young shall lie down together; and the lion shall eat straw like the ox. The nursing child shall play over the hole of the asp, and the weaned child shall put its hand on the adder's den. They will not hurt or destroy on all my holy mountain; for the earth will be full of the knowledge of the Lord as the waters cover the sea. (Isa 11:6–9)

> They shall build houses and inhabit them; they shall plant vineyards and eat their fruit. They shall not build and another inhabit; they shall not plant and another eat; for like the days of a tree shall the days of my people be, and my chosen shall long enjoy the work of their hands. They shall not labor in vain, or bear children for calamity; for they shall be offspring blessed by the Lord—and their descendants as well. Before they call I will answer, while they are yet speaking I will hear. The wolf and the lamb shall feed together, the lion

17. Yoder, *Shalom*, 69.

shall eat straw like the ox; but the serpent—its food shall be
dust! They shall not hurt or destroy on all my holy mountain,
says the Lord. (Isa 65:21–25)

While these passages are familiar to our ears, we do not often give our full
attention to the implications of Isaiah's oracle. What I see as I read these
Scriptures is the end of predatory violence not only in a literal sense—the
wolf and lamb are amiable companions—but also in a figurative sense.
The events leading up to Jesus's crucifixion also describe predatory violence within the human community that we should also read metaphorically. Jesus's enemies sought after him in a way that is analogous to both
big game hunters tracking a lion and wolves breaking into a sheep pen.

Jesus did not resist predatory violence in an immediate sense by
outrunning his "predators." It is in his resurrection that Jesus challenges
this pattern of the stronger overcoming the weaker. He overcomes the
personal, structural, and predatory violence of his death. From a point
of view that combines theology and ecology, the community Christ calls
us to serve is a community full of plants and creatures—human and
nonhuman.

Conclusion

I think of the Bible as feast and the interwoven cultural and theological
ideas I have discussed in this essay become culinary utensils. As we survey
the table, we must determine (*a*) if what is on the table conforms to our
dietary standards, (*b*) if we want to eat the things that do fit our diet and
lifestyle, and (*c*) if what we find to eat will provide us with nutritional
balance. Like ladles, spatulas, knives, forks, and spoons, I believe the
ideas and concepts I have introduced in this essay—the theologies of the
ancient Near East; a view of nonhuman animals known as "instrumentalism"; violence in its personal, structural, and predatory forms; relationship expressed through sacrifice; and our view of Jesus's death on the cross
as a form of sacrifice—help us serve ourselves manageable portions of
Scripture. This is not simply picking and choosing what we like from what
is on the table!

Even though the Bible is full of promise, it is often a challenge to know what to do with the biblical materials because we are never quite sure what is in front of us, what it will do to us if we eat it, or if it is even edible. Indeed, Christian tradition has often dished up Scripture as heaping portions of inedible stone rather than the bread of life. And yet, when we read the Bible today, we have the chance to revive ancient teachings by bringing new insights to the table, namely, a renewed vision of God's love and care for us as a community of creatures. When this is our hermeneutic, I do not believe we will ever be sent away empty or improperly nourished when we feast on the text. As mature believers who care about nutrition, health, and wellness, we come to the table for soul-nourishing food that meets the body's needs in a holistic way. This too is part of God's great *shalom*.

4

Doesn't the Bible Say that Humans Are More Important than Animals?

Nekeisha Alexis-Baker

VEGANISM IS AN INTEGRAL part of my Christian faith and witness, consequently, I often have to explain my decision in light of the Bible's apparent distinction between human and nonhuman animal value. Usually, the person asking the above question is already convinced that Scripture affirms God's preferential option for people, that it supports putting the needs and desires of humans over those of nonhuman animals, and that it extends moral consideration to humans that it denies other animals. At best, these presumptions cause Christians to be "nice" to other creatures while insisting that people and animals are not the same and should be treated accordingly. Such is the case when Christian environmentalist Rusty Pritchard positively describes a prestigious Southern Baptist anticruelty advocate as "neither a radical animal rights activist nor a vegetarian," but a man who is "crystal clear on the distinction between humans, created in the image of God, and animals."[1] At worst, Christians who believe the Bible says nonhuman animals are less important than humans adopt theologies and practices that treat other animals as mere resources.

1. Pritchard, "Different Shade of Green," 9.

Such is the case with Christian environmentalist Holmes Rolston III, who claimed that "the cow is a meat factory . . . Cows cannot know they are disgraced."[2] Unsurprisingly, how we answer the question, "Doesn't the Bible say that humans are more important than animals?" has grave consequences for how we treat them. Therefore, it is essential that we look at Scripture carefully.

In this chapter, I will show that the Bible has multiple perspectives on human and nonhuman animal worth. At times, it claims that humans are more valuable than other animals. In other instances, it suggests that nonhuman animals are superior and worthy of imitating. In still other situations, it refers to human and nonhuman animals as equals under God and describes their differences as degrees on a spectrum instead of rungs on a ladder of worth. All of these positions are held together by the Bible's overall narrative that God loves each creature and intends for all to live in mutual relationship with one another.

Creation as Community

The dominant view in Western society is that humans are more important than other animals. At the heart of this argument is the incorrect belief that rationality, language, and skills like tool-using are desirable traits unique to our species.[3] These and other similar ideas were perpetuated in part by influential Christian thinkers like Augustine and Aquinas, and philosophers like Descartes and Spinoza.[4] Although many Christians

---

2. Rolston, *Environmental Ethics*, 83.

3. Many biologists, behavioral scientists, linguists and others in the scientific fields have demonstrated that many of the traits we think unique to humankind exist in other animal species. For compelling evidence that many supposedly human traits are indeed shared by other animals, see Shumaker, Walkup, and Beck, *Animal Tool Behavior,* and de Waal, *Age of Empathy*. For a compelling and entertaining documentary, which also records the heartbreaking way in which scientists have treated chimpanzees as property, see *Project Nim*.

4. In this essay, I have limited the conventional "human-animal" pairing in favor of using "humans" or "people" on one hand, and "other animals" or "nonhuman animals" on the other to acknowledge the biological reality that human beings are a kind of animal. I will primarily use the term "animal" in reference to other-than-human creatures when quoting from other sources.

read the Bible through this lens, this worldview actually departs from the Jewish tradition of which Jesus was a part and from which the earliest Christians came. The Bible in no way justifies Christians abusing other animals.[5] Instead, Scripture sees human and nonhuman animals as part of the same community that God has established.

In Genesis 1, the Creator makes the world and everything in it and has an intimate relationship with creation. God speaks water creatures into being before telling them to "be fruitful and multiply." God also creates land animals and people on the same day, testifying to the closeness between the two kinds of creatures.[6] In Genesis 1:29–30, God gives plants, seeds, and fruit as food to everyone with breath, making nonhuman and human animal diets free of any bloodshed. On each day, God alone determines the goodness of the creatures and does so independently of human beings, who do not yet exist.[7] Genesis 1:31 might even suggest that humanity's goodness is tied to the goodness of everyone and everything else God creates.[8]

The connection between God and creation as well as between all members of creation is also apparent in Genesis 2. In Genesis 2:7 and 2:18, God forms the man from the ground, then shapes each living creature from the same earth. In Genesis 2:19, God responds to the man's loneliness by creating land and air animals to be his helper-partners and brings them to the man for him to name. This naming ceremony symbolizes the man's deep understanding of each animal's place in and worth to creation—not domination.[9] When the man cannot find a fitting companion, his relationship to the creatures does not disappear. Instead, the man's need for deeper relationship sparks even more creativity from God, who forms the woman out of the man's dust-formed rib. On the surface, this story seems to suggest that nonhuman animals are inferior to humans because the man cannot commune with them as he does with the woman.

5. Birch and Vischer, *Living with the Animals*, 2.

6. Webb, *On God and Dogs*, 20.

7. Birch and Vischer, *Living with the Animals*, 49. See also Webb, *On God and Dogs*, 20.

8. Spanner, "Tyrants, Stewards—or Just Kings," 217–18.

9. Moritz, "Animals and the Image of God," 136. See also Spanner, "Tyrants, Stewards—or Just Kings?" 218–19.

However, another interpretation sees all the earth's animals as part of a continuum in which the man opens the circle, the land, and air creatures continue the circle; and the woman closes the circle alongside the man.[10]

Other clues in Genesis point to the close relationship between human and nonhuman animals. The man, woman, and animals are all "living souls" or "living beings" (*nephesh*), suggesting an intimate bond between them. Likewise, the words "all flesh" (*kol basar*) refer to both humans and other animals, forming "a basic kinship of creatureliness under the shared providence of a merciful God."[11] Human and nonhuman animals also share the "spirit of life" (*ruach hayyim*).[12] Even the idea of humanity bearing the image of God suggests mutuality between human and nonhuman creation when we realize this mark does not place us over creation, but instead calls us to a special role within it. Consequently, we act in God's image when we love and care for nonhuman animals—and we act against God's image when we abuse and neglect them. For Christians, Jesus exemplifies how we must live out the image of God with other animals. He was born among sheep and oxen; began his post-baptismal ministry amidst wild nonhuman animals;[13] used animals as examples in his teaching and as part of his witness; and lived, died, and rose again to restore *all* of creation. Jesus did not regard divine status as "something to be exploited, but emptied himself, taking the form of a slave" (Phil 2:6–7). His example of servant leadership calls us to exercise our distinguished role using justice, mercy, and humility—not abusive power and control. Through his example, we can also better understand his statements about human and nonhuman animal value.[14]

---

10. As biblical scholar John Eaton explains: "They have a companionship to offer, and *in their own way are necessary for human happiness.*" See Eaton, *The Circle of Creation*, 7–8. Emphasis mine.

11. Webb, *On God and Dogs*, 20. See also Moritz, "Animals and the Image of God," 135.

12. Moritz, "Animals and the Image of God," 135. See also Spanner, "Tyrants, Stewards—or Just Kings?" 221.

13. Bauckham, *Living With Other Creatures*, 111–32.

14. Spanner, "Tyrants, Stewards—or Just Kings?" 223.

"Are you not of more value than they?"

In Matthew 6:26, Jesus asks his disciples a question that strongly implies human preeminence over other animals. The passage is part of his lesson on material possessions where he cautions his hearers against accumulating wealth and serving mammon instead of God. He then reminds his listeners not to fret about their daily bread or clothing, but to trust God for their needs. Within this context, Jesus uses birds as models of creatures who do not worry about their lives or what they will eat because they receive food from their Creator. His rhetorical question, "Are you not of more value than they?" helps his hearers see the birds as witnesses to God's care and sure provision. Unlike some rabbinic texts, which described other animals as useless beings or humanity's servants, Jesus testifies to our similarities as fellow creatures of God who receive God's care.[15]

Unfortunately, people have instead used Matthew 6:26–30 to denigrate other animals. In his commentary on Matthew, Thomas Long writes:

> Jesus, however, is not suggesting that human beings can be like birds or lilies. Indeed, he means to emphasize the difference between birds and lilies, on the one hand, and human beings, on the other. Compared with human beings, birds are insignificant creatures and lilies are trifling weeds . . . If God cares so lavishly for inconsequential creatures, how much more will God provide for human beings.[16]

Such a human-centered interpretation is questionable on several points. First, Jesus does not say that the birds are insignificant, inconsequential, or unlike human beings. Instead, he insists that God feeds every hungry bird, demonstrating that they—like people—are valuable enough to deserve God's individual attention and provision. Second, Jesus's comparison between his hearers and the birds reflects their kinship and shared origins. His words remind his hearers that "they are dependent, like the birds, on the resources of creation without which no one could sow, reap or gather into barns."[17] Finally, the birds teach the disciples and the crowd

---

15. Bauckham, *Living With Other Creatures*, 94–98.
16. Long, *Matthew*, 75.
17. Bauckham, *The Bible and Ecology*, 74.

what it means to depend on God. Jesus strongly encourages his hearers to study the birds because they are witnesses to God's care and a concrete sign that his followers need not worry.[18] Therefore, the birds are not only valuable in God's eyes, they are also essential to Jesus's call to trust the Father more fully.

Another assumption about Matthew 6:26 is that God is the one who values humans more than other animals. However, looking at similar "lesser-to-greater passages" might offer us a different interpretation. In Matthew 6:28–30, Jesus points to the grass of the field, "which is alive today and tomorrow is thrown into the oven," as evidence that God clothes the faithful. He then argues that because the Father provides so lavishly for the grass that humans value only as fuel, his hearers can be assured that God will also provide for them. In Matthew 10:29–31, Jesus makes a similar statement as he cautions his disciples not to fear persecution. As part of his teaching, he asks his followers, "Are not two sparrows sold five for a penny? Yet not one of them will fall to the ground unperceived by your Father." Here again, he reassures his disciples of the Father's provision using "a creature which is valued very cheaply *by humans,* of course on the basis of its limited usefulness to them."[19] In these instances, Jesus's message is that the Father's care extends even to the nonhuman creation that *humans* devalue. Therefore, his listeners should have more faith that God will take care of them as well.

Jesus's debate with the Pharisees in Matthew 12:12 might also be helpful for rereading Matthew 6:28–30. In those verses, Jesus confronts the Pharisees for allowing people to help a fallen sheep on the Sabbath while refusing to help a man in need. He then reestablishes the original intent of the Sabbath as a time of rest that nonetheless permits kindness and care toward humans and animals alike. Jesus's question, "How much more valuable is a human being than a sheep?" prompts the Pharisees to acknowledge the man with the withered hand toward whom they showed no mercy. Here again, the argument is not about creating a hierarchy between people and other animals but is an appeal to common sense and a call to the Pharisees to widen their circle of compassion. Jesus's question implies that willingness to aid a nonhuman animal on the Sabbath should

18. Bauckham, *Living With Other Creatures*, 88.

19. Ibid., 92. Emphasis mine.

lead a person to do the same for his or her fellow humans. The critical issue in this verse is not that God prefers humans to sheep but that the religious leaders do not make room for all God's creatures.

With these examples in mind, we can approach Jesus's words in Matthew 6:26–30 differently. Like the lilies of the field, the sparrows sold in the market, and the man with the withered hand, the birds are of little value to the civilized society around them. They do not grow and harvest food like humans, which was a highly valued practice in that society, and some birds were considered unclean, like the ravens in Luke's version of this story. When viewed in this way, Jesus's question, "Are you not of more value than they?" is not about affirming a hierarchy of God's creatures. Rather, it is a challenge to his followers' lack of faith: "You see that God cares for those whom you value so little. Why would you be surprised that God can take care of those you value more?" Jesus invites his followers to look to creation to better understand how God works in the world. In so doing, they will be better prepared to seek the kingdom.

Even if we forego the above reinterpretation and insist that the above passages affirm human superiority over other animals, it is still crucial for Christians to understand what that difference in value does and does not imply. First, the Greek words for "more value"—*mallon diaphrete*—likely reflect superiority as embodied in the ideal Israelite king.[20] On this point, it is important to remember that monarchy was not God's original intent for the people, and kingship (ideal or otherwise) is not our primary or only model for relating to other creatures. Instead, 1 Samuel 8 describes the Israelite's demand for a king as a rejection of divine leadership. Similarly, Judges 9:7–15 portrays kingship as a power grab by the prideful and undeserving.[21] Even when the Israelites adopted monarchies, kings did not emerge from a royal bloodline, but from within the common community.[22] Furthermore, God expected kings to practice mercy and justice toward their subjects and condemned those who did not. Therefore, even if being of "more value" implies human superiority over other animals, we should remember that such superiority ultimately requires service.

---

20. Ibid., 95.

21. Ellul, *Anarchy and Christianity*, 47–48.

22. Spanner, "Tyrants, Stewards—or Just Kings?" 223.

Jesus's story about a shepherd who leaves ninety-nine sheep to search for the lost one is particularly instructive for understanding "more value" in our relationship to other animals.[23] Economically speaking, leaving ninety-nine sheep unattended to recover only one is financially irresponsible. It would be less costly to forget about that one and pay closer attention to the more valuable remaining investment. Yet, Jesus speaks highly of the shepherd's decision and likens his actions to God's! Therefore, "the first lesson we can take away from this story is that the interests of the 'less valuable' should not be sacrificed to the interests of the 'more valuable'"[24] (see also Matt 5:5; 20:16). Even if we think that humans are more valuable than other animals, that higher status does not give us permission to impose our will over them. If anything, our greater importance may well call us to greater respect and responsibility for their well-being.

"But ask the animals, and they will teach you"

Although Christians can readily cite Scriptures to defend human supremacy, we are less familiar with those Scriptures that directly challenge this view of ourselves. Consequently, many Christians know that God allowed nonhuman animal sacrifice; that a person who killed a nonhuman animal faced less severe punishment than someone who killed another person; and that God delivers nonhuman animals into human hands after the flood.[25] Yet, many are unaware that God later condemns animal sacrifice and, through Isaiah, compares it to killing a human being; likens animal slaughter outside the ritual offering to murder; and promises to make peace between people and other animals.[26] In many ways, our blindness to the diverse perspectives on human and nonhuman animal value in the Bible is like the blindness of Job, who understandably but incorrectly let his situation determine the way he perceived God's intent for creation. Like God's speech from the whirlwind, the Bible beckons us to a broader and deeper understanding of nonhuman animals and greater humility about our place among them.

23. See Matthew 18:12–13.

24. Phelps, *Dominion of Love*, 145

25. Genesis 9:5–6; Exodus 21:12–14, 33; and Genesis 9:2.

26. Isaiah 1:11–13; 66:3; Leviticus 17:34; and Hosea 1:18.

Nonhuman animals are crucial to Job's argument with his friends and especially in his final confrontation with God. Throughout the drama, Job's peers see the nonhuman animal world as evidence that God afflicts the wicked and that Job's disobedience has led to his suffering. Job also uses the nonhuman animal world to describe his suffering, to defend his innocence, and to demand that God explain his condition. When God finally responds to Job, it is clear that God has listened closely to both sides of the argument. God uses the very same animals as examples "to decentre [Job] away from his preoccupation with his own case. He is taken out of himself and given a broader vision of the universe and God's way with it."[27]

Earlier in the book, Job suffers so intensely that he not only accuses God of hunting him like a lion (Job 10:1, 16), he also wonders whether God finds it good to oppress and despise creation while favoring "the schemes of the wicked" (10:3). From Job's limited vantage point, the entire earth "is given into the hand of the wicked" (9:24) because they grow old and powerful, their families prosper, and their domestic animals breed successfully (21:7–13). As Job compares the good fortune of evil people with his inexplicable loss, he decides that God does not defend the innocent but threatens creation. Although Job and his friends base their arguments on what they have observed around them, God mines the nonhuman creation to defy their understanding of the cosmos. Rather than a simplified view of the earth as one in which God punishes wicked people and rewards those who are obedient, Job 38–41 introduces us to a God who creates and sustains creation in ways that Job and his friends cannot begin to know. He and his peers have only an incomplete picture about what makes the world turn. That his affliction results, not from sin or disobedience, but from a test of faithfulness, shows that God often orders the world in complicated and unknowable ways.

God's response confirms that Job and his peers do not have all the answers. Furthermore, it subverts Job's—and our—human-centered view

---

27. Bauckham, *Bible and Ecology*, 45. For examples of God using the same animals to respond, see the lion of 4:10–11 and 10:16, the wild ass of 11:12 and 24:5, the ostrich of 30:29, and the eagle of 9:26 in the whirlwind speech in verses 38:39–40; 39:5–8; 39:13–18; and 39:27, respectively.

of creation.[28] In chapter 39, God describes the divine care for, attention to, and delight in wild animals in ways that contradict Job's sense of safety, control, order, and boundaries.[29] There are deer and mountain goats who give birth beyond the human gaze (39:1–2). There is the wild ass who scorns the city and ignores the human taskmaster. There is the wild ox who rejects servitude and refuses agricultural labor. There is the ostrich who lacks wisdom when nesting but nevertheless laughs at horse and rider. There is the lion and the raven whose appetites only God can satisfy. All of them are created by and provided for by God, even when they live in areas where no humans live. All of them confront Job with the message that "humanity is no longer the measure of the creaturely world."[30]

Perhaps this lesson is best learned when Job is introduced to one of the wildest of the wild, named Behemoth. Although the mythical creature likely represents a chaos monster, it might also refer to the hippopotamus or to "'The Animal' or 'the beast *par excellence.*'"[31] In Job 40:19, God declares Behemoth to be one of the first great acts. God may have made Behemoth just as God has made Job (40:15), but Behemoth is preeminent and the most powerful (40:19). Katherine Dell suggests that God's words from the whirlwind

> serve to overwhelm Job with the wonders of creation, to make him see other possibilities that lie outside a human-centered worldview, hence to displace him from his usual "world," and to teach him more about God's created world, particularly a world that is on the margins of his experience.[32]

The barrage of examples of God's provision beyond human experience puts Job in his place as a fellow creature and shrinks his importance in the drama of creation.[33] The list of nonhuman animals reminds human hearers (and we Bible readers) that an entire world exists in which other creatures are independent of us and in which God takes pleasure.

28. Dell, "The Significance of the Wisdom Tradition in the Ecological Debate," 56.

29. Ibid., 66. See also Balentine. "'Ask the animals, and they will teach you,'" 6.

30. Ticciati, *Job and the Disruption of Identity*, 108.

31. Bauckham, *The Bible and Ecology*, 55.

32. Dell, "The Significance of the Wisdom Tradition in the Ecological Debate," 66.

33. Ibid., 64. See also Bauckham, *The Bible and Ecology*, 51.

Moreover, God's response moves God as well as God's creative desire and sustaining activity to the center where Job and his friends previously placed themselves.[34]

Like Job, the book of Proverbs often places humans in learning positions while elevating nonhuman animals as teachers and models. Tova Forti catalogs the nonhuman animal imagery in this text, including passages encouraging people to adopt the ways of smaller, easily overlooked animals. One such creature is the industrious ant of Proverbs 6:6–11 who is sustained by the food she diligently harvests and prepares. To the lazy person who repeatedly neglects his labor, the ant is both an example of self-sufficiency and a moral agent. According to Forti, the "ways" in this passage "can be taken literally as the trail blazed by the harvest ants carrying their burdens, but it can also be understood as the path of moral rectitude. . . . The warning against laziness calls on the sluggard to imitate the ant's diligence in pursuit of an ordered and upright life."[35] The observation that the ant has no ruler or chief, though incorrect, also conveys a sense of dissatisfaction with hierarchical human society as compared to the ant's apparent freedom.[36]

In Proverbs 30:24–28, the scribe similarly praises the wisdom of ants, badgers, locusts, and lizards, and contrasts their powerlessness with their ability to do great things. The ants are "a people without strength" (30:25), yet they still find and store their food. The badgers are "a people without power," but they make their homes in hard rocks. Like the ant in 6:6–11, the locusts are small but they can organize themselves without a leader or hierarchy. Even the lizard manages to enter royal places where some people cannot go. These detailed descriptions "initiate an educational example that begins with empathy for the tiny creatures, evokes admiration for the instinctual behavior that compensates for their handicap, and finally urges readers to adopt such modes of behavior. The numerical saying . . . calls not for observation, but rather for applying the lessons learned to the human social order."[37]

---

34. Bauckham, *The Bible and Ecology*, 50–51

35. Forti, *Animal Imagery in the Book of Proverbs*, 103.

36. Ibid., 104.

37. Ibid., 118.

Even more importantly, these and other passages in Proverbs suggest the closeness the scribe shared with the nonhuman animal world. Such proximity reveals our distance from other animals whom we are more likely to learn about by reading Wikipedia or watching YouTube than through direct observation. Unlike our technological gaze, which views nonhuman animals as experiments or entertainment, the scribe watchfully records the other animals as subjects with their own lives—not objects for his use. Although their insect and reptilian virtues are useful for human flourishing, he does not devalue them into mere resources.

"You Save Human and Animal Alike"

In addition to Scripture passages that suggest humans are more important than animals, and those that elevate nonhuman animal value, there are still others that make no distinctions between the two. In the striking example of Ecclesiastes 3:18–21, the scribe reflects on God's judgment, saying:

> I said in my heart with regard to human beings that God is testing them to show that they are but animals. For the fate of humans and the fate of animals is the same: as one dies so dies the other. They all have the same breath, and humans have no advantage over the animals; for all is vanity. All go to one place; all are from the dust and all turn to dust again. Who knows whether the human spirit goes upwards and the spirit of animals goes downward to the earth?

This passage testifies to the shared essence of human and nonhuman animal beings as ones who are made of dust, who return to dust, and whom God animates with a common breath. Like Job, the text also exposes the limits of human knowledge and directly challenges the belief that humans are more privileged than other animals.[38] In describing the profound connection between people and other animals, he goes so far as to call humans "animals" as a comment on our shared creatureliness before God. In a few short sentences, the scribe echoes some of the key creation-as-community motifs found in Genesis 1 and 2.

38. Dell, "The Significance of the Wisdom Tradition in the Ecological Debate," 64.

Similarly, the book of Psalms uses equally descriptive imagery as Ecclesiastes and avoids distinguishing between human and nonhuman animal importance before God. For example, Psalm 104 beautifully describes how all creation—cattle, wild asses and goats, young lions, people, and even plants—depend on God's nourishment. In verses 27–30, in particular, the psalmist describes how *all* of God's manifold works look to God for every good thing: "When you hide your face they are dismayed; when you take away their breath, they die and return to their dust. When you send forth your spirit, they are created" (Ps 104:29–30). Likewise, Psalm 33:13–15 speaks of God watching over all humankind and all the earth's inhabitants, and professes that God "fashions the hearts of them all and observes all their deeds" (Ps 33:15). Meanwhile, Psalm 36:6 reminds us that the Lord saves "humans and animals alike," and Psalm 145 speaks of the Lord showing compassion toward all creation, raising up all who falter, and satisfying the wants and needs of all living things (Ps 145:9, 14–15). The confession of these and other passages sprinkled throughout the Psalms is one of shared vulnerability before and mutual dependence on the Creator. At several points, the psalmists envision human and nonhuman animal beings sharing the same origins and the same destiny before the One who delights in us all, regardless of our species.

While there are many other Scriptures that emphasize mutuality among human and nonhuman animals, two additional examples should suffice. In the book of Jonah, human and nonhuman animals both respond to and participate in God's purposes. When Jonah refuses to bring news of God's judgment to Nineveh, God enlists a whale to help him comply. After Jonah calls the city's inhabitants to repent of their wickedness, the king issues an edict stating that "no human being or animal, no herd or flock" was to eat or drink water (Jonah 3:7). From that moment, everyone from the king himself to all the domestic animals begins fasting and wearing sackcloth. God, in turn, shows mercy to the entire city and relents, which ironically makes Jonah quite unhappy. When God explains the decision to Jonah, God credits the obedience of the vast number of people *and* the many animals with averting the disaster (4:11).

The second and final example, from Luke 13:18–19, brings Jesus, the birds, and the disciples back to the fore. In this parable, Jesus compares God's kingdom to a mustard weed that grows and attracts the wild birds.

The most obvious meaning of this passage is that the people who come into the kingdom are like the "wild birds" of Matthew 6:26 (*ta peteina tou ouranou*), who are worth little to human society but are nonetheless cared for by God. Though neighbors may reject the disciples, they still have a witness for the world and are still important to God's work. Yet, a second layer of meaning may also be present. Perhaps Jesus is also saying that even birds will have a place in the kingdom alongside their human counterparts. Given the biblical examples above, this way of reading the text is quite possible.

Conclusion

What this brief survey shows is that the Bible does not allow a simple yes or no answer to one of the common questions asked of Christian vegans, vegetarians, and advocates for nonhuman animals. The easy answer that questioners often assume to exist simply is not there. Instead, Scripture contains multiple perspectives on differences in value between people and other animals, all of which elevate nonhuman animals far above the status they currently have in our society. At minimum, we can conclude that "the Bible treats animals as others who are really different and yet similar enough to merit kindness and to be included in God's plan for the world."[39] This alone should give us pause as we decide how to think theologically about animals and how to interact with them on a daily basis.

---

39. Webb, *On God and Dogs*, 20.

5

Didn't Jesus Eat Lamb? The Last Supper and the Case of the Missing Meat

Stephen H. Webb

JESUS PREACHED ABOUT LOST sheep, but did he eat one during his last meal with his disciples—and if he did, why don't the Gospels mention it? You can scour the secondary sources, the countless commentaries on this meal, and you would have a hard time finding any reference to what was served other than bread and wine. This is the most famous meal in history, and over a billion people reenact it every Sunday. Yet the menu is an historical blank page. Nevertheless, any time a Christian vegetarian makes the case that the only meat Jesus was known to have eaten is fish, someone is sure to reply that Jesus ate lamb at the Last Supper. In my experience, many people think that the lamb is missing in the text due to simple oversight. The Gospel writers just chose not to mention the obvious. After all, if the Last Supper was a Passover meal, then the main course would have been slaughtered at the temple, taken to the upper room, and served by Jesus to his disciples before he turned to all of the theological business involving the bread and the wine. Even those scholars—and they are probably in the majority—who doubt that this occasion coincided with Passover rarely if ever raise any doubts about whether lamb was served. It was supper, after all, and Passover was in the air, along with the scent of savory mutton cooked in herbs and spices. Besides, wouldn't the disciples have been hungry that night if they didn't eat meat?

I want to argue that the Gospels neglected the lamb because *it was not there.* That is the simplest hypothesis, but it also makes the most sense. Far from being an accidental omission from the text, its presence at that dinner would have spoiled what Jesus was trying to say. Indeed, I want to defend the following rather bold claim: the missing lamb is a crucial ingredient for understanding not only the meaning of the Last Supper but also the significance of Jesus's life, death, and resurrection.

Of course, it is only natural that Jesus's followers remembered his words from that evening more than his dishes. This was his farewell banquet, consumed on "the night when he was betrayed" (1 Cor 11:23), so the mood was somber, intense, and even frightening; every word counted, not every bite. Nonetheless, Jesus made sure that the disciples did not entirely forget what they ate that night. Jesus was approaching his death and wanted to leave his followers with food for thought so that they would remember him in a special way. Food gives us life, so what better way to remember Jesus's life? To accomplish this purpose, Jesus focused on bread and wine, the basics of any meal—the essence, we could say, of food itself, except that bread and wine leave out the category of meat. What, however, if that was the very point that Jesus wanted to make? What if meat and all that it symbolizes could not have contributed anything to Jesus's message? And if the bread and wine were enough to dramatize the death that Jesus faced as well as to anticipate the joy that his resurrection would create, why would meat have been present at the meal at all?

Think about it: Would the disciples have been full of lamb, the epitome of ritual sacrifice, just at the moment when Jesus was instituting a new sacrifice of his own body and blood? And if lamb had been present at the very meal during which Jesus defined his ministry, wouldn't he have commented on it as he explained his upcoming death? How could he have ignored such a great potential symbol simmering right in front of his face?

To answer these questions, we need to consider what kind of meal Jesus shared with his disciples and what kind of ritual he instituted to help them understand his approaching death. We should first of all pause to dismiss out of hand all skepticism that attributes the Last Supper to the later, post-resurrection imagination of the disciples. Jesus spent his entire teaching career using food to convey his message's power. People followed him to be fed both physically and spiritually. In the ancient world, meals were a time for reestablishing familial and social boundaries, but Jesus used meals to critique retrograde taboos and erect new orders of socially inclusive belonging. Jesus's ministry was wrapped up in food practices that provoked the religious and political authorities.[1] Even if we bracket the question of his divine status, Jesus demonstrated a mastery of symbolism as well as a deep awareness of the provocative consequences of his teachings and the disturbing range of his prophetic power. He did not need to be God to figure out that his days were numbered and that his disciples needed a graphic way of recollecting the meaning of his death. What better way to bring his ministry to its culmination?

Next we need to address the crucial question of whether the Last Supper was a Passover meal, because if it was, that would seem to lend credence to the assumption that lamb was served. The most succinct answer to that question is: nobody knows. It is absolutely inscrutable. Indeed, the dating of the Last Supper is one of the most complex puzzles in the New Testament. Scholars have debated this question for over a century, and the closest thing to a conclusion that they have reached is to agree that no satisfactory conclusion is possible. And, as anyone knows who has debated in high school or served on a jury, an inconclusive result is itself a kind of conclusion, since a case that has not been proven must be abandoned, even if there is some evidence in its favor.

The evidence in this case is all over the place. The earliest reference to the Eucharist is from the Apostle Paul in 1 Corinthians 10–11. Scholars debate whether these chapters are unitary or composite, but they agree that they were written around 53 or 54 CE, which places them only twenty years or so after the famous meal. Paul addresses the problem of meat bought from the market that has been sacrificed to pagan idols. His concern is to keep dietary issues from dividing the fledging church. He is especially incensed that some believers were bringing food from home that they refused to share with others (1 Cor 11:21). The Lord's Supper was dividing the rich from the poor and the well-fed from the hungry.

---

1. There is little question among scholars that Jesus ate fish, but the ancients did not consider fish to be on par with meat that had (more) blood in it. For the social context of eating fish in Jesus's day, see Webb, *Good Eating*, 129–32; 223–26.

Paul does not explicitly say that meat was the divisive issue, but he does frame his discussion of Corinthian rudeness and gluttony in the context of meat-eating and idolatry. Meat was a rare commodity for most people in the ancient world. If some Christians were bringing food to church and hoarding it in separatist cliques, it makes sense to speculate that this food was meat. Only meat has the capacity to bring out our worst expressions of ravenous hunger, and thus meat frequently spawns tension over who gets the biggest cut and the best pieces. The smell of meat would have overwhelmed the aroma of the bread and wine and distracted from the meager and frugal meal that bread and wine represent. When Paul reminds the Corinthians that they have "homes to eat and drink in" (1 Cor 11:22), he is obviously not saying that they should not eat anything in church. He is telling them to leave certain foodstuffs at home, and the most likely candidate for the kind of food that was causing all the trouble is meat.

The full social and theological context behind the Corinthian fellowship troubles is hard to figure out from the text, but Paul is clearly dealing with an eating practice that is both a real meal and a charged symbolic ritual. In giving the Corinthians the proper way to celebrate the Lord's Supper, Paul writes that he is handing on to them what he received from the Lord. What he goes on to describe is "the earliest account of the Last Supper, and there is a prima facie case for its authenticity."[2] Most likely, he received this tradition from Peter, from whom he learned about the details of Jesus's ministry not too long after his conversion. What Paul describes is a Jewish meal custom used for solemn occasions that Jesus has modified to meet the specifics of his lesson for the disciples. The bread is blessed and broken before the meal and the cup is passed around "after supper" (1 Cor 11:25). That still leaves open the question of what was served for dinner, but since Paul does not describe a Passover meal, lamb, which was expensive and ordinarily saved for special occasions like Passover, is unlikely to have been the main course.

Paul does not portray the Last Supper as a Passover meal, but the Gospels complicate the question. Luke 22:15 records Jesus saying, "I have eagerly desired to eat this Passover with you before I suffer," although that saying is not decisive since Jesus could have been speaking in terms of the

---

2. Jones, *Study of Liturgy*, 195.

season of Passover and not the specific meal, or he could have moved up the meal with his disciples in anticipation of his growing conflict with the religious authorities. Moreover, it is rarely pointed out that the wording of Jesus's statement in Luke raises the question of whether he even partook of the dinner that evening at all, since he goes on to say that "I will not eat it until it is fulfilled in the kingdom of God" (Luke 22:16). It seems that Jesus might have distributed the bread and wine without consuming either of them; perhaps he was fasting in preparation for the night ahead.[3] In any case, Jesus looked forward to the transformation of the temple from an abattoir to a place of God's perfect presence "not made with hands" (Mark 14:58), and the New Testament follows his eschatological vision of Edenic peace by portraying the new Jerusalem as a city where the life of Christ has replaced the temple altogether (Rev 21:22).

The chronology of those crucial three days is difficult to establish with any confidence. All the early Christian texts seem to agree that Jesus was crucified on a Friday afternoon, but they disagree about when Passover was celebrated that year. The Gospel of John puts the events leading up to the crucifixion before Passover (John 13:1). For John, the crucifixion coincided with the slaughtering of the lambs at the temple, which vividly underscores how Jesus's death took the place of the temple sacrificial system. Scholars used to dismiss John's chronology out of hand, but recently some have been defending John's rootedness in the earliest Jesus traditions.[4] If John's chronology is correct, and given the fact that the lambs were slaughtered the day before Passover was kept, it is highly unlikely that lamb was eaten at the Last Supper. Unblemished male yearlings were the only sheep sacrificed at Passover, and with all of Israel busy in their transportation, preparation, and slaughter, it is unlikely that mutton from rams or ewes (which does not taste nearly as good) would have been available in the markets.

Let us suppose, however, that the Last Supper was either a Passover meal or, more likely, a quasi-Passover meal (a meal that reflected some

3. Horton Davies draws the conclusion from Luke that Jesus might not have eaten the meal, though he does not speculate that Jesus might have been fasting. See Davies, *Bread of Life and Cup of Joy*, 84. I have also benefitted in this essay from Welker, *What Happens in Communion?*

4. See, for example, Bauckham, *Testimony of the Beloved Disciple*.

Passover elements since it was held so close to the actual Passover date). Does this mean that Jesus ate lamb? Actually, if the Last Supper was a Passover meal, then the evidence against Jesus eating lamb is even stronger, because Jesus makes no reference to the lamb while contemplating his own death. Jesus could have turned meat into a staple of Christian remembrance, elevating lamb to a required sacramental means of worshipping God, but he did not. He also passed on other foods uniquely related to the Passover ritual, like the unleavened bread and the bitter herbs. He focused instead on the bread and wine, which are not unique to the Passover meal at all. The Passover meal looks back to the liberation from Egypt but also forward to the journey ahead. It is a meal that was originally supposed to be eaten in haste (Exod 12:11), and there must have been something of that same urgency in the Last Supper. The difference, of course, is that the Israelites were readying themselves to escape from Egypt, while Jesus was preparing himself to walk straight into a trap—and one that was being set by one of his own followers. Betrayal and not just danger was in the air. He was going to be handed over, which makes his passing of the cup and plate all the more poignant. This was no time for looking back to the bitterness of the Egyptian bondage, nor was it time for a festive dinner with meat at the center of every plate. Clearly, Jesus was taking the spotlight off of the lamb and putting it onto himself. He was giving his disciples his body and blood; the lamb was rendered worse than redundant. Its presence would have been a contradiction of the central action of the meal. Its presence would have said that there was still value in the old system—and said it at the very moment when Jesus was saying something utterly new.

For these reasons, the lamb was most likely eliminated from the meal altogether. Besides, there were plenty of other food items to eat. Deuteronomy 8:8 describes the bounty of the promised land as including plenty of water and wheat, barley, figs, grapes, olives, pomegranates, dates and honey (but not meat!).

To put my position on firmer ground, however, we need to think more carefully about what Jesus was trying to do during that meal. Jesus preached through meals, and his message was one of a coming divine judgment that would disturb this world to its very core by replacing it with a peaceable kingdom of godly rule. He understood that transformation requires challenging and painful changes. Rather than excusing people from being responsible for their sins, he held up forgiveness as the foundation of true community. These themes dominated his teachings and were at the forefront of his message at the Last Supper. He was about to be betrayed but had no anger in him. He was about to be killed but gave his life voluntarily, hoping to reconcile the whole world to God. He was thinking about all people, of course, since his message was a universal one, but he was particularly concerned for his followers, who were given the task of continuing his ministry. He wanted to leave them with symbols that cemented their relationship to each other and to God. He wanted to give them his own life so that they could have him, after his death, in the most intimate and appropriate form.

Bread and wine accomplish those goals perfectly. Bread is the most basic food, we could say, since people can almost live on bread alone! In any case, in the Middle East and for much of the West, bread provides the foundation of any meal, and as such it is the most basic gift of God for human nourishment. Bread sustains us physically just as Jesus has the whole world in his hands. The *Didache* ("The Teaching of the Twelve Apostles"), one of the earliest church documents, describes—in an image used in many hymns and liturgies—the bread as being "scattered over the hills" and then gathered to become one loaf, just as the church is one body. The fact that bread can be broken before it is distributed only heightens its symbolic representation of unity and new life. (The brokenness of bread finds a parallel in the natural association between wine and blood.) Bread is also a symbol that unites the Old and New Testaments, especially in the Gospel of John, which talks about Jesus as the bread of life. Indeed, some scholars have speculated that the Jewish people at the time of Jesus expected the Messiah to reenact the miracle of the manna, which is precisely what Jesus did in making his body the substance of that supersubstantial bread of the angels (Ps 78:25).[5]

Wine also has appropriate religious connotations. Wine is the symbol of festivity and joy, and every happy occasion should evoke gratitude to the divine. More than a symbol, however, wine literally provides life-enhancing properties that not only alleviate thirst but also elevate the spirit. If the bread recalls the body of Christ given to us on the cross, the

---

5. See Pitre, *Jesus and the Jewish Roots of the Eucharist.*

wine lifts up the glad tidings of the resurrection and the sanctified community poured out by the Holy Spirit.

Both elements also represent a gradual and peaceful transformation of nature, and this is a crucial point that is lost if reconciliation between God and humanity is made the exclusive focus. The Eucharist demonstrates how God's gifts are also gifts of nature—or, put better, how God gives to us through nature. We can come to God only as a people who also, at the same time, learn how to come together in a human community that is working its way toward peace with all of nature. Bread is possible only as the product of planting, harvesting, and baking, while wine is both an incentive and a reward for labor. Wine, too, from the cultivation of the grapes to their fermentation, is a product of careful and delicate interaction between humanity and nature. Animals, however, ordinarily must be killed for meat to be eaten, which is surely why their death is so carefully regulated in the Old Testament. When meat is produced on a large scale, that regulation becomes more necessary but harder to monitor and enforce. So many lambs had to be "processed" at the temple, for example, that the scene there must have been chaotic with flowing blood and overworked priests. In any case, cutting a lamb's throat is never a peaceful act, and if it is impossible to imagine Jesus doing it, then it should also be hard to imagine Jesus contributing to a system that did it in a rushed and messy manner. The point I want to make, however, is that lambs could function as a sacrifice for human wrongdoing only because we can identify with them and thus imagine them as innocent substitutes for our waywardness. At the Last Supper, Jesus was putting himself forward as a substitute for this substitution and thus an end to violence as the means of reconciling humanity and God.

So what led Jesus to this meal of bread and wine? Here I want to draw from the portrait of Jesus's last days presented by Bruce Chilton in his book *Rabbi Jesus*. Chilton puts Jesus's food ministry at the center not only of his theology but also of his conflict with the Pharisees. The Pharisees are easily and unfairly caricatured as self-righteous busybodies, but in fact they were motivated by some of the same passion that guided Jesus. Both Jesus and the Pharisees were bold and aggressive in challenging the spiritual milieu of their day, but they looked for solutions in different directions—the Pharisees toward renewed ritual purity and Jesus toward a new moral community. Jesus enjoyed arguing with the Pharisees and typically called them out for emphasizing outward, visible actions over inward, invisible intentions. To make his point, he was often rather cavalier about Jewish food rituals. He did not go out of his way to provoke and annoy, but he let it be known that meals were primarily about restoring broken fellowship rather than, as with the Pharisees, reinforcing family traditions and social boundaries.

According to Chilton, Jesus initially thought the kingdom of God would come in the form of a new Jerusalem temple, and only after his plan to reform the temple failed did he come to understand that he himself was to replace the temple sacrifices. His plan to reform the temple, however, was nothing less than a religious revolution. He was guided by a prophecy found in Zechariah 14, which states that the end will come when all the families of the earth bring their offerings to this sacred place. Zechariah also predicts that this culmination of worship will bypass the priests and traders by accepting as holy all the cooking pots across the land of Jerusalem and Judah. Zechariah pictures this event happening during the feast of Sukkoth (or the Festival of Booths), a seven-day family ritual. For Zechariah, the coming kingdom of God will turn this family feast into a truly universal meal.

If Chilton is right, Jesus was pitted against the temple authorities from the very beginning of his ministry. Just as the Pharisees had no intention of permitting family customs to be transformed into inclusive and universal practices, the temple authorities tolerated no challenge to their symbolic role at the center of Jewish life. The temple, we must remember, was, in Chilton's words, "an incredibly complex barbecue pit."[6] The altar, according to Josephus, was twenty-five feet high and seventy-five feet wide, and the priests were skilled in keeping the fire going and the meat cooking, but they had to be even more careful to accomplish their tasks in strict accordance to the rules of Leviticus. In the temple's great court, vendors turned a profit selling animals to those who had brought none of their own.

Zechariah was especially critical of the vendors and saw no place for animal sellers in the time when God would restore the temple practices to their proper holiness. Jesus shared Zechariah's passion enough to act on it

6. Chilton, *Rabbi Jesus*, 217.

in a way that sealed his fate with both the religious and political authorities. He visited the temple at Sukkoth and staged a symbolic demonstration of its corruption and need for transformation. Jesus drove out those selling animals and overturned the tables of the moneychangers. He even drove out the sheep and the cattle. These were obviously symbolic acts. Nobody was hurt—the money could easily be picked up and the animals collected and returned. In fact, Jesus was careful to tell those selling doves to take them out of the temple; opening the cages would have subjected the birds to all of the chaos and confusion.[7]

Chilton argues that after the temple incident, Jesus was a wanted man. Chilton thinks that the Last Supper was a change of direction in Jesus's ministry (from reforming the temple to replacing it with himself), while I think it not only continues his earlier teachings but brings them to a fitting culmination. Either way, this supper was the final event that sent him to the cross. By identifying the wine with his blood and the bread with his flesh, he was overthrowing the temple in his words, just as his earlier action symbolized the destruction of the temple with his deeds. "The radical meaning of his words was that wine and bread replaced sacrifice in the Temple, and that was a direct challenge to established ritual practice in Israel."[8] The Eucharist was the new altar, with Jesus himself functioning as the lamb.

In sum, the Lord's Supper enacted a logic of sacrificial substitution that rendered the lamb not just redundant but insufferable. Compared to Christ, no sacrifice is worthy of the name. Animals are freed to be what they are rather than what the ritual system turned them into. The idea that the bloody death of a mere animal could redeem us looks, in retrospect, absurd. Jesus died to save humans from their sins, but his death also saved in a quite literal way countless animals from being killed in our place. Judaism did away with the temple sacrifices when the Romans destroyed the temple in 70 CE, but this custom continued in pagan Rome. Indeed, it took the Christian church several centuries to stamp out animal sacrifices as part of its mission to preach the good news of the cross. Christians did

7. For this insight about the doves, I am in debt to Alexis-Baker, "Violence, Nonviolence and the Temple Incident in John 2:13–15," 94.

8. Ibid., 255. I disagree with Chilton's suggestion that mutton would have been cheap and plentiful in the market leading up to Passover (ibid., 256).

not always follow through on the logic of this religious revolution—they could treat animals as poorly as anybody else—but buried deep within the Christian message was a compassion for animals that would express itself in the behavior of many of the saints and in the meatless diets of the monks. But that is another story.[9] The case of the missing meat can now be closed, and we can keep it closed when we learn to approach every meal as a thanksgiving without animal sacrifice.[10]

9. See Danielle Nussberger's chapter in this volume for some of that story.

10. For my prior reflections about this topic, see Webb, "Whatever Happened to the Sin of Gluttony," 243–50; *On God and Dogs*, 155–67; and *Good Eating*, 141–59.

6

Didn't Jesus Eat Fish?

Andy Alexis-Baker

Ever since I became a vegetarian/vegan, other Christians frequently ask me, "Didn't Jesus eat fish?" The assumption behind the question, of course, is that refusing to eat animal flesh contradicts Jesus's own practices and that vegetarianism cannot be linked to Christ's example or teachings. Most of Jesus's interactions with fish in the Gospels revolve around using them for food. He cooks fish for his disciples (John 21:9–13), multiplies fish and bread to feed a large crowd (Matt 14:13–21; 15:32–39), helps his disciples catch fish (Luke 5:4–6; John 21:6–8), and tells Peter to retrieve a coin from a fish's mouth (Matt 17:24–27). In a single passage in Luke, Jesus even eats a piece of fish after the resurrection to prove his return in bodily form (Luke 24:42–43).

Do these passages mean that advocating Christian-based vegetarianism inadvertently charges the Prince of the peaceable kingdom with the sin of violence? Is Christian vegetarianism a form of arrogance considering that even the Son of God ate, captured, cooked, and distributed fishes? In this chapter, I will examine six perspectives on Jesus's actions in the above passages. Some of these perspectives can be held together, but for the purpose of clarifying different moral reasons, I will keep them separate. This array of views shows that, like many of the biblical and theological questions about vegetarianism, veganism, and animal advocacy more broadly, interpreting these texts is not always as straightforward as the asker presumes.

Option 1: Jesus Ate Fish; Therefore I Can Too

One way to interpret the Gospels' fish stories is to claim that it is fitting for the Prince of Peace to eat fish. This position is often based on the argument that nonhuman animals are created for human use. Therefore, it makes perfect sense that Jesus would use fish to feed himself and others because that is animals' purpose. Jesus participates in dominion and shows us what it means. Thus, since Jesus ate fish, we can too. Some Christians go even further, claiming that Jesus's fish-eating entitles us to eat any animal.

However, as other chapters in this book argue, dominion should be understood as service, not domination.[1] This view also presupposes an unbiblical view of other animals' purpose, which is not for human use, but for God's glory.[2] The third problem is the one-to-one correspondence this view presupposes but upon which it does not follow through. To consistently follow Jesus's diet suggests that the only animal we have grounds to eat is fish, which is still too broadly construed. In Jesus's time, water creatures without fins and scales were expressly off limits to all Jewish sects. Therefore, we can cautiously assume that Jesus likely did not eat catfish, shrimp, crab, and shellfish, just as he did not eat pigs, ducks, rabbits, and other land animals that Mosaic dietary laws explicitly or implicitly forbade (Lev 11 and Deut 14). Consequently, "seafood" is far too large of a category for a truly biblical "pescatarian," and the adage "What would Jesus eat?" actually prevents Christians from eating much of the popular Western menu.

---

1. In particular, see chapter 1, "What About Dominion in Genesis?" and chapter four "Doesn't the Bible Say that Humans Are More Important than Animals?"

2. See chapter 10, "What's the Point of Animals?"

Option 2: Luke Does Not Mean for Us to Read Jesus's Eating Fish Literally

A second option, which Gerald O'Collins, SJ, argues, is that because Luke tells the story of Jesus's appearance in different ways, we are not meant to read Jesus's fish-eating in Luke 24:42–43 literally.[3] In Acts 1:4, Luke describes the disciples eating with Jesus, whereas in Luke 24, only Jesus eats.[4] In Acts 10:41, Peter says that the disciples ate and drank with Jesus, but in Luke 24, Jesus does not drink anything. Even more problematic, according to O'Collins, Luke's account conflicts with Paul's description of the resurrected body, which does not in any way eat or drink (1 Cor 6:13).[5]

O'Collins maintains that the differences between Luke and Acts are like the difference between the ascension as described in Luke 24:50–51 and the ascension story in Acts 1:6–11. In Luke, Jesus lifts his hands and blesses the disciples and while doing so ascends into the heavens. Meanwhile, in Acts, Jesus converses with the disciples, but he does not bless them or raise his hands. Instead, a cloud takes him into the heavens where two men tell his followers not to be dismayed. The "simpler story" in Luke, O'Collins states, "forewarn[s] the reader not to interpret in a wooden literalistic way" the more elaborate ascension story in Acts. Luke "self-corrects" himself.

Because O'Collins's purpose was not to argue about the propriety of eating fish, *per se*, but about the nature of the resurrected body, the nonliteral reading doesn't really help us with the image of Jesus being presented in Luke 24 or in other parts of the Gospels in which Jesus feeds fish to others. Nevertheless, it is important to remind ourselves that Luke 24:42–43 at least is not necessarily to be taken in a rigid fashion.

---

3. See O'Collins, "Did Jesus Eat the Fish?" 65–76.

4. O'Collins follows the majority of commentators in interpreting Acts 1:4 as "eating with." However, *synalizomenos* can simply mean "gathered together" or more likely here it is an alternate spelling of *synaulizomenos*, "staying with" (NRSV), which better suits the context of Acts 1.

5. Many commentators do not think that Paul means to say that the resurrected body will not have a stomach or eat food in 1 Corinthians 6:13 since he is talking about the pre-resurrected body and death. Yet it is hard to avoid the conclusion that the destruction of the stomach and food that Paul mentions does not have some bearing on the resurrected body that he calls "spiritual" in chapter 15.

Option 3: The Texts Are Part of an Early Christian Debate

Ever since the early church, there have been Christians who have claimed that Jesus abstained from animal flesh. For example, a second-century Gospel called the *Gospel of the Ebionites* depicts Jesus informing his disciples, "I do not earnestly desire to eat meat with you this Passover."[6] Many early Christian authors thought the disciples ate only plant-based food as well. Eusebius mentions a long tradition that claimed that Jesus's brother James "drank no wine nor strong drink, nor did he eat flesh."[7] Accounts like these may have been inspired by the widespread practice of abstaining from nonhuman animal flesh during Christianity's earliest centuries. Clement of Alexandria (150–215 CE) and Tertullian (160–220 CE) argued that Christians have good reasons to abstain from eating meat provided that abstention is not tied to various heresies.[8] Some unorthodox thinkers argued that Christians should not eat animal flesh because the material world is evil and because flesh-foods cling to the soul, keeping a person from full spiritual salvation. However, not all Christian-based abstention devalued the material world or linked the practice to salvation. According to Augustine (354–430 CE), many orthodox Christians did not eat animal flesh because abstaining was cheaper, because it aided a "tranquil life," and because they wanted to respect "weaker" Christians who thought flesh-eating was sinful.[9]

This brief history shows that questions around eating animal flesh were part of early Christian disagreements about Jesus's relationship to the material world. Thus, some scholars suggest that Luke portrayed Jesus eating fish to oppose those groups who thought Jesus's physical body was an illusion and who abstained from flesh-foods. Although John's Gospel shows Jesus cooking fish for the disciples, no other writer shows him eating one. We should also consider that Jesus called the disciples away from their fishing occupations—which they eagerly abandoned—both before

6. See Epiphanius, *Panarion* 30.22.4. Greek text and English translation in Klijn, *Jewish-Christian Gospel Tradition*, 76.

7. See Eusebius, *Ecclesiastical History*, 2.23. Clement of Alexandria said that Matthew "used to make his meal on seeds and nuts and herbs, without flesh meat," (*Christ the Educator*, 2.1.16).

8. See Tertullian, *On Fasting*.

9. See Augustine, *On the Morals of the Catholic Church*, 33.

and after the resurrection (Matt 4:18–20; Mark 1:16–20; Luke 5:1–11). In John, Jesus asks Peter, "Do you love me more than these?" which probably refers to Peter's fishing occupation.[10] Thus, Norm Phelps maintains that regardless of whether Jesus thought fishing was cruel or simply a distraction, "he insisted that they choose between fishing and preaching."[11]

Option 4: In a Fallen World, Sometimes We Have to Kill Other Animals to Survive

In his book *Animal Theology*, Andrew Linzey claims that "it can sometimes be justifiable to kill fish for food in situations of necessity," such as survival.[12] Jesus and the disciples must have faced such situations. But because there is a presumption in Christianity for life and against taking it, those of us who can live without recourse to violence should and must do so, even if there are borderline cases where violence and killing are necessary in a fallen world.

However, it is not immediately apparent in the text that Jesus and his disciples needed to eat fish to survive. They were never in danger of starving. Even when Jesus was tempted in the wilderness, he did not hunt the wild animals that were with him, despite his severe hunger. Instead, he stayed among them and inaugurated the peaceable kingdom when non-human and human animals would not destroy one another.[13]

Although Linzey's argument does not apply to the biblical texts, it is relevant to the rest of us. People such as the Inuit and Aleut, who live in places like the Arctic, and Western people who have severe food allergies must depend on animal flesh. Most Westerners don't need animal flesh to survive though.

10. On this see Phelps, *The Dominion of Love*, 120–22.

11. Ibid., 122

12. See Linzey, *Animal Theology*, 134–35.

13. See Bauckham, *Living With Other Creatures*, 111–32.

Option 5: Jesus's Diet Is Not Normative for Us

A fifth possible reading is that Jesus's fish-eating is not normative for us. We must carefully identify the practices in Jesus's ministry that we are called to follow and imitate. We are called to follow his example in forgiving others (Eph 4:32; Col 3:13); loving one another (John 13:34; 15:12; 1 John 3:11–16); serving others (Mark 10:42–45; Matt 20:25–28; John 13:1–17); giving our lives and loving as he did (Eph 5:1); accepting suffering for doing the right thing (1 Cor 4:9-16; 11:1; Phil 3:7–17; 1 Pet 2:21); and suffering the world's hostility to the barrier-breaking, nonviolent kingdom (Matt 10:38; 16:24; Luke 14:27). There is no place in the New Testament, however, that calls us to imitate Jesus in terms of itinerancy, dress, modes of transportation, or diet.

Ironically, instead of providing Christians with greater freedom, the question, "Didn't Jesus eat fish?" threatens to bind us to practices that Jesus did not explicitly direct us to imitate. Unlike the passages immediately above, there is no place in the Gospels where Jesus commands us to eat, catch, and cook what he did—except of course in the celebration of the Last Supper, in which he replaced animal flesh with plant-based food. Consequently, the question, "Didn't Jesus eat fish?" is akin to the church asking people who wear shoes, "Didn't Jesus go barefoot?" or asking people who drive cars, "Didn't Jesus walk or ride a donkey?" Asking what Jesus wore, rode, and ate as a way to determine what we should wear, drive, and eat today establishes rules that Jesus himself did not establish. However, being vegetarian does not conflict with or diverge from following Jesus in the ways that Jesus expects. Indeed, as we will see below, abstaining from fish *in our context* can be a way to faithfully perform the things Jesus *does* call us to do, given the threat facing our oceans due to mass consumption of fishes.

Option 6: The Modern World Requires a Different Approach to Fish-Eating than the Biblical World

A final interpretative option is to appeal to the cultural differences and similarities between Jesus's time and place and our own.[14] In the first

14. For another perspective like the one I am developing, see Clough, "Why Do

century, people rarely ate animal flesh; at most, people ate animal flesh a few times a year during an annual festival. Fish, on the other hand, was more available. The Roman occupation dramatically increased the accessibility of fish in Palestine, seen in the increased number of fish bones at archaeological sites during the period of Roman occupation. The Romans had large fleets to fish the Mediterranean Sea, built some *piscina* pools to breed fish in aqua farms, such as those at Caesarea Maritima and Tel Tanninim,[15] and imported large amounts of fish to Palestine. Roman fish sauce was as common then as is ketchup in American households today. Nevertheless, fish was not so available or cheap to have in daily meals. At most an average Jewish person could acquire a few bites of fish a week for their Sabbath meal.[16]

Although there are similarities between the Roman fishing industry and today's practices, the widespread industrialization of our current system and the damage it has done to our seas is nowhere near the same scale. Roman vessels could not capture anything close to the *one hundred tons* of sea animals that a single modern ship can process *per day*. Likewise, residents of the Roman Empire could not eat as much fish as we can now or eat them as cheaply. Modern industrial fishing has done something the Roman Empire could never have done: it has depleted the ocean such that for every ten fish that were in the ocean a hundred years ago, there is now only one.[17] That means 90 percent fewer of the world's sea creatures are now swimming the oceans, and the numbers are expected to continue shrinking. Bluefin tuna, Chilean sea bass, orange roughy, and Atlantic halibut, among others, may well go extinct within the next few years,[18] and some estimates predict that most of the world's fisheries will utterly collapse by the year 2050 due to extinction from overfishing, which kills not only the animals that Westerners normally eat but also those we do

---

Some People Eat Meat?" 32–40, available also on his research page at http://chesterrep. openrepository.com/cdr/researcher?action=viewResearcherPage&researcherId=5281.

15. See Stieglitz, "A Late Byzantine Reservoir and Piscina at Tel Tanninim," 54–65.

16. On the fishing industry in Roman Palestine, see Safrai, *The Economy of Roman Palestine*, 92–93.

17. See Clover, *The End of the Line*, 18, 37, 62.

18. "IUCN Red List of Threatened Species." Online: www.iucnredlist.org. See also "Last Act for the Bluefin."

not, like turtles and dolphins. This is not a far-fetched alarmist call. Local areas fisheries have already collapsed, such as the 1992 collapse of the fisheries in Newfoundland, Canada, which led to a moratorium on fishing and a loss of forty thousand jobs, devastating the local economies. The cod population there has never recovered despite the government ban on catching them instituted in 1993.[19]

Today, 40 percent of fish sold in US supermarkets come from aqua farms, which need several pounds of wild fish to produce one pound of farmed fish. That is unsustainable and only quickens the extinction rate. Moreover, aqua farms breed diseases that threaten wild fish populations. For example, farmed salmon have developed a lethal virus called "infectious salmon anemia" due to the overcrowded conditions in the farms, and they also are very prone to flesh-eating sea lice. Millions of the afflicted salmon have escaped into open waters, causing the virus to spread among salmon populations in the northwestern United States and southwestern Canada, which could wipe out the wild population.[20] The same virus threatens the salmon runs in Maine.[21] One response to these aqua farms and to industrial fishing is to catch one's own fish. However, it is nearly impossible to get fish that is not tied to this industrial system since even the fish used to stock ponds and lakes usually come from commercial farms.

The industrial-scale fishing industry has not only devastated aquatic life, but it has also destroyed human livelihoods and communities. After utterly depleting fish populations in European zones, fleets of European, Chinese, and Russian fishing boats have moved their operations to Northwest Africa to meet Western consumers' appetites. The rampant overfishing that ensued has since crippled local African economies, triggering a flood of immigrants into Europe. In 2007, over thirty-one thousand Africans tried to reach Spain's Canary Islands on nine hundred boats. Approximately six thousand of those people died or disappeared.[22] In a *New York Times* exposé on the issue, Ale Nodye, a Senegalese man who braved the dangerous waters, said that his primary reason for leav-

---

19. See Arms, *Servants of the Fish,* and Harris, *Lament for an Ocean.*

20. Yardley, "Knot of Worry Tightens for Fishermen."

21. See Molyneaux, *Swimming in Circles,* 101–38.

22. See Lafraniere, "Europe Takes Africa's Fish, and Boatloads of Migrants Follow."

ing home was that "there are no fish in the sea here anymore."[23] This is a common refrain. In a United Nations' news report on African migration, another Senegalese man who attempted the perilous voyage, Pape Seck, explained, "Look here on the beach. You can see all of these men, with their boats, and how few fish we catch after a whole day's efforts. There's no living off the sea these days. The fish are gone, and hard work won't change that."[24] Both of these men, like thousands of others, were caught and deported back to their homes to face the worsening conditions. Meanwhile, commercial fishing continues.

Fish, once a source of food and survival for the local populations of North Africa, has now become so rare and expensive that poor people can hardly access them. Meanwhile, Europeans and African governments have colluded by buying and selling fishing rights for industrial-scale fishers, while poorer Africans are left with a choice of migration to the richer nations. Yet even this arrangement is unsustainable. According to a European Commission report, many of the North African fish are also near extinction due to overfishing. As Moctar Ba, a scientific researcher in Mauritania and West Africa, said, "The sea is being emptied."[25]

"What Did Jesus Eat?" Or "What Should Jesus's Followers Do?"

Given the impact the fishing industry has on our world today—an industry whose destruction far surpasses that of Jesus's time—how should Christians decide whether or not to eat fishes? Should we decide by the food Jesus ate? Or is it reasonable to decide in light of the practices that Jesus called us to imitate? Among Jesus's explicit ethical instructions, he commanded his followers to live lives of love for our neighbors, service to others, and sacrifice—even suffering—for what is righteous and just. Abstaining from fish flesh in today's world is one way in which we can live out Christ's example given the damage that eating fish does to God's creation, both to the sea creatures and to human beings. Even if the Gospels do not call upon us to imitate Jesus in what we eat, when our diets destroy

23. Ibid.

24. IRIN, "West Africa: Poverty, search for status driving migration to Europe." Online: http://www.irinnews.org/report.aspx?reportid=73079.

25. Ibid.

human communities in other parts of the world, create economic havoc, and threaten people's (and other creatures') survival, then I contend that choosing not to eat any fish is one way that we can live out Christ's love, service, and sacrifice. How can it ever be wrong to expand our love and service to an ever widening circle of creatures and to change our own habits, even ones we believe we are free to practice, when those habits harm others?

Efforts to preserve the vast diversity in the world's oceans and lakes have a strong biblical basis in the Noah's ark story. God commanded Noah to conserve every kind of animal by building an ark and bringing aboard two of every creature.[26] We face a similar situation when it comes to the world's oceans. Ironically, Noah did not need to protect the fish from the rising tides of water.[27] Today, however, the rising tide of human violence threatens animals that the floodwaters in the Genesis story did not. Would Jesus call upon us to make efforts to safeguard the world's ocean creatures? If so, how would we do that? One thing would be to stop eating them. Other actions would be to help stop the pollution that destroys vast stretches of reef and other fish habitat and creates giant dead zones in which no creatures can survive. Another possibility is to support with time and money those groups helping to rescue and save the rich diversity that so awed the psalmist: "Here is the great immeasurable sea, in which move creatures beyond number" (Ps 104:25, NEB). Conservation work is an effort against human pride, which risks nullifying such passages. Like the work of Noah, this work is not optional but mandatory in a world like ours. And it can and should start on our plates first and foremost.

Conclusion

Out of the six options I have listed, I think that the first option is too simplistic and limited to be much use for interpreting the texts and for Christian life. The rest of the options, which can be held together, all have strengths and weaknesses that help us read the passages and live more faithfully. Particularly when we see that Jesus called us not to imitate his

26. Southgate, "The New Days of Noah?" 251.

27. I owe this insight on Noah and fish to Stephen Webb, who commented on an earlier draft of this chapter.

dietary habits but to love and serve others, not only does expanding that love and service to other creatures make sense, but in our world where fishing is destroying the oceans and human communities, it is a way to concretely practice that which Jesus calls us to imitate.

7

Does Christian Hospitality Require that We Eat Meat?

Laura Hobgood-Oster

TODAY WAS THE SIXTY-EIGHTH day with temperatures reaching above 100 degrees in central Texas during the summer of 2011 (actually, we were hitting 100 before summer technically even started). Couple that heat with an "exceptional drought" stage—twenty inches below normal rainfall for the previous twelve months—and this landscape is crunchy, brown, and increasingly scary. Everyone appears to be a bit dazed, even the native animals who have made their home here for centuries. Living in this intense, hot, dry place requires new ways of thinking about hospitality. But this summer, one of the hottest and driest on record, if not *the* hottest and driest, has required hospitality at an unprecedented level.

With so little water around, humans and other animals alike try to find it wherever they can. So we decided to extend our normal wildlife outreach to include more water holes, compost scraps, and birdseed than usual. As a result, a community of critters gathers in the shady space in the middle of our backyard (our yard borders on a small protected area that includes a cave with endangered species). A cardinal pair comes and goes, splashing in the birdbath; squirrels lie relaxed under the trees, finding some relief in the cool ground cover; deer finish off scraps and a big tub of water each day; hummingbirds find the red blossoms of the salvia; sparrows tend a nest on an eave under our porch cover; various tree lizards come and go. And then there are the cottontails, precious little rabbits born under the shade of a live oak tree right behind our porch.

But the cottontails complicate our seeming oasis of hospitality. If one member of the community is determined to eat another member, hospitality becomes, well, less hospitable. And since my primary community activist work involves dog rescue, the dogs who inhabit my yard and house are not the best hosts for cottontails.

Early one Sunday morning one dog was nosing around the ground cover in the center of the backyard with too much intensity. Up she popped with a screaming baby rabbit in her mouth; the race was on for me to get her to drop the bunny. She did eventually let go, but not before breaking the bunny's back leg. So I headed out to Wildlife Rescue with this ten-week-old cottontail. They took the bunny in, and hopefully this little critter will live. Of course, I cannot be upset with my dog who tried to eat the bunny; that is nature at work. Some animals eat other animals; some humans eat other animals. Such is the world. Or might Christian hospitality call that assumption into question?

Indeed, what does this whole series of events and the resulting realization of the way the world works suggest for Christian hospitality? And, more specifically, what does it mean in light of the question, "Does Christian hospitality require that we eat meat?" I think that, somehow, cottontails, canines, humans, and a dry, crunchy, steamy backyard in central Texas come together with the prophets and saints in Christian history when we pose those questions. And as the dogs (now cloistered in the house and relegated to leashes until all the baby bunnies hop away) might respond, Christian hospitality is not easy, and it requires rethinking some of the ways we live.[1] Before delving into that question specifically, it is helpful to provide a background in Christianity and hospitality. Why and how is hospitality such a central component of the Christian tradition?[2]

1. Later in the essay, I will address the question of real animals and of not projecting human ideas on them; anthropomorphism can be dangerous if taken to certain extremes with other animals.

2. Three studies have been published in the last fifteen years on Christian hospitality; they provide excellent overviews: Russell, *Just Hospitality*; Pohl, *Making Room*; and

The Roots of Radical Hospitality in the Christian Tradition

> Then the righteous will answer him, "Lord, when was it that we saw you hungry and gave you food, or thirsty and gave you something to drink? And when was it that we saw you a stranger and welcomed you, or naked and gave you clothing? And when was it that we saw you sick or in prison and visited you?" And the king will answer them, "Truly I tell you, just as you did it to one of the least of these who are members of my family, you did it to me." (Matt 25:37–40)

As Amy Oden points out, "the word 'hospitality' has lost its moral punch over recent centuries."[3] But since hospitality is almost indisputably a central tenet of Christianity, the possibility of reclaiming that punch is always present. A quick glance at early Christianity's sacred texts—from those of the Hebrew Bible to those of the Christian Apocrypha and of the eventual New Testament—reveals how pivotal this radical form of welcoming was in the tradition's development.[4]

The Hebrew Bible, coupled with the hospitality culture of the ancient Mediterranean world, significantly influenced ideas about hospitality for this new religious movement. In the Torah, foundational ideas for hospitality are evident. Abraham and Sarah, understood by many as the "parents" of the Israelites, set the standard in Genesis 18, which recounts the day when three strangers wander past their home. Abraham immediately runs to greet them and together they prepare a marvelous feast for the strangers. In addition to that passage, the list of texts related to hospitality in the Hebrew Bible is lengthy: Genesis 19, Joshua 2, 1 Kings 17, Leviticus 19, Exodus 23, and more. Some accounts even extend hospitality to ani-

---

Oden, *And You Welcomed Me.*

3. Oden, *And You Welcomed Me*, 15.

4. The Christian canon (the New Testament as it was later designated) was not formally established until the fourth century CE. Before that time, and even subsequently, numerous texts were central to the religious life of different Christian communities. In other words, during the first three hundred years of Christianity, many texts not included in the New Testament had a major impact on the belief systems that were developing in this new religion. While many of these are no longer extant, others are. It is necessary to take all of these texts into account, not just those that eventually formed the canon.

mals. For example, Genesis 24 and 29 emphasize the urgency of watering camels and sheep from the few wells in the dry landscape. The flocks were even watered before the people drank from these wells.[5]

The earth is also portrayed in the Scriptures as a place where God offers hospitality to all creatures, not just to humans. Arguably, Psalm 104 provides the most powerful example. Here "birds of the air have their habitation" by the streams, and the springs give "drink to every wild animal." All of the creatures look to God "to give them their food in due season." This theme is echoed throughout the Bible.

Ancient Mediterranean culture as a whole was a complicated world of hospitality, which was at times given and at other times strategically withheld. It was a reciprocity culture, so the guests welcomed were frequently influential community members who might benefit the host in the long run. But ancient Greek literature also included the idea that travelers might be divinities in disguise, so one should extend a hospitable hand to any wanderer. Still, Hellenistic forms of hospitality were most often connected with reciprocity culture—or, as Lactantius (d. 325), an early Christian thinker, framed and criticized it, "ambitious" hospitality.[6]

As Christianity developed, notions of hospitality within the tradition challenged both the Hellenistic practices of "ambitious hospitality" and Jewish laws categorizing clean and unclean. For Christians, ideal hospitality became something quite distinct from those practices. Matthew 25, quoted above, and Luke 14 express central ideas of the more radicalized notion of hospitality that became integral to Christianity. What was it that changed and made Christian notions and practices of hospitality more radical? New Testament scholar John Dominic Crossan calls it a shift to "open commensality."[7] The table of fellowship, which both physically enacts and simultaneously symbolizes ideas of hospitality, was open to everyone. In a culture where notions of clean and unclean, pure and impure marked societal relations, Christianity challenged those dichotomies. So in Matthew 25, even those who would have been considered unclean (sick, naked, imprisoned) were welcomed to the table. Indeed, Jesus himself ate

---

5. For more on this topic, see Hobgood-Oster, "For Out of the Wells the Flocks Were Watered."

6. See Pohl, "Responding to Strangers," 91.

7. See Crossan, *Jesus*, 54–74.

with sinners, with those who were considered unclean, and with women, who were always potentially unclean (see Matt 9; Mark 2; Luke 5). Jesus elaborates on this concept with the parable of the Great Feast, recalled in Luke 14:

> When you give a luncheon or a dinner, do not invite your friends or your brothers or your relatives or your rich neighbors, in case they may invite you in return, and you would be repaid. But when you give a banquet, invite the poor, the crippled, the lame, and the blind. And you will be blessed, because they cannot repay you, for you will be repaid at the resurrection of the righteous. (Luke 14:12–14)

This description of guests at a feast firmly establishes the framework for hospitality practices. In this parable, Jesus reinforces the radical notion that the host should never expect repayment from the guests. It is no longer reciprocity; hospitality is now the end in itself without reward.

But are animals ever included when Jesus sits at a table or is involved with hospitality in general? In the canonical texts, they are, though admittedly rarely. In Matthew 15 and Mark 7, Jesus acknowledges that even the dogs below the table deserve crumbs. In other passages (Mark 6; Luke 12), Jesus recognizes that God provides sustenance for the entire creation. All are to be welcomed and fed. So animals are at least considered, even if not a focus of the canonical texts.

While early Christianity obviously approaches hospitality from a different and radical perspective, nothing is that simple, and Christians continued to debate notions of hospitality throughout history. Unfortunately, and indeed tragically, many Christians did not always practice or even approach this ideal. As people connected with the tradition grew in power and influence, those who were different or other were often not welcomed and were even deliberately excluded or killed (consider the Inquisition, the Crusades, witch trials, and executions). Still, the ideal remained and was often exemplified by the saints.

Several stories of saints highlight practices of hospitality for even the very least among them—other animals. Saint Jerome reportedly opened his monastery to an injured lion, and they lived together for the rest of their lives. Saint Francis of Assisi, patron saint of ecology, invited animals back into the sanctuary to reenact the scene of Christ's birth in which animals hospitably shared their home with the baby Jesus. And Saint Martín de Porres, a sixteenth-century Peruvian saint, invited diverse animals to eat with him. For example, one of St. Martín's fellow monks observed the following scene in the monastery's kitchen:

> At the feet of St. Martín were a dog and a cat eating peacefully from the same bowl of soup. The friar was about to call the rest of the monks in to witness this marvelous sight when a mouse stuck his head out from a little hole in the wall. St. Martín without hesitation addressed the mouse as if he were an old friend. "Don't be afraid, little one. If you're hungry come and eat with the others." The little mouse hesitated but then scampered to the bowl of soup. The friar could not speak. At the feet of the servant St. Martín, a dog, a cat, and a mouse were eating from the same bowl of soup.[8]

This story of St. Martín offers a powerful transition to reconsidering specific issues about hospitality and eating in Christianity. So I come back to the overriding question: does Christian hospitality require that we eat meat?

Earth Community, Meat-Eating, and Hospitality

> Better is a dinner of vegetables where love is than a fatted ox and hatred with it. (Prov 15:17)

Hospitality is only complete when everyone gathered around the table, in whatever form that table might take, is at peace and unafaid. That might seem like an obvious statement, but when considered in the context of nonhuman animals and humans, it becomes much less obvious and much more complicated. And when one intersects this aspect of hospitality with the history of eating in Christianity, layers pile upon layers. Where do these intersections emerge?

As mentioned above, one of the ways early Christianity began to differentiate itself from Judaism focused on the rules of eating, particu-

8. García–Rivera, "Come Together," 48.

larly those rules associated with clean and unclean, pure and impure. For Judaism, Leviticus 11 and Deuteronomy 14 categorize those animals who are clean and therefore can be consumed and those who are unclean and therefore must be avoided. While these laws still allowed for the slaughter of animals as food, they restricted how that practice would take place and which animals could be eaten. Just as some animals were clean or unclean, so were some humans. Laws delineating with whom one could eat also revolved around these categories. Early Christianity recalled consistent accounts of Jesus challenging some of these laws, particularly when the issue was inclusivity around the table.

Other accounts in the New Testament grapple directly with the issue of animals as food, or at least that seems to be the case. The book of Acts, for example, describes the Apostle Peter who, while on the roof praying, becomes hungry and asks for food to be prepared. While waiting, he fell into a trance and had a vision:

> He saw the heaven opened and something like a large sheet coming down, being lowered to the ground by its four corners. In it were all kinds of four-footed creatures and reptiles and birds of the air. Then he heard a voice saying, "Get up Peter; kill and eat." But Peter said, "By no means, Lord; for I have never eaten anything that is profane or unclean." The voice said to him again, a second time, "What God has made clean, you must not call profane." This happened three times and the thing was suddenly taken up to heaven. (Acts 10:11–16)

Interpretations of this vision vary widely, and even Scripture states that Peter was "greatly puzzled" about what to make of it. As always, understanding the text's context sheds light on the particular passage.

Peter's vision is preceded by the story of Cornelius, a centurion and a Gentile. Cornelius had a vision as well; in it he was told to invite Peter to his home. Now this was problematic because it was unlawful for Peter to go into a Gentile's home since Gentiles were considered unclean. Moreover, for a Jewish rebel like Peter, who would take up arms to defend Jesus in the Garden (only to be rebuked), going to the home of an occupier or collaborator with that regime was even more problematic (the far right and far left rarely eat together at home if they are strangers). Nonetheless, Peter accepts the hospitality, enters Cornelius's home, and proclaims that "God has shown me that I should not call anyone profane or unclean" (Acts 10:28). Eating with the uncircumcised is the issue; the vision of the animals is the vehicle to present that complicated purity rule. As Chris Miller states in his study of this passage:

> Peter's apparent violation was entering the house and enjoying the hospitality of people whose only unique feature was their uncircumcision. Reading the charge of "eating with the uncircumcised" as if it meant "Peter ate pork" is ill-advised and is a weak foundation for saying that the vision refers to food.[9]

As a matter of fact, the text does not mention what food was served. It could be assumed that Cornelius, quite familiar with the laws of his Jewish neighbors since he is described as a devout man, would have served kosher food to Peter.[10] Most telling, perhaps, is the final section of this chapter in Acts where Peter begins to share the good news with Gentiles. The vision, it seems, is not about eating animals; rather it is about extending hospitality to all humans. While animals in sacred texts are often real animals and should be considered as such, in this particular case it seems that in Peter's vision animals symbolized human categories that exclude other humans from community.[11] One response of early Christians to this broader Mediterranean culture of exclusivity and more specific encounter with Gentiles was to offer table fellowship and thus hospitality to everyone.

That does not mean, however, that early Christians were not struggling with the issue of whether or not to eat meat. Decisions about eating meat automatically connect to situations of hospitality in that historical context. In letters to churches in Corinth and Rome, Paul warns that nothing is inherently unclean and that one must not injure one's brothers or sisters "by what you eat" (Rom 14:14–17; 1 Cor 8:8). These statements from Paul, combined with a particular interpretation of Peter's vision

---

9. Miller, "Did Peter's Vision in Acts 10 Pertain to Men or the Menu?" 316.

10. For more on this argument, see ibid., 302–17.

11. For more on animals as real or as symbol, see the introduction to (and some subsequent sections of) Hobgood-Oster, *Holy Dogs and Asses*.

cited above, have been used in tandem to stress that Christians should eat meat in order to fulfill the obligations of hospitality.

But the answer is not that simple, and other Christian practices reveal different paths. So, in contrast to the ideas that Paul expressed, the next four centuries witnessed the development of various ascetic practices in Christianity. For a variety of reasons, many of the desert ascetics abstained totally from meat, preferring to eat and share vegetables instead. Reports on the life of Pachomius (ca. 290–346)—frequently considered the father of desert monasticism—state that he embraced this practice after he had found a spot in the wilderness in which to live:

> The thing pleased him and he settled down there, growing some vegetables and some palm-trees in order to feed himself or some poor man of the village or again some stranger who should happen to pass by in a boat or on the road.[12]

Generations of desert ascetics have followed Pachomius's pattern. The *Historia Monachorum*, a late fourth-century work that describes ascetic life, reveals a desert of "flourishing agricultural projects—gardens of vegetables for the use of the monks and their visitors, green plants growing which were never there before." And hospitality is extended to the city of Alexandria, where larger communities of people in need of food resided; "whole ship-loads of wheat" were shipped to Alexandria "because it is rare for anyone in need to be found living near the monasteries."[13]

While this pattern of hospitality offered by formal religious communities (monks and nuns) extends into the Middle Ages, the usual suspects are not always rigid when sharing vegetarian fare. In a fascinating study on Saint Francis of Assisi and meat-eating, David Grumett points out that even Francis ate meat. This saint, so often equated with living in total harmony with animals, would "eat of everything set before him" when he was a guest.[14] Not only when they were guests in wealthier homes, but also as mendicants who lived by begging for their food, Francis and his brothers were often confronted with the choice to eat meat. Grumett suggests that, when placed in its historical and religious context, Francis's decision

12. Oden, *And You Welcomed Me*, 155.

13. Ward, *Lives of the Desert Fathers*, 13.

14. Grumett, "Vegetarian or Franciscan?" 452.

to occasionally eat meat becomes clear and the saint is able to place this choice in relationship to evangelism. For one thing, during the twelfth and thirteenth centuries when the Franciscan order was established and growing, many new sects that were deemed heretical were associated with vegetarian diets. At the least, it would have been a dangerous claim to associate with a new group. It seems that Francis placed his emphasis elsewhere.

One final and intriguing note before turning to the question for the contemporary audience is that animals also offered hospitality. Paul the Hermit, an early Christian ascetic, had lived alone in the wilderness for years. One day Saint Anthony Abbot, who later became the patron saint of animals, decided to visit Paul. A series of animals then began to welcome him. First, a wolf met him and led him to Paul's cave; then a crow flew in with bread for the two men to share (Paul informed Anthony that the crow brought his food to him each day); finally, when Anthony returned for a second visit and found that Paul had died, two lions helped him bury the hermit. This series of hospitality stories is mirrored in other accounts as well.[15]

With all of these precedents in mind, it is appropriate to turn to the question of hospitality and eating meat for contemporary Christian practice. Obviously, throughout its history, Christianity changes depending on the context while taking into account the tradition and the Bible. But the idea of radical hospitality, in whatever age and in whatever form, remains. The practice changes depending on the context, but the underlying idea is still intact. As Christine Pohl claims, "Hospitality to the least, without expectation of benefit or repayment, remained the normative commitment by which each generation measured its practice."[16]

In the twenty-first century, then, how must this radicality be practiced, and to whom should hospitality be extended? In other words, who are "the least"? From my study of Christian history and from my experiences with the best of Christian practices (there are indeed not so welcoming versions and incidents in Christian history), I have concluded that when any guest appears, expected or unexpected, similar or quite dif-

15. For a more elaborate description and additional sources, see Hobgood-Oster, *Holy Dogs and Asses*, 63–80.

16. Pohl, *Making Room*, 35.

ferent, Christianity insists on an open table and an open door. Christianity compels an invitation to come to safety, to find the calm harbor where life will be nurtured. Central to this is a requirement on the host to welcome, with no requirement on the guest either to reciprocate or to (necessarily) accept everything that is offered.

In an increasingly interconnected world marked by a period of massive extinction of species, it is also imperative to extend Christian hospitality beyond humans. Again, this is not unprecedented in Christian history; it is a thread throughout. As claimed above, radical hospitality requires an entirely new relationship with all creatures and, following through with the metaphor (and reality) of the feast, that relationship must embrace the notion of a safe place at the table for all of the guests present. Just as it did in early Christian practice, this extension of hospitality means subversion in a society that thrives on walls and barriers. In the first and second centuries, those walls were constructed between Jews and Gentiles, rich and poor (as they still are), male and female (as they still are). But one wall that is even more daunting than in past generations is that erected between species. Like the barriers between different classes and races and sexualities of humans, the barriers between species are harmful and even deadly. Subverting these categories can be a dangerous and unstable position to take. I contend that this is particularly the case when one breaks down the binary of human/animal.

It is also a dangerous way to practice hospitality. As Jacques Derrida claims, the seemingly benign ideas of hospitality must be complicated: "Hospitality, therefore—if there is any—must, would have to, open itself to an other that is not mine, my hôte, my other, not even my neighbor or my brother."[17] John Blevins elaborates on the ideas here by reminding the reader that the French term *hôte* does not have an equivalent in English. It subsumes the meanings of guest, friend, enemy, and host into one term. The key moment of hospitality, according to Derrida, is when the guest (whoever that might be) shows up, uninvited and unexpected. The guest may well be the enemy, or may be another species, but hospitality requires an open door.[18]

17. Derrida, "Hospitality," 363.

18. For more on this, see Blevins, "Hospitality Is a Queer Thing," 105–10.

The only way to break down this wall is to remove meat from the table. Why? If there are any "guests" who are not safe, then hospitality is incomplete. And if all the sentient beings who share the world are guests, then all must be safe from the most basic of threats—death at the hands of the host. Yes, this is a radical and potentially revolutionary suggestion, but one that is compelled by the current state of both meat production in the developed (and developing) world and of all animals outside of this domesticated system of factory production as well. When animals who are still in their natural habitats are threatened with death at the hands of humans, and domesticated animals are raised in inhumane conditions only to be killed and eaten, then the host is anything but hospitable.

While the host is then called to welcome guests without question, what is required of the guest? Recall the shift away from reciprocity in early Christianity; the guest was no longer expected to repay the host in some way. In Greek and Roman hospitality cultures, the idea of a grateful response was central: the host expected some benefit. Significantly, this concept changes in early Christianity. Once again the text from Luke 14 is crucial—"do not invite your friends or your brothers or your relatives or your rich neighbors, in case they may invite you in return, and you would be repaid." Early Christians were frequently in a marginal position. They were vulnerable. Hospitality was requisite for survival in a sometimes hostile environment before Christianity was recognized as a legal religion; therefore, no repayment was ever expected—hospitality was a gift with no debt accrued.

But, again, what of the idea of being grateful? If, for example, the host offers meat to the guest, is the guest required to eat all of the food provided? Here it is helpful to return to some interesting ideas that Derrida suggested. He claims that "absolute hospitality requires that I open my house and that I give place not only to the foreigner, but to the absolute, unknown, anonymous other, and that I let them arrive, and I let them take place without asking of them either reciprocity or even their names."[19] In this scenario, no requirement is placed on the guest. Indeed, the requirement is placed on the host to provide appropriate sanctuary for the guest. To clarify this idea, thinking about nonhuman animals is helpful.

19. Derrida, *Of Hospitality*, 25.

Humans are omnivores, as are some other animals; but many other animals have very particular food requirements. There must be adequate bamboo for pandas to survive, oceans full of krill for blue whales, lush grass for cattle, plentiful nectar and pollen for bees. Providing hospitality entails offering the appropriate welcome, a gracious welcome that includes food that will nourish the guest. A host would not offer a hot dog to a cow. When we "host" other animals, we consider carefully what they naturally eat and plan accordingly. The burden—and in Christianity this is a positive burden willingly accepted—is not on the guest, but on the host.

Along these lines, the question that is sometimes posed is whether or not a guest, when offered meat, should graciously accept and eat it. From the perspective of Christian hospitality, the answer might be situational, but can certainly be no. Particularly in the United States, where confined animal feeding operations supply most of the meat that is eaten, there are myriad reasons not to eat (or to serve) meat. The system of meat production itself is so inhumane to animals that it is offensive to consider that meat as worthy fare for a guest. It highlights the lack of hospitality humans offer to other animals on the planet. But in any setting, a guest can graciously decline to eat meat while sharing in the rest of the feast provided. As a matter of fact, in some settings this might even relieve the burden of the host, who can then save that food for another meal. Still, the essential foundation of this idea is that radical Christian hospitality is incumbent on the host without any requirement placed on the guest.

This idea is further illuminated by Letty Russell, who celebrates what she calls "riotous difference." She claims that God "just does not like uniformity in human life and community and in nature."[20] The current system of industrialized factory farming focuses on uniformity. The diversity of species is sacrificed for a standardized production system that functions as an assembly line of chickens, pigs, and cows (with farmed fish being added rapidly). In addition, the plant-based agricultural system that supports factory farming narrows the range of plants to corn and soy, significantly decreasing biodiversity.[21] It has been suggested that agriculture is the enemy of biodiversity; while that might be a harsh assessment,

---

20. Russell, *Just Hospitality*, 53.

21. For specific figures, see http://www.epa.gov/agriculture/ag101/cropmajor.html.

it is easily recognized when examining industrialized plant and animal production.[22]

So, what does this mean for other animals who, most certainly, eat each other? A major and valid critique of some animal activists is that animals are no longer allowed to follow their own nature and eat other animals. The notion of hospitality suggested here does not necessarily extend to placing restrictions on the ways that other animals live; rather it is a suggestion that humans (as the quite powerful host) provide a safe sanctuary for all of the guests, no matter how different or other.

Still, I am intrigued by the eschatological vision of Isaiah 11, which others in this volume point to but which is worth quoting again here:

> The wolf shall live with the lamb, the leopard shall lie down with the kid, the calf and the lion and the fatling together, and a little child shall lead them. The cow and the bear shall graze, their young shall lie down together; and the lion shall eat straw like the ox. The nursing child shall play over the hole of the asp, and the weaned child shall put its hand on the adder's den. They will not hurt or destroy on all my holy mountain; for the earth will be full of the knowledge of the Lord as the waters cover the sea. (Isa 11:6–9)

This is the vision of complete, revolutionary, radical hospitality never attained—but always sought. It is the vision expressed in stories of Jesus when he eats with those who are unclean. In essential ways, it is also Peter's vision, accepting of all people by joining them at the table.

So, does Christian hospitality require that we eat meat? In our little backyard oasis, do the dog and the bunny lie down together? No, and I would not expect them to do so. But in a world where wild rabbits have very few places left to graze, Christian hospitality requires a safe harbor. And in a world where animals are treated like inanimate objects in a factory until they are slaughtered and wrapped in cellophane to be purchased from the meat counter in a huge grocery store, Christian hospitality requires that such meat be banished from the table. And until there is rain in

---

22. This claim can be found in environmental studies literature broadly; for a recent report, see Picone and van Tassel, "Agriculture and Biodiversity Loss," 99–105.

central Texas, water and bread and seed must be provided for the guests, however unexpected, who knock at my door.

8

Doesn't Romans Say that Vegetarians Have "Weak Faith"?

Michelle Loyd-Paige

When I became a vegan in 2005, I didn't do so because of poor health, food allergies, or the influence of people within my social circles. Although I knew a few people whose doctors had told them to eat less animal-based protein, at the time, none of them had made any changes. All of my friends and family ate meat. In fact, meat-eating has continued to be a significant part of their lives, particularly in my African American family and church. So when I shifted away from eating animal flesh, I expected my fellow Christian brothers and sisters to give me a lot of push-back at common meals and potlucks. To my surprise, however, they were willing to accommodate me and were even eager to try "the greens that didn't have any meat." Even more affirming is the fact that my pastor recently presented a month-long sermon series on creation care, during which he encouraged the congregation to eat more plants and less animal flesh.

Having encountered little resistance within the African American church, my first encounter with significant opposition to veganism occurred within a college setting that is predominately white.[1] The ques-

1. At Calvin College, however, I have also met other Christian vegans among the faculty and students whose support prepared me for questions others might ask about

tioning I have encountered in that setting has not been an attempt to understand why I became a vegan, nor has it been a curiosity about what I eat; even less is this questioning about how I survive traditional African American social and celebratory gatherings that involve food. The questions and resistance I have encountered have been an attempt to persuade me to accept as true that it is impossible to be a Christian and embrace a vegan lifestyle—an idea based on vague notions that supposedly derive from Scripture.

Before I became a vegan, I paid little attention to what the Bible did or did not say about what I put on my plate. My change to a vegan lifestyle, therefore, did not begin as a response to a particular interpretation of Scripture. Instead, my change began when I participated in a church-sponsored Daniel Fast and culminated several months later when I began to wonder what happened to the rest of the chicken as I stood in line at a chicken wing fast-food restaurant.[2] The only biblical passages about dietary choices I had ever heard were related either to the Jewish dietary restrictions mentioned in Leviticus 11 or to the words Peter heard in his vision: "Get up, Peter, kill and eat" (Acts 10:13). Because I am not Jewish, I did not think that the Levitical guidelines pertained to me; and when people cited Acts 10:13, the challenge was always spoken as a lighthearted prayer by a family member, who was not thinking with theological depth but merely wanting to start eating from a bountiful table. Even though my family was at first concerned that my new way of eating would mean that I would become malnourished, no one in my circle of family and friends ever brought up Scripture to either challenge or support my dietary choice. Challenges to the possibility of my being a vegan *and* a Christian would come from a stranger who contacted the college where I work.

In March 2011, writer and speaker Carol J. Adams came to Calvin College and spoke about veganism. My office—the Office for Multicultural Affairs—was one of several sponsors for Carol's two-day lecture series. We were pleased to support her because she would speak about the intersections of diet, sexism, and racism, as well as the connection (or lack thereof) between how we view God and how we view animals. As one of

becoming vegan.

2. For a more comprehensive telling of my vegan journey, see my essay "Thinking and Eating at the Same Time."

the sponsors, the Office for Multicultural Affairs was listed on the promotional posters generously placed around campus. A parent of a student had read the poster and was upset that the college (and my office) would support a lecture that so actively promoted veganism. The parent sent an angry e-mail to the college president, whose administrative assistant in turn passed the e-mail on to me for a response. The parent did not think that a person could be healthy if she did not eat meat, nor did the parent think that a person could be both a Christian and a vegan. Furthermore, the parent thought that I, as a college representative, was being irresponsible by affording an opportunity for someone to come to a Christian campus to promote a vegan lifestyle. This parent maintained that God created animals for humans to eat and that if we did not eat them our health would be compromised. The person even cited a news story about a French vegan couple who had recently been charged in the death of their eleven-month-old child, who had only been breastfed, as evidence of the human need for animal-based protein. The overriding sentiment was that a Christian who became vegan was far less faithful than one who continued to eat other animals. In response to this parent's concern, I shared Paul's words: "Those who observe the day, observe it in honor of the Lord. Also those who eat, eat in honor of the Lord, since they give thanks to God; *while those who abstain, abstain in honor of the Lord and give thanks to God*" (Rom 14:6; emphasis added).

What Does Paul Say in Romans 14?

However, in using Romans 14 to respond to the challenge to Christian veganism, I recognize that Paul says things in that chapter that could be taken out of context as proof-texts against being Christian and vegan. After all, somebody might ask, "Doesn't Paul say in Romans that those who do not eat meat have a weaker faith?" It is a strange question because, according to Paul, what we choose to eat should line up with our convictions: "I know and am persuaded in the Lord Jesus that nothing is unclean in itself; but it is unclean for anyone who thinks it unclean" (Rom 14:14). As Christians it is natural and good to anchor our convictions to the biblical text; however, we must clearly understand a particular passage before we use it to prove a point we are trying to make. We have to examine not only what Paul said, but also why he said it. Additionally, it may be helpful to review what meat is, what it symbolizes, and whether or not Paul was talking about a pattern of eating found among believers in the twenty-first century.

In his letter to the Romans, Paul responds to reported conflict and misunderstanding about fasting, eating, and observing certain days. In chapters 1 to 13, Paul traverses a wide range of theological issues, including salvation by faith alone, being dead to sin, life through the Spirit, being living sacrifices, and submission to authorities. In Romans 14 and 15, Paul speaks of charitable living, the duty of self-sacrifice, and rejoicing in a universal gospel. In the fourteenth chapter, where it would seem that he associates eating only vegetables with weaker faith, he is writing about conscientious differences of opinions. More particularly, Paul writes about whether or not it is proper for Christians to eat food (meat, in some translations) that had been offered to idols.

In this context, Paul says, "Some believe in eating anything, while the weak eat only vegetables" (Rom 14:2)—and "anything" refers to eating food, including meat, that had been offered to idols. This is important because in addition to animal flesh, vegetables were offered as sacrifices to Greco-Roman deities. The issue here is idolatry and what constitutes participating in such worship. Paul touches on this in 1 Corinthians 8 as well. In his appeal to the Corinthians, he addressed both those who were worried ("their conscience being weak") about eating food offered to idols and those who were not worried. To those worried about eating food that had been offered to idols—which often included animals, but clearly included vegetables as well—Paul's goal was to remind them that there is only one God. The idols that pagans worshiped had no real power over their lives, and so anything they regarded as food—meat or vegetable—that had been offered to idols had no religious significance. Paul instructed those Christians who could, with a clear conscience, eat animal flesh that had been offered in pagan temples not to create barriers that would prevent new converts from experiencing the fullness of salvation. To offer vegetables or meat from an animal that had been sacrificed in a pagan temple to someone who earnestly thought that by doing so they were honoring a pagan idol was to create a "stumbling block" (1 Cor 8:9). Yet, Paul did not say that all believers could eat whatever they desire.

Paul's central point in both 1 Corinthians and Romans was that idols are not gods at all but demons (1 Cor 10:20); therefore, we should eat to the glory of the one and only God.

Moreover, one of the central issues in these texts is how we address one another when our viewpoints differ so dramatically. So Paul encourages each group to extend grace to the other: "Those who eat must not despise those who abstain, and those who abstain must not pass judgment on those who eat; for God has welcomed them" (Rom 14:3). Paul uses eating food that had been offered to pagan idols as an illustration of conscientious differences, just as he used the contentious point of which day of the week a person considered to be sacred to illustrate differences of opinion: "Some judge one day to be better than another, while others judge all days to be alike. Let all be fully convinced in their own minds" (Rom 14:5).

Daniel: An Old Testament Vegetarian of Great Faith

In Romans 14, Paul's statement that "the weak eat only vegetables" is not really about whether the person has a feeble and insufficient faith. After all, Paul claims elsewhere that "God chose what is weak in the world to shame the strong" (1 Cor 1:27). In fact, we could say that in Romans 14, Paul is referring to people who have a solid and enduring faith. After all, Paul no doubt was aware of a wonderful story from the book of Daniel that really challenges the notion that veganism is for the spiritually and physically unfit.

Daniel, Hananiah, Mishael, and Azariah were young men of nobility whose faith in God was so strong that even though they were forcibly taken from their homeland and enslaved, they resolved not to defile themselves by eating food from the king's table but to eat only vegetables. The king had provided a Babylonian education for Daniel and his friends, in which they learned the language and stories of the Babylonian Empire, so that they would be fit for serving in the royal household. After three years of instruction, they would graduate to full servant status. The king assigned a ration of food and wine for them, but this was food that was contrary to Jewish law. So Daniel requested that they be allowed to eat only vegetables, and if this would be a problem, to just allow them to test it out for ten days, after which the king's steward could examine their health and appearance. The result was that "at the end of ten days it was observed that they appeared better and fatter than all the young men who had been eating the royal rations. So the guard continued to withdraw their royal rations and the wine they were to drink, and gave them vegetables" (Dan 1:15–16).

This story was the basis for the above-mentioned forty-day Daniel Fast that members of my church practiced in January 2005. The Daniel Fast was encouraged for members but required of the leadership. This kind of fast is not unusual among Black churches (usually, however, the fast lasts only ten days). The fast began with a sermon series on the book of Daniel and was viewed as a way to "start the new year off right" with a clean mind, body, and soul. No one saw eating only vegetables, fruits, nuts, and whole grains as a sign of weak faith or as an affront to our Christian walk. On the contrary, given the strong cultural preference for meat within the traditional African American diet, it takes much more faith to resist the comfort foods of our communities. Many participants, even those who did not complete the full forty days, reported feeling better and vowed to make more permanent changes to the way they ate. For this congregation—and for me—this fast was a spiritual discipline that helped us better respect our bodies as temples of the Lord. Although the participants did not claim that as Christians, based upon Daniel's story, we should always eat only vegetables and drink only water, we did claim that abstaining from animal-based protein was a legitimate spiritual discipline that had benefits for both our physical and spiritual health. In fact, the Daniel Fast is only a small part of a larger Christian tradition of abstaining from meat as a spiritual discipline.

A case in point is *The Rule of St. Benedict* (written in the sixth century). Within the seventy-three chapters of wisdom and instructions for monastic living, one finds these words: "Let everyone, except the sick who are very weak, abstain entirely from eating the meat of four-footed animals."[3] For St. Benedict and many of his followers, abstention from red meat was a key marker for monasticism, and they did not think it meant that they had a weaker faith or that they could not be Christian, as the man who wrote to Calvin College thought. Rather, *The Rule of St. Benedict,*

---

3. Benedict, *Rule of St. Benedict,* 62.

which most monastic communities eventually followed, saw red meat as particularly inessential for people's physical and spiritual well-being. They did not interpret Paul as mandating a meat-eating diet for all believers. Quite the contrary—red meat was for the ill and for children, and eating it was a sign not of physical and spiritual fitness, but that something was wrong. This long-standing and long-practiced rule fits very well with the contemporary experience of African Americans who experiment, however briefly, with the Daniel Fast.

Extending Grace

Food is an integral part of our daily lives and is filled with much symbolism. Unsurprisingly, therefore, Christians in the past and present have based their notion of appropriate and inappropriate food choices on their understanding of Scripture, religious tradition, and/or some other form of spiritual revelation. I believe this is why Paul encourages believers with differing convictions about eating animal flesh and grains that were used as offerings in pagan temples to remember what God's kingdom is really about, to resist judging one another in the body of Christ, and to conduct ourselves in ways that bring people together for fellowship rather than excluding members over issues that are not in direct violation of biblical commands.

> If your brother or sister is being injured by what you eat, you are no longer walking in love. Do not let what you eat cause the ruin of one for whom Christ died. So do not let your good be spoken of as evil. For the kingdom of God is not food and drink but righteousness and peace and joy in the Holy Spirit. The one who thus serves Christ is acceptable to God and has human approval. Let us then pursue what makes for peace and for mutual upbuilding. Do not, for the sake of food, destroy the work of God. Everything is indeed clean, but it is wrong for you to make others fall by what you eat; it is good not to eat meat or drink wine or do anything that makes your brother or sister stumble. The faith that you have, have as your own conviction before God. Blessed are those who have no reason to condemn themselves because

of what they approve. But those who have doubts are condemned if they eat, because they do not act from faith; for
whatever does not proceed from faith is sin. (Rom 14:15–23)

Is the Question Genuine?

In saying that we must extend grace to one another, however, we have to
be careful not to short-circuit genuine discussion and challenges. "Did
Paul say in Romans that people who do not eat meat have weaker faith?"
is a question that some Christian believers have asked out of a genuine
concern for wanting to live correctly before God. Some of these Christians
have read the Holy Scriptures and located passages that would indicate
that Jesus ate fish or that seemingly suggest that meat-eating is symbolic
of stronger faith, as Romans 14:2 does. Consequently, they may conclude
that meat-eating is the morally correct path for believers who strive to
imitate Christ. Yet others who ask this question out of the same desire to
do what is right will not take the literal words of Paul as a proof-text, but
will also seek to understand the cultural context and the purpose of Paul's
words and conclude that eating animal flesh is not a deal breaker for the
Christian life. They may conclude that Paul was talking about a specific
religious practice that is no longer followed today, and therefore vegetarianism is the path of their Christian journey. It is clear that there was then,
as there is now, a difference of opinion. In response to this difference, Paul
was seeking to ensure that these differences did not lead to one group
condemning the other and breaking off fellowship. Rather, people were
being called to treat each other with respect and dignity.

Yet I cannot help thinking that often the question about whether
Christian vegetarians have "weaker faith" already judges Christian vegetarians as weaker. The person asking the question is not really looking for
an answer but rather is trying to remain comfortable eating in a way that
pleases him or herself. Consequently, he or she uses a passage of Scripture
to support already held convictions and therefore does not allow Scripture
to challenge comfortable practices and lifestyles. But if it were true that
the person asking the question really did believe that the non-meat-eating
Christian is someone of weaker faith, Paul's instructions are clear:

> Let us then pursue what makes for peace and for mutual upbuilding. *Do not, for the sake of food, destroy the work of God.* Everything is indeed clean, but it is wrong for you to make others fall by what you eat; *it is good not to eat meat* or drink wine or do anything that makes your brother or sister stumble. The faith that you have, have as your own conviction before God. Blessed are those who have no reason to condemn themselves because of what they approve. But those who have doubts are condemned if they eat, because they do not act from faith; for whatever does not proceed from faith is sin. (Rom 14:19–21; emphasis added)

In other words, if one indeed holds the conviction that Christians who are vegan or vegetarian have a weaker faith, the burden is on the meat-eater to abstain from those dietary practices that would make his or her vegetarian sisters and brothers falter.

More than Individual Conscience

The seeds of my journey into veganism started with my participation in a Daniel Fast. Although the fast lasted only forty days, concluding in mid-February, by Thanksgiving of that year I was a committed vegan. One could say that I have been on a Daniel Fast since 2005. But being vegan is not just about how I personally benefit. How I eat, and what I believe Paul was trying to convey, is a community matter—not just a matter of individual conscience. After all, Paul maintains that the ritual communal meal we call the Lord's Supper has enormous consequences for community life. The rich and poor alike eat from the nonviolent Eucharist (1 Cor 11:23–34). I have remained committed to a vegan lifestyle because I see this as a spiritual discipline that coincides well with my convictions to actively resist sexism and racism, and because it is a way to advocate for more conscientious eating (which has global implications) and for a healthier diet within the African American community (many of the diseases within the African American community could be avoided or made less severe with a plant-based diet). When we are so privileged as to be able to choose how we eat, we need to be mindful that the choices we make have implications far beyond what we put in our mouths. Ordering multiple chicken wings, I found out after my initial puzzlement, has implications for how chickens are treated and for consumers in a nation that tends to have a high rate of obesity. The high US demand for meat has global implications, too, as our collective prosperity often comes at the expense of those in developing countries. The Amazonian rainforest, for example, is currently being cut at a rapid rate in order to raise cattle for consumption by North Americans and Europeans. For the most part, people in the developed world are not mindful eaters; they eat thinking only about what they want at that moment.

For these reasons I am eager to find ways to raise the collective consciousness of people in my sphere of influence by educating them about becoming vegan. Whether it is writing an essay for a book, sponsoring a nationally known vegan advocate, insisting that vegan (not just vegetarian) offerings be available at campus events, or bringing a vegan option to an African American church potluck, I am intentional about my actions and seek ways that invite people to become a more mindful and hospitable community—especially within the body of Christ.

Conclusion

In Romans 14:2, Paul says that "some believe in eating anything, while the weak eat only vegetables." However, stopping at verse 2 and failing to explore the context and purpose of Paul's observation is to overlook that he was striving to address a conflict that had resulted from differing convictions about special days, fasting, and food among believers. The conflict in Paul's day is, in some ways, similar to conflicts in our day. We experience passionate disagreements and concerns within the body of Christ about the appropriateness of meat-eating, factory farming, and animal rights. We are concerned about how such an integral part of our lives as eating is or should be reflected in our spiritual practices. We wonder how to express our convictions without judging others or how to enjoy our liberties in Christ without becoming a stumbling block for others.

These struggles are real—but need not be a source of division. "For the kingdom of God is not eating and drinking, but righteousness and peace and joy in the Holy Spirit" (Rom 14:17). These words promote unity rather than division, insightful conversation rather than uninformed attacks, and community rather than individuality. Again, these struggles are real, but with the careful study of Scripture and a spirit of grace that expands with never-ending bounds, we will find the way of peace and peaceful living with all of creation.

9

Doesn't Jesus Treat Animals as Property?

Annika Spalde and Pelle Strindlund

ACCORDING TO MARK'S GOSPEL, Jesus met a man possessed by "unclean" spirits, who recognized Jesus and begged him not to destroy them but to send them instead into a large herd of swine that was feeding nearby. "And the unclean spirits came out and entered the swine; and the herd, numbering about two thousand, rushed down the steep bank into the sea, and were drowned in the sea" (Mark 5:13; cf. Matt 8:28–34 and Luke 8:26–39).

Critics of Christianity have pointed to this text as an example of a moral flaw in Jesus. For instance, in a 1927 pamphlet titled "Why I Am Not a Christian," the prominent English philosopher Bertrand Russell wrote: "There is the instance of the Gadarene swine, where it certainly was not very kind to the pigs to put the devils into them and make them rush down the hill into the sea. You must remember that He was omnipotent, and He could have made the devils simply go away; but He chose to send them into the pigs."[1] Likewise, contemporary philosopher Peter Singer, who has been dubbed the father of the animal rights movement, has said in reference to this story that "Jesus himself is described as showing apparent indifference to the fate of non-humans."[2]

1. Russell, "Why I Am Not a Christian," 575.
2. Singer, *Animal Liberation*, 191.

While critics have been quick to point fingers at Jesus's apparent callousness, Christians have also used this story to justify their own coldness toward nonhuman animals. In a recent book, Mark Driscoll, pastor of the megachurch Mars Hill in Seattle, writes mockingly that when Jesus sent the demons into the pigs, he sent "the animal rights blogosphere into a panic" and created "a bacon famine only rivaled by the great Irish potato famine."[3] With less sarcasm but no less dismissiveness, biblical scholar I. Howard Marshall maintains that there is no moral problem at all with Jesus's sending the demons into the pigs: "The moral problem can be safely dismissed: one man is of greater value than many swine."[4] These pastors and scholars stand in a long tradition of using this passage to justify violence against animals. Augustine of Hippo (354–430 CE), whose writings were very influential in the development of Western Christianity, cited this story, and another episode in which Jesus cursed a fig tree, to argue that Jesus cared for neither animals nor plants.

> Christ himself shows that to refrain from the killing of animals and the destroying of plants is the height of superstition, for judging that there are no common rights between us and the beasts and trees, he sent the devils into a herd of swine and with a curse withered the tree on which he found no fruit. . . . Surely the swine had not sinned, nor had the tree.[5]

In the thirteenth century, Thomas Aquinas answered the objection that it is not "fitting" for Jesus to work miracles that harm humans or other creatures. Thomas replied that "Christ came specially to teach and to work miracles for the good of man, and principally to the salvation of his soul. Consequently, he allowed the demons that he chased out to do men some harm, either in his body or in his property, for the salvation of man's soul—namely, for man's instruction."[6] The pigs, in other words, were killed to teach humans a lesson.

3. Driscoll and Breshears, *Vintage Jesus*, 43.

4. Marshall, *Gospel of Luke*, 336.

5. From Augustine's *The Catholic and Manichaean Ways of Life*, quoted in Singer, *Animal Liberation*, 129. On Augustine's view of animals, see also Sorabji, *Animal Minds and Human Morals*, 196.

6. Aquinas, *Summa Theologiae*, III-II 44, ad. 4.

Can it really be the case that Jesus, in this encounter, demonstrates how little regard we should have for animals? While Christian history is full of examples that use the passage to answer yes to that question, behind Aquinas's answer lies an uneasy objection that it is not fitting for the "Lord of Glory" to so callously kill innocent creatures. So there have always been parallel readings: a literal reading that sees the killing of the pigs as a demonstration of God's power, and a figurative reading that sees not a cruel God who kills pigs but rather a God who liberates—and thus the story stands as a code for other issues. For example, Chromatius of Aquileia (d. 407 CE), an influential churchman from the fourth century, maintained that the pigs stand in for a point about humans:

> The swine to which the demons fled symbolize the unfaithful and unclean people who, feeding at some distance by the sea, were living according to the sins of the world. Thus the swine showed themselves to be a ready residence for the demons. Living nearby this worldly sea they are steeped in error and inordinate desire. This made it easy for them to be overcome by the demons.[7]

What would a parallel reading to those which justify killing animals look like today though? In what follows, we will outline one of the most prominent ways that Christians have begun to read this story: a political reading that sees imperial imagery and resistance to domination behind the text. This reading further opens up the issue of property: are animals merely human property? In our time, any animal, whether a pet or a farm animal, can be killed without giving any reason or account because that animal is by law the property of her owner. Like in Jesus's time, killing pigs without reason is just part of the property game. If this imperial reading, however, holds, then such acts of domination run counter to the story's main thrust.

The Anti-Imperial Reading of Mark 5:1–20

Against a literal reading of this story stands a more nuanced and careful reading: this is a coded political tale that grew out of anti-Roman sentiment. The demon tells Jesus that its name is "Legion"—the name for the

7. Quoted in Simonetti, *Matthew 1–13*, 171.

largest Roman military unit. Nobody who heard this at the time Mark's Gospel was written could have failed to recognize that this name referred to Roman troops. New Testament scholar Hans Leander maintains that "once the name Legion has been revealed several other military allusions are displayed."[8] Here are some examples:

- the Greek term behind "to send them" (*apostellō*) can also mean "dispatch," as when an officer dispatches a soldier (5:10);

- the Greek word used for "herd" (*agelē*) was also a local term for a band of trainees (5:11);

- "He gave them permission" (*epetrepsen autois*) can also denote that a military command has been given (5:13); and

- the Greek term behind the English "rushed" (*hormaō*) connotes a troop rushing into battle (5:13).

The spirits beg Jesus not to "send them out of the country." The pigs, considered unclean animals, can be interpreted as symbols of the "unclean" conquerors that had occupied Jewish lands. The self-destruction of the possessed swine, then, is a symbol of the end of the occupation, when the Roman soldiers have been sent "out of the country."[9] Moreover, this passage echoes the exodus drama, as the possessed pigs "rush" headlong into the water and drown, just as Pharaoh's army had done at the Red Sea.

Moving beyond the text itself to the historical context, the Tenth Roman Legion that was stationed in Decapolis (the region where the story takes place) at the time Mark wrote his Gospel had a boar as their ensign, and the number two thousand corresponds to the size of a Roman legion that had been detached to fight against the Jewish insurgents.[10]

In an occupied country, "Mark's depiction of 'Legion' as inferior to Jesus evidently has subversive potential," writes Leander. Maybe, as Leander suggests, the story was written down and spread as a way for an oppressed people to resist the occupying forces without actually risking their lives; the story then tells us that "the Romans are not as powerful as they think."

8. Leander, *Discourses of Empire*, 248.

9. Lattea, "Say to this Mountain," 59. Phelps, *The Dominion of Love*, 139–42.

10. Leander, *Discourses of Empire*, 257–58.

Coded political messages are not unheard of in biblical times. The book of Revelation, for example, contains many allusions to Roman politics. It characterizes the Roman Empire as a leopard with bear's feet and a lion's mouth (Rev 12:18). J. Nelson Kraybill notes that this is similar to how modern cartoonists depict political parties and politicians as different animals (like elephants and donkeys).[11] Kraybill methodically compares the images of worship in Revelation to those depicted on Roman coins, artwork, and literarature in which emperors were worshipped or hailed as gods, and concludes that Revelation deliberately parodies that imperial imagery to build up a church with allegiance to God alone and that resists emperor worship.

Even in modern times, coded political imagery has been an important part of many peoples' spiritual experience. African American spirituals, for instance, contain many layers of meaning, including coded messages about liberation from slavery. Consider the lyrics to "Steal Away," written by Wallis Willis, who had himself escaped slavery:

Steal away, steal away,

Steal away to Jesus!

Steal away, steal away home,

I ain't got long to stay here.

My Lord, He calls me,

He calls me by the thunder,

The trumpet sounds within my soul,

I ain't got long to stay here.

While the message is spiritual from a white perspective, from the perspective of a slave longing for freedom, this song carries a very different connotation. Fredrick Douglass expressed this double meaning well when he noted that "a keen observer might have detected in our repeated singing of 'O Canaan, sweet Canaan, I am bound for the land of Canaan,'

---

11. Kraybill, *Apocalypse and Allegiance*, 42–43.

something more than a hope of reaching heaven."[12] Douglass also said that as he and other slaves were planning their escape, the following song was their favorite:

> I thought I heard them say,
>
> There were lions in the way,
>
> I don't expect to stay
>
> Much longer here.
>
> Run to Jesus—shun the danger
>
> I don't expect to stay
>
> Much longer here.[13]

Many slaves sang "The Drinking Gourd," which refers in a coded way to the Big Dipper, the constellation that contains Polaris, the North Star, which would guide escaping slaves northward: "Follow the drinking gourd, for the old man is awaiting to take you to freedom, if you follow the drinking gourd." The song mentions a "big river," commonly thought to be the Tennessee River, and a "little river," commonly considered to be the Ohio River.

So, coded political imagery is common. Therefore, it does no violence to Mark's Gospel to see the very explicit military imagery in Mark 5:1–20 as a coded depiction of Jesus battling the Roman Empire. In addition, there are other facts that push us toward a political reading.

A herd of two thousand pigs would be the equivalent size of a factory farm today—but would obviously not have been run like one since these pigs were free-ranging. Such a herd would require enormous resources to maintain since pigs take up to four times as many caretakers as other domesticated animals, like sheep. It is questionable whether anybody in Jesus's time could take care of that many pigs. The typical herd of pigs at that time consisted of between 100 and 150, which makes it all the harder to believe that the Scriptures meant for readers to take "several

12. Douglass, *My Bondage and My Freedom*, 203–4.

13. Ibid., 203.

thousand pigs" as a realistic number.[14] Also, the English term *herd* may mislead modern readers who have little knowledge of pig behavior. Pigs are not herd creatures in the sense that they bunch up together and move in a pack. They are more independent-minded, even though they are very social and stay close together in small groups. Perhaps a more appropriate term would be *flock* since it better connotes the pig's free-yet-social nature. When herd animals are frightened, they gather closer together and run as a group. But when pigs are frightened, they don't stampede like cattle; they scatter in all different directions. All of this points away from seeing the story as having anything to do with actual pigs.

That Mark and the other authors depict the destruction of animals is unfortunate. Yet it is also the case that no moral lesson regarding our relationship to animals can be derived from this text since it is really about Jesus's interaction with a powerful military regime. Neither does the story reveal any unseemly details about Jesus's character. This text is about a person possessed by a military spirit, whom Jesus freed; God Almighty versus imperial might—that is the structure of this text. To have a callous attitude toward sentient creatures based on this passage would certainly go against the trajectory of the gospel, which is about expanding love and mercy. Interpreting the text in favor of animal cruelty also goes against other sayings of Jesus, such as his assertion that God is concerned with every sparrow and his affirmation that we should rescue human and non-human animals that need help, even on the Sabbath. An alternative reading to the dominant interpretation of Mark 5:1–20 and parallel passages in Matthew and Luke strongly suggests that this story was not meant to be read literally but as coded politics: the description of the pigs does not match the reality of pig behavior and animal husbandry at the time.

14. For the typical number of pigs kept, see Fussell, "Farming Systems of the Classical Era," 35. We are grateful to Andy Alexis-Baker for these insights into pig behavior and classical animal husbandry, and also to Carly Sinderbrand for her comments. For further reading on farm animal behavior, see Hatkoff, *Inner World of Farm Animals*, 92–121; Masson, *Pig Who Sang to the Moon*, 15–53; and Grandin and Johnson, *Animals Make Us Human*, 173–206.

Humans and Nonhumans as Property

Besides a reading that simply sees the story as teaching us that one human is more important than thousands of pigs—a lesson not supported by the coded imagery—a more sympathetic reading comes from liberation theology, which sees a lesson about modern corporations who care more about profit than people. When he was a theology student, Pelle read a prominent liberation theologian who reflected on the story of the possessed man and the herd of pigs. Through his action, the theologian claimed, Jesus showed that he values human life more than personal property. Two thousand pigs, though historically unrealistic, would have cost a lot of money. Pelle thought that this was a good interpretation. It didn't cross his mind until much later in life that the pigs could be viewed as anything other than some rich person's possessions. The thought has not crossed a lot of people's minds; a great many people in history have reduced animals to someone's property.

In the second century BCE, the Roman statesman Cato the Elder (234–149 BCE) counseled that a wise farmer should sell worn-out cattle as well as any "old cart, old iron tools, *an old slave, a sickly slave*, and anything else surplus."[15] What could be done to domestic animals could also be done to slaves. In the 1700s, British newspapers ran ads like this one: "For sale at The Bull and Gate Inn, Holborn: A chestnut gelding, a Tim whiskey [a light carriage] and a well-made good tempered Black Boy."[16] At the same time, in the American South, slaves were sold at auctions along with dogs and horses.

Slavery is based on the idea that people can be property. The basic principle of the abolitionist movement was that a person cannot hold another human being as property. When activists were criticized for helping slaves from the South flee to the North, they responded that the persons who escaped, and the people who assisted them, certainly did not deprive

15. Cato, *De Agricultura*, 2.7; emphasis added.

16. Hochschild, *Bury the Chains*, 35–36. An American slave trader described in a letter in 1756 how a doctor had visited the ship and said that the men were a fine batch of slaves. "We shall hope to rend you an agreeable sale." And in a later letter: "I make no doubt that this will be the best Market for Africans all the next [year], of any in America." Similarly, there is now a market for cows, chickens, and pets from which people profit.

the white men of any property. Instead, the act restored the property to its rightful owner; the slaves were restored to themselves. They were the owners of their bodies.

Today's advocates for animals question the habit of regarding chickens, cows, dogs, and other animals as property because property by definition is something of which the owner disposes at his or her will. This means, for example, that the owner of a farm can breed pigs for a few months and then have them killed (given that the killing is done in accordance with the law). That animals are considered the property of their "owners" also means that someone can take a perfectly healthy dog to the vet and ask that the animal be killed. The "owner" does not have to give any justification whatsoever. The person's reason might be extremely trivial; perhaps the master got tired of the dog or is going on a long holiday trip. Most laws would allow this under the idea that the dog is the human's property, nothing more. "I'm amazed at how many people come to kill their healthy animals," reflects a woman who works as a veterinary nurse at a small Swedish animal clinic.[17]

An alternative approach would be to think of humans as "guardians" of animals, analogous to being a child's custodian. It is the responsibility of a child's custodian to care for him or her and to provide a safe space as well as a good upbringing. The guardian need not be a natural parent. The courts can take children away from those who abuse or neglect them. In that case, another person is then appointed to take care of the child. Of course, there are differences between being the guardian of a child and being the guardian of a dog or a few cows or chickens. According to the United Nations Convention on the Rights of the Child, every child has the right to an education. Being educated in a school is not necessary for animals, but the principle remains the same: you are responsible for ensuring the welfare of the child or animal, and if you fail at the task, society has an obligation to intervene.

Seeing animals as property supports the present order where humans, in many situations, are allowed to harm and kill other creatures. The prevailing attitude toward animals may be summed up thus: "I get to do what I want with what is mine!" In many countries there are laws

17. Emmy Melander, in the Swedish animal rights magazine *Djurens Rätt*, no. 1 (2005) 24.

that limit what the owner of a pet may do to the animal, but these meager regulations do not apply to animals who are not pets—for example, those in factory farms. You would risk legal consequences if you put a cat in a small mesh cage for six months and then killed her to make a hat of her fur. But doing the same thing to a mink is perfectly legal in most places in the world.

The Way of Service

Rather than seeing animals as property, there are at least two other ways of relating to nonhuman animals, rooted in the Christian faith and tradition. One of them is offered by Andrew Linzey, an Anglican priest and pioneering theologian in the field of animals and theology. He does not agree with those who argue that "rights" terminology is "a secular import into moral theology." Instead, Linzey argues, "the whole debate about animals is precisely about the rights of the Creator." For this reason, he coined the term "theos-rights," which means that animals have rights as God's creatures; they belong to God. "From a theological perspective, rights are not something awarded, granted, won, or lost but something *recognized*. To recognize animal rights is to recognize the intrinsic value of God-given life."[18] We often think of rights as something given by states and governments—and therefore easily trampled upon, if not taken away. Yet in this way Linzey connects rights to God and limits the power of the state to give and take away rights. Rather than a thin veneer to mask state power, theos-rights are part of a robust discussion about what human and non-human animals are for: they are created for God's good purposes, and for that reason how we treat animals must be in harmony with God's good purpose.

The second way is to focus on humanity and to see our calling as one of service. We tend to think that greatness means power over others, but Jesus had a radically different idea. "The greatest among you must become like the youngest," he said, "and the leader like one who serves" (Luke 22:26; see also Mark 10:42–44). Jesus directed this teaching to his closest disciples—those who held or wanted to hold leadership positions in the new Christian community. The established social order of Jesus's

18. Linzey, *Animal Gospel*, 40.

day—with those at the bottom of society serving those at the top—was turned on its head.

At the end of the Gospel of John we find one illustration of this new, subversive order put into action: Jesus washes his disciples' feet. Using this story as a lens, a Christian social framework based in service becomes clear, which should have consequences for how we treat animals.

> After he had washed their feet, had put on his robe, and had returned to the table, he said to them, "Do you know what I have done to you? You call me Teacher and Lord—and you are right, for that is what I am. So if I, your Lord and Teacher, have washed your feet, you also ought to wash one another's feet. For I have set you an example, that you also should do as I have done to you. (John 13:12–15)

Some cultural context can help us understand just how remarkable it was for Jesus to wash his disciples' feet. Biblical scholar Luise Schottroff explains that within the strict division of labor practiced in Jesus's time, only women and slaves (usually female slaves) performed the task of footwashing. In other words, those at the very bottom of the social order washed the feet of those at the top. Jesus overturned this hierarchy of gender and social class when he—a free man—washed the feet of his disciples, including the women. It was unheard of for a teacher to wash the feet of his followers. Yet this was the kind of power that Jesus wanted his disciples to practice. "Power shall no longer be power from up to down," writes Schottroff. "Power exists only where it emanates out of the relationship to God and Jesus. And this presupposes a clear step: to refrain from dominion, in the sense of the hierarchies' meaning."[19]

Another hierarchical order exists today: our absolute dominion over animals. What could Schottroff's analysis mean for this relationship? Most Christians think that animals should be treated humanely. But

19. Schottroff, "Om att avstå herravälde och om försoningens tjänst," 57. In this we follow the analysis of contemporary feminist theologians and biblical scholars, who argue that Jesus presented a radical critique of social inequality, including gender inequality. See, for example, Fiorenza's *In Memory of Her*. These views are not universally held, however. As Kathleen Corley concludes in her book *Women and the Historical Jesus*: "Jesus' teaching clearly involved critique of rank and class, but it included no recognition of sexism in his culture," 145.

isn't it going too far to talk about serving them? After all, humankind is supposedly the pinnacle of creation. Serving animals, we might protest, would be to lower ourselves to a level where we do not belong. But what is God's revelation in Christ? God stooped down, so to speak, to the level of creation. As Paul writes in his letter to the Philippians: "[Christ Jesus], though he was in the form of God, did not regard equality with God as something to be exploited, but emptied himself, taking the form of a slave, being born in human likeness" (Phil 2:6–7).

We believe that the spirit of Jesus calls us to a relationship with other creatures that is characterized by service and caregiving. Throughout the history of the church, many people have applied this evangelical attitude. Some may even have applied the "washing of feet" service to animals. According to a story from the early church, Saint Jerome (347–420 CE) and his monks washed the feet of tired camels and other animals that found refuge at their monastery in Bethlehem.[20] But what could it mean for us today to serve animals? First and foremost, it would mean to end the institutionalized oppression of raising them for food in cramped spaces and harming them in scientific and industrial experiments. It would mean to stop hunting and fishing out of sport rather than out of necessity. And it would mean no longer clear-cutting forests and polluting oceans—that is, we would respect animals by respecting their habitats, letting them live on their own terms, for their own sake. It could also, for us as individuals, mean adopting an abandoned dog from a local animal shelter, or taking an injured wild bird to a vet or wildlife rehabilitator.

It is difficult to resist power's corrupting influence. It is difficult to support social change when the status quo protects our privilege and props our egos. It was in the selfish interest of free men that female slaves were at hand to wash them, but Jesus challenged this custom. Many people today feel that it is in their interest that hot dogs and steak be available in the grocery store.[21] As Christians, we should ask ourselves if this is a responsible exercise of power.

20. Waddell, "St. Jerome and the Lion and the Donkey," 35.

21. We write "feel" because it is not obvious that meat is in the interest of meat eaters. The high consumption of animal-based food among Westerners is not ideal from a human health perspective.

In many ways, our societies are more egalitarian today than in Jesus's time. The labor, civil rights, and women's movements, among others, have helped us correct some power imbalances and have helped those who were once held as property regain their status as God's beloveds who deserve fair and equal treatment. In our relationship to animals, however, this imbalance persists. Couldn't things be otherwise? What role do Christians have in creating another reality? Mark 5:1–20 points us toward something very different than a dominion of violence. So, why should we not expand a dominion of love to all creatures?

10

What's the Point of Animals?

David Clough

WHEN I TALK TO members of my church about my interest in how Christians understand and treat nonhuman animals,[1] one response is striking in its frequency and consistency: Christians believe that God gave other animals to human beings to use. Therefore, I am often told, we might have responsibilities to not treat other animals cruelly, but we should not have moral qualms about accepting God's gift of them to us. God's purpose in creating animals, on this account, is to make life more convenient for human beings by providing us with food, clothing, labor, entertainment, companionship, subjects for experimentation, or anything else we might find useful. Henry More gave dramatic expression to this position: he wrote in 1653 that the only reason God gave life to cattle

---

1. In this chapter I use 'animal' to refer to the biblical category of *nephesh hayyah*, or creatures with the breath of life (e.g., Gen 2:7, 19), which therefore includes human beings. It is striking that there is no biblical term that means all animals except human beings. The English word 'animal' has been ambiguous about whether it includes human beings from its earliest usage in the sixteenth century. It is not present in the King James Version of 1611. I prefer to use 'animal' as including humans so as to reflect the biblical language and to keep in focus our commonality with God's other creatures with the breath of life. For further discussion of this, see the Introduction to Clough, *On Animals*.

and sheep was to keep their meat fresh until we need to eat them.[2] In this view, then, the divinely ordained point of other animals is to provide for humans.

I have three reasons for questioning this position. First, I am troubled by the astonishing scale of the exploitation of other animals it seems to justify: for example, each year sixty billion animals are killed worldwide for human consumption, the majority of which are raised, slaughtered, and processed in novel industrial facilities far from the sight of their consumers.[3] It seems to me out of keeping with a faith that teaches compassionate care for the neighbor to think that nonhuman neighbors are entitled to little or no care at all. One could argue in response that God provides other animals for human use, and that we need to treat them much better than most are currently kept today. If the final truth about other animals is that they are for us, however, any consideration of human convenience—most crucially, access to cheap meat—will trump concerns about their welfare at every point. We would need to be very sure of our interpretation of biblical texts and the Christian tradition to use them to undergird a position with such devastating implications for all other-than-human animals.

My second reason for doubting the position that Christianity teaches that the point of nonhuman animals is to provide for human beings, is that it is so obviously in our own interests to believe that our God gives us license to exploit other creatures for our own ends. Whenever we are tempted to use our faith to advance our own interests, we should be especially alert to the dangers of self-deception. In 1864, John Henry Hopkins, the Episcopal Bishop of Vermont, reissued a pamphlet defending slavery on the basis of the divinely instituted order, where "we behold a grand system of ORDER and GRADATION" with some races higher and some lower in the scale, with "some being born to commanding authority and influence, while others are destined to submit and obey."[4] It is hard to conceive of a more blatant and transparent use of Christian faith for selfish human ends, but clearly this is not an isolated example of the Christian

2. Cited in Thomas, *Man and the Natural World*, 20.

3. Compassion in World Farming, *Global Warning*, 6.

4. Hopkins, *A Scriptural, Ecclesiastical, and Historical View of Slavery*, 21, quoted in Meeks, "The 'Haustafeln' and American Slavery," 236.

God being invoked to defend social injustice. Given how clearly it serves human ends to believe that God gave us permission to make use of all other creatures, we should be especially careful to ensure we are not employing the kind of self-serving theological arguments white Christians used to defend slavery.

The two preceding reasons for doubting that the purpose of other animals is to provide for human animals lead to a third: that the biblical and doctrinal bases for this position are by no means clear. Most of the remainder of this chapter is devoted to refuting biblical and doctrinal arguments purporting to show that other animals are merely for human use: I argue that neither the Genesis 1 identification of humanity as the image of God and associated command to have dominion, nor the Genesis 9 permission to eat the flesh of other animals, nor the creaturely hierarchy suggested in the opening of Psalm 8, nor Jesus's affirmation that humans are worth more than sparrows and sheep, nor the various other grounds many theologians cite, are sufficient, individually or in combination, to establish that the point of other animals is providing for humanity. Instead, I will argue that a Christian theological account suggests that the point of other animals is much the same as the point of us: to glorify God and participate in the divine triune life.[5]

Biblical Texts on the Point of Animals

The Bible is remarkably quiet about God's purpose in creating the universe as well as about the point of creating any particular creature or kind of creatures. Psalms such as 104 and 148 celebrate the majesty of God's creative acts, but make no claim to comprehend the intention that lay behind them. Genesis 1 reports what took place, rather than scrutinizing God's motivation. In this chapter it is notable that the nonhuman animals of the sea, air, and land are pronounced good in themselves without further reference to any other creatures (vv. 21, 25), whereas human beings are pronounced good only in relation to the whole (v. 31). At the end of the chapter human beings are uniquely identified as imaging God in the world and given the task of dominion over the other animals and sub-

5. Clearly, within the confines of this chapter, my argument will be of summary form. For a more detailed engagement with these themes, see Clough, *On Animals*.

duing the earth (vv. 26–28), but this imaging is a role they are given in relation to the other creatures, not a statement that other creatures only have meaning in relation to the human. The chapter concludes with God assigning food to different groups of animals: humans are given plants yielding seed and trees with seeds in their fruit; other animals of the land and air are given green plants (1:29–30). However we are to interpret the image of God and dominion, therefore, the role envisaged for humans here is a limited one. The work of creation reaches its climax not with the creation of human and nonhuman land animals on the sixth day, but with the seventh, blessed and hallowed by God (Gen 2:3). Human beings find their place alongside the other land animals of the sixth day, and are directed, with all that God has created, toward the Sabbath blessing and rest, which points forward to God's redemption of creation.

Genesis 2 takes a different perspective on the creation narrative to the first chapter: here the order of creation is reversed, with God forming Adam to look after the Garden of Eden and then producing plants for Adam to tend. Given this reversal between chapters 1 and 2, it is clear that we cannot derive conclusions as to the significance of particular creatures merely from their place in the order of creation. The other animals are formed by God in response to God's observation that it is not good for Adam to be alone (2:18), with each brought before Adam in turn. Adam names them all, which could be taken to be a sign of power over them but could also be an indication of Adam's careful attention to the particularity of each of the other animals. However we read it, chapter 2 provides no more grounds than chapter 1 for deciding that human beings were God's sole object in creation: even more clearly than in chapter 1, human existence is seen in relation to others of God's creatures. This is also evident in the story of Noah, who is given by God the task of preserving the full diversity of God's animals (6:19–21). Even Genesis 9, where God, after the flood, for the first time allows humans to use other animals for food (9:3), does not suggest that this new permission means that other animals have meaning only in relation to humans: indeed, the instruction that an animal is not to be consumed "with its life, that is, its blood" (9:4) suggests that blood indicates the commonality between humans and other kinds of animals.

Beyond Genesis, Psalm 8 declares human beings to be "a little lower than God . . . crowned with glory and honor" with the other animals put under their feet (8:5–8), but the context here seems to be a reassurance to a downcast people—"what are human beings that you are mindful of them?" (8:4)—that, despite the seeming insignificance of human beings in the context of the universe, God has given them their own particular place of honor. The remarkable closing chapters of Job echo the opening of Psalm 8 in picturing human beings as a small and incomprehending part of an immense whole (38–41), and Ecclesiastes declares that the fate of humans and others animals is the same (Eccl 3:18–21). Jesus declares that humans are of more value than the birds of the air (Matt 6:25–30; Luke 12:24–28), of more value than many sparrows (Matt 10:29–31; Luke 12:6–7), and of more value than a sheep (Matt 12:11–12; Luke 14:5), but the first two of these examples affirm God's attentive providential care for birds independent of any reference to human beings and the latter acknowledges the need for humans to rescue domestic animals on the Sabbath. These Gospel texts might be used, therefore, to argue for the greater value of human beings, but cannot be used as evidence that other animals have importance only in relation to human beings.

This brief tour of biblical texts treating the relationship of human and nonhuman animals to God and each other suggests that there are grounds for affirming that human beings have a relationship to God that is unique in particular respects, but do not make the case that Christians should understand that all other animals were created *only* for the sake of human beings. Quite the reverse seems clear even from this brief survey: God creates, declares good, and sustains a great diversity of animal life, human and other-than-human. We cannot quickly determine the purpose of the lives of other animals from the biblical texts, but we should understand that God determined to create and sustain them just as God determined to create and sustain human animals.

Theologians on the Point of Animals

The lack of biblical foundations for the view that God created other animals for the sake of human beings has not prevented a number of Christian theologians from asserting this position. Many critics of Christianity have noticed the assertion. The eighteenth-century atheist geologist George Hoggart Toulmin criticized Christianity on the basis that "the whole magnificent scene of things is daily and confidently asserted to be ultimately intended for the peculiar convenience of mankind," and the quotation from Henry More with which this chapter began demonstrates that this view was not without foundation.[6] In the following century, Ludwig Feuerbach made a similar complaint: "Nature, the world, has no value, no interest for Christians. The Christian thinks only of himself and the salvation of his soul. . . . The practical end and object of Christians is solely heaven."[7] The roots of this view run deep. For example, the first-century Jewish thinker Philo of Alexandria wrote commentaries on the book of Genesis that were highly influential on later Christian interpretations. Philo is troubled by the fact that humans are created last in the Genesis 1 account, whereas in Plato's *Timaeus* the world is constructed around them. He responds by arguing that being created last demonstrates the particular dignity of human beings, because just as a banquet host ensures that everything is prepared before his guests have arrived, so God wanted humanity to encounter a feast and sacred theater.[8] In commenting on why God destroyed the other animals along with human beings, Philo notes that when a human being's head is cut off, the rest of the body dies with it; so it is not strange if other animals died along with their head, humanity.[9] Similar positions are taken up by Christian theologians such as Lactantius, Gregory of Nyssa, John Chrysostom, Bonaventure, Luther, Calvin, and William Kirkby in the nineteenth-century *Bridgewater Treatises*.[10] More broadly, Justin Martyr, Origen, and Irenaeus of Lyons seem to accept that

6. Toulmin, *The Antiquity and Duration of the World*, 73, cited in Thomas, *Man and the Natural World*, 17. Thomas provides many other contemporary examples to support Toulmin's complaint.

7. Feuerbach, *The Essence of Christianity*, 287–88.

8. Philo, *On the Creation of the Cosmos*, ch. 14, §§ 77–84.

9. Philo, *Philo Suppl. I*, "*Quaestiones et solutiones in Genesim*," bk. II, qu. 9 (cf. the similar question in bk. 1, qu. 94). For more discussion of Philo's thought in this context, see Clough, "All God's Creatures," 145–61.

10. Lactantius, *Divine Institutes*, bk. 2, ch. 8; Gregory of Nyssa, On the Making of Man; Chrysostom, *Homilies on Genesis*, Homily 8, §5; Schäfer, "The Position and Function of Man in the Created World," 316; Luther, *Luther's Works*, 1:39; Calvin, *Genesis*, 64; Kirby, *On the Power, Wisdom and Goodness of God*, ch. 1.

creation was for the sake of human beings.[11] Karl Barth seems to echo a similar view in his position that "the purpose and therefore the meaning of creation is to make possible the history of God's covenant with man," though as I note below and argue elsewhere this is only one element of many in his consideration of the place of other animals before God.[12]

We can see, then, that it is not difficult to find Christian theologians *asserting* that God's creation, and therefore the existence of all other animals, is for the sake of human beings. It is much harder, however, to find persuasive biblical or theological *arguments* for taking these positions. Sometimes, it seems that theologians have been motivated by allegiances with philosophical schools: for example, Origen seems to be siding with a Stoic view of the providential place of human beings in God's purposes against views that pictured the gods as disinterested in events in the world. Sometimes, it seems that theological grounds are given for obvious human interests, such as the rationale theologians provided for the dramatic expansion in human exploitation of the natural world in the early modern period. Most significant, however, may be the proclamation of God's grace in a context in which the natural world seems a constant threat and the situation of human beings precarious. In Martin Luther's commentary on Genesis, for example, he repeatedly notes the similarity between humans and other animals in the spirit of the author of Ecclesiastes (Eccl 3:18–21), suggesting that this shared animal nature inclines us to think we are no more than animals. After each of these comparisons, however, Luther declares that the Genesis text communicates the gospel good news that human beings are distinct in origin and destiny.[13] Here, then, unflattering comparison with other animals and a sharp differentiation between the fate of humans and other animals are Luther's means of making a rhetorical point about Christian hope. Nonhuman animals themselves are clearly not the focus of his attention: he is simply seeking to communicate the gospel to his readers. The primary motivation behind the claims of

11. May, *Creatio Ex Nihilo*, 31; Origen, *Contra Celsum*, bk. 4, §74; Irenaeus, "Against Heresies," bk. 5, ch. 29, §1.

12. Barth, *Church Dogmatics*, 3/1, 42. Hereafter cited as *CD*. For further discussion of Barth and animals, see Clough, *On Animals*, ch. 4.

13. Luther, *Luther's Works*, 1:56, 85, 121, 230. For further discussion of this theme in Luther, see Clough, "The Anxiety of the Human Animal," 41–60.

the centrality of humanity to God's purposes, seems to be *pastoral*, rather than biblical or systematic. It may be that this is the motivation for other theological accounts as well, which highlights the novelty of the theological question that asks about the place of other animals before God in their own right.

Alongside the theologians that considered the point of other animals to be exhausted in the service they provided to human beings, it is important to recall the strands of Christian theology where a different answer is given. Alongside Barth's affirmation of God's covenant with humanity as the purpose of creation, for example, he also notes the profound theological danger of claiming that human beings are central to God's creative purpose and wants to avoid replacing theology with anthropology.[14] Instead, Barth argues, we should declare with the *Didache* that "Thou didst create all things for Thy name's sake."[15] Aquinas similarly argues that since "each and every creature stretches out to its own completion, which is a resemblance of divine fullness and excellence . . . divine goodness is the final cause of all things,"[16] and Bonaventure affirms that the final end of creation cannot be anything outside God.[17] Other theologians have seen difficulties in the claim that God made everything for God's own glory. Wolfhart Pannenberg states that "the creature was not created in order that God should receive glory from it"; God has no need of glorification by creatures.[18] Instead, Pannenberg sees creation as an expression of God's free love in which God's action is oriented wholly to creatures who are "the object and goal of creation."[19] This echoes Basil of Caesarea's enthusiastic celebration of the diversity of God's creatures in his *Hexaemeron*, in which he instructs his congregation that "the world was not devised at random or to no purpose, but to contribute to some useful end and to

14. Barth, *CD* 3/1, 46–47; *CD* 2/2, 136–37.

15. Barth, *CD* 3/1, 47.

16. Aquinas, *Summa Theologiae*, 1.44.4. Aquinas does also argue that within the created order lesser creatures exist for the sake of the nobler, but recent interpreters of his thought in relation to nonhuman animals suggest that this should not be taken out of context: see Barad, *Aquinas on the Nature and Treatment of Animals*; Berkman, "Towards a Thomistic Theology of Animality." .

17. See Schäfer, "Position and Function of Man," 271.

18. Pannenberg, *Systematic Theology*, 2:56.

19. Ibid.

the great advantage of all beings."[20] For Pannenberg, the corollary of this broader understanding of the significance of all creatures to God is that for God "no creature is merely a means"; rather, the existence of every creature is ordered to "the *kairos* of the manifestation of the Son" so that "each creature has a part in the saving purpose of the Father."[21] Christoph Schwöbel recognizes the dangers of identifying God's glory as the purpose of creation, but maintains that creation cannot be understood as an end in itself. Instead, we should say that "including creation into the mutuality of communicating and communicated glory is the end of God's creating, which in this way defines the destiny of creation to join with the Spirit in the glorification of the Father through the Son."[22]

Rethinking the Point of Animals for Christians

In this brief overview, we have seen that despite popular Christian under-standings concerning the point of animals, informed by many claims of Christian theologians in the past, there are no good biblical grounds for the assertion that God made everything for the sake of humanity—but there *are* good theological reasons for arguing instead that the only adequate vision of God's creative purposes is the inclusion of all creatures into the life of the triune God. The best available theological account of the point of nonhuman animals, therefore, is identical with that of all other creatures, including human beings: we exist through God's creative and sustaining grace to glorify God through living out our particular creaturely lives in response to God and one another, and to come to participate even in the life of God—Father, Son, and Spirit.

We may be able to understand why theologians have sought to reas-sure church members in the past as to the importance of human beings before God in the face of natural threats, but the way these traditions of thought have rendered other animals as merely instrumental for human ends is a highly problematic theological legacy that Christians have good reason to rethink. Especially at a time when the major problems con-fronting humans, other animals, and the earth itself have arisen from the

20. Basil, "On the Hexaemeron," 1.6.

21. Pannenberg, *Systematic Theology*, 2:7.

22. Schwöbel, "God, Creation and the Christian Community," 169.

consequences of human activity, it is crucial to recognize God's creative intention that human beings exist alongside other creatures, rather than that all else exists to serve their interests.

If Christians were to take the theological point of other animals seriously, the consequences for Christian practice would be revolutionary. If we paused to reflect on the theological insight that there is a God-given purpose to the life of every creature, a very great deal of what passes for acceptable Christian behavior would be revealed to be the most flagrant and disobedient disregard for the workings of God in our world. If chickens, cows, sheep, fish, and pigs are intended by their Creator to live lives that glorify God and fit them for inclusion in the trinitarian life, then Christians should be the first to recognize that cruelly constraining, reshaping, and curtailing their lives for our convenience frustrates their Creator's intention for the ways they should be creatures before God. If God intends rats, mice, dogs, and monkeys to fulfill their particular creaturely callings, then breeding them as raw material for experiments intended only to make improvements in human lives would be recognizable as a failure of Christian discipleship. If horses, greyhounds, elephants, whales, and dolphins have lives of their own to live before God, then Christians have reason to object to keeping them for human entertainment in conditions where they cannot live those lives to the full.

These seem like radical transformations of what Christians have understood as their responsibility towards other animals before God, but they arise clearly and obviously from the basic recognition that the point of their lives is not exhausted in their relationship to us. Once we have understood that we are not the point of the lives of other animals and that each animal's life has a point of its own in relationship to God (who is their God as much as ours), how could we not act differently in relation to these our fellow creatures?

11

Are We Addicted to the Suffering of Animals?
Animal Cruelty and the Catholic Moral Tradition

John Berkman

WE ARE ALL OPPOSED—at least ostensibly—to mindless animal cruelty. Almost no one defended Michael Vick and his cohorts when they tortured and killed dogs for their dog fighting ring. Imagine Michael Vick had been selling a product—say dog-skin handbags from the "losing" dogs—that financially supported and enabled the continued torture of more dogs. We would not only *not* buy these dog-skin handbags, we would boycott the handbags and urge others not to buy them as well.

Michael Vick grew up in an American subculture where dog fighting was socially acceptable. What was introduced to him at age seven as a diversion and entertainment, became for him as an adult an addiction. At twenty-one, as soon as he became wealthy, he set up his Bad Newz Kennels near Surry, Virginia, and oversaw its operation for six years until he was arrested. For his financing and leadership in a particularly socially unacceptable form of animal cruelty, Michael Vick went from the pinnacle of success—the highest paid football player in America at the time—to bankruptcy and a twenty-three-month prison sentence. When Vick arrived in prison, he still didn't think he had done anything wrong. Only while he was in prison did he come to see the cruelty of his dog fighting.

Since his release from prison, in talks to youth about his dog fighting, Vick readily admits that he was addicted to it, saying that he spent more time on his dog-fighting business than he did preparing to play football. For Vick, it took many months in prison to see the wrongfulness of his addiction to dog fighting.

Vick is by no means the only person who has failed to see his involvement in animal cruelty and the wrongfulness of it. In fact, Vick's Bad Newz Kennels was simply a drop in the animal cruelty bucket compared to that being perpetrated by his neighbor, Smithfield Foods.[1] Joe Luter III, CEO of Smithfield Foods from 1975–2006, created the world's largest (and most notorious) factory farming system for pigs. Reading an interview with Luter, you would not even know he is talking about live animals, much less intelligent and feeling creatures, as he refers to them only as "raw materials" for his business.[2] Clearly, Luter does not think he is doing anything wrong, much less engaging in boundless animal cruelty.

This essay argues that we are a lot more like Michael Vick and Joe Luter than we care to imagine. No, we're not highly paid football players and we won't go to jail or go bankrupt for our participation in animal cruelty. But like Michael Vick and Joe Luter, we participate in animal cruelty, and we are similarly raised in a way that we do not see its wrongfulness.

How do we participate in animal cruelty? By spending billions of dollars each year financially supporting an incredibly common and pervasive form of animal cruelty: factory farming, which involves raising pigs, cows, chickens, turkeys, and other animals in deplorable conditions. And, like Michael Vick, we financially support it in part because we have an addiction. More specifically, we are addicted to the taste of low-cost industrial meat. As a result, we refuse to see our financial support of large-scale cruelty to animals.

And yet, in the last fifty years, factory farming has become the dominant form of "raising" animals in America. If you buy chicken, pork, or

1. Less than twenty miles from Surry is Smithfield, Virginia, birthplace and headquarters of Smithfield Foods. Founded in 1936, Smithfield Foods was a small pig slaughtering and packaging company for fifty years. However, in the 1980s, Joseph Luter III embarked on a plan to expand Smithfield Foods into the raising and intensive confining of pigs. In doing so, Luter expanded and perfected factory farming with pigs, vaulting his company into the largest producer of pig meat in the world in less than twenty years.

2. See Miller, "Straight Talk from Smithfield's Joe Luter."

eggs from your local grocery store, the animals that make up this food have almost certainly been inflicted with gross suffering that in truth is nothing other than institutionalized cruelty on a vast scale.

Thinking of Michael Vick and Joe Luter reminded me of how almost thirty years ago, Bob Dylan sang the words, "Steal a little and they throw you in jail; steal a lot and they make you king."[3] Dylan could equally have said this about the factory farming industry. If you treat a few animals callously, whether it is training your dog for fighting or torturing a few cats, you can be cited for animal cruelty. However, if you cage millions of animals in small spaces where they can hardly move; mutilate them by cutting off their beaks, tails, and/or horns; brand them with hot irons; castrate them; genetically engineer their bodies; and breed them with techniques that result in a lifetime of severe pain, you are unlikely to ever get penalized. In a cruel twist of fate, those at the forefront of these enterprises, like Joe Luter, are often rewarded with significant wealth and influence. Corporations that typically run factory farms have become powerful enough to persuade many US state legislatures to explicitly exclude all farm animals from any kind of animal cruelty legislation. Even with government protection, factory farms typically operate under a cloak of secrecy. They are set up in remote places and surrounded with fences and barbed wire so that no outsiders can see what goes on. Recently, industry supporters have also convinced US state legislatures to pass laws against photographing or taking videos of the conditions in these places. And you wonder why you don't know where your meat comes from and how it was produced?

In the face of these harrowing conditions and the industry's attempts to hide their vast animal cruelty, this essay contends that factory farming is immoral. Furthermore, once we become aware of this wanton cruelty, we must refuse to participate in it, in part, by choosing not to buy or eat meat from factory-farmed animals. Factory-farmed meat is, if we are honest, "cruelty meat," and it behooves us to find alternatives wherever possible.

The first half of the essay begins the argument by describing the history and character of factory farms in America, making it clear that animal cruelty is as necessary in North American factory farming as animal

3. From "Sweetheart Like You" (*Infidels*, 1983).

cruelty is necessary in dog fighting. In the second half of the essay, I will develop the argument as to why all of us—especially Christians—ought not to participate in this widespread and mindless cruelty to animals. Turning to an argument that has historically been a part of Christian social teaching, especially in the Catholic tradition, I will argue that supporting factory farming by buying and/or consuming its products is a form of what the Catholic moral tradition has called "cooperation with wrongdoing," which no morally serious person ought to do. Christians have a particular obligation not to cooperate with the wrong of factory farming, not only out of respect for God's laws, but also because such participation, once recognized and understood, corrodes their character and undermines their ability to criticize or resist other kinds of evils. To be clear, the point of this particular chapter is not to oppose meat-eating *per se.* My objection here is not with the Inuit who eat seals as their primary (or only) food source, nor with aboriginals who hunt and kill wild boars for the same reason. Rather, my objection here is to wanton cruelty and to Christian acceptance of, and collusion with, enterprises that engage in that kind of action, whether the perpetrator is Michael Vick or Joe Luter.

What Is Factory Farming, and How Are Factory-Farmed Animals Actually Treated?

So, what is factory farming? To answer this, we also need to ask two other questions: How are factory-farmed animals actually treated, and when did this system come about? In order to keep my argument narrow and focused, I will discuss the factory farming of pigs only, since among the various farm animals (*a*) they are the most consistently factory-farmed after poultry—more than 95 percent of pigs in America alone are on factory farms; (*b*) they are very harshly treated; and (*c*) they are the most social, loyal, and intelligent (evidently more intelligent than dogs, for example) of factory-farmed animals. As such, factory-farmed pigs arguably suffer the most from their harsh treatment, and along with poultry probably receive the cruelest treatment.

A factory farm, also known as an Animal Feeding Operation (AFO), a Concentrated Animal Feeding Operation (CAFO), or an Industrial Farm Animal Production (IFAP), is a highly intensified system for raising animals for meat, dairy, or egg production. The basic philosophy is to turn the farm into a mechanized system that needs as little labor and skill as possible to produce the greatest quantity of meat for the lowest cost. Typically, this means a large-scale economy: "Get big or get out" has been the mantra of farming for decades. What is perhaps hard to believe and thus important to note, is that in the logic of factory farms, the welfare of animals receives *no* intrinsic consideration. The only reason to halt or lessen cruel treatment of animals is if the degree of mistreatment leads to an increase in cost of the end product. If the pigs are stuffed so close together that some are regularly smothered, just toss the dead ones into a dumpster. If disease breaks out, give them antibiotics to stave off the illness until the upcoming slaughter. If a pregnant sow has a broken leg, leave her in her pain until the piglets are born, then kill her because mending her leg is not cost effective. Are the pigs so crowded, hungry, and stressed that they start chewing on each other's tails? Dock their tails and grind down their teeth—without using anesthetics.[4] Worried that a sow might smother her piglets when she rolls over in her sleep because her space is too small? Rather than give her more space, make her completely immobile by putting her in a metal crate for months, perhaps even strap her down to the floor; that way she cannot roll over at all. Although giving more room to her and her piglets would reduce their suffering, such a move adds to costs and cuts into profits. Such is the inexorable logic of the industrial production system when applied to intelligent mammals who have emotions, habits, desires, and needs, and yet who are nevertheless made to suffer *ad nauseum* in this system.

The situation actually worsens when it comes to slaughtering factory-farmed pigs. Even though pigs can live from ten to eighteen years, and do not reach maturity till they are three or four years old, most pigs sent to slaughter are only six months old. They are still piglets. But selective breeding and intensified feeding cause them to grow faster than their bones naturally allow. This fast growth causes enormous stress on a pig's body. But waiting even three years is not economically desirable for large corporations.

---

4. "Docking" is clipping a pig's tail to make it highly sensitive, because if a pig allows its tail to be chewed, the pig is likely to get infected and sick and thus must be killed.

Although slaughterhouse conditions differ, we can get a clear picture of the production line logic in which "economically required" modes of transport to slaughter and "disassembly line" speeds lead inexorably to massive cruelty. To transport them to the slaughterhouse, pigs are often beaten to force them into a severely overcrowded trailer. Some fall and suffocate when others are crammed in on top of them. Even though the journey may be hundreds of miles, the pigs typically receive no food or water. These journeys often have temperature extremes. In the summer, since pigs cannot sweat, many die from heat exhaustion. In the winter, many freeze to death, or more often their bodies are frozen to parts of the unheated trucks. One transporter notes that "in the wintertime there are always hogs stuck to the sides and floors of the trucks. [Slaughterhouse workers] go in there with wires or knives and just cut or pry the hogs loose. The skin pulls right off. These hogs were alive when we did this."[5] According to a 2006 industry report, more than one million pigs die every year in these transport trucks.[6] Another industry report notes that as many as 10 percent of pigs arriving at US packing plants are "downers," which means that they are so ill or injured that they are unable to stand and walk on their own.[7] These sick and injured pigs will be kicked or struck with electric prods to get them to move, and if that fails, drivers will grab their legs with winches to pull them, often pulling their legs right off in the process.

As awful as the transportation conditions may be, the pigs that die in transport may be the fortunate ones. When they arrive at the slaughter-house, the unloading is often a witness to the sustained cruelty inherent in these pigs' short lives. Having been kept basically immobile for their entire lives and fed a drug-riddled diet to make their bodies grow faster than their bone structure can handle, their legs and respiratory systems are so weak or deformed that in most cases they cannot walk very far. When they come off the truck, they can see more open space in the herding pens than they ever have. Those that can will try to run for the first time, mistaking the slaughterhouse pen with freedom. But some collapse

---

5. Eisnitz, *Slaughterhouse*, 133.

6. Goihl, "Transport Losses of Market Hogs Studied."

7. Gonyou, "Stressful Handling of Pigs."

and cannot get up, their bodies racked with weakness and pain. They will be dragged.

A typical slaughterhouse "disassembles" up to eleven hundred pigs an hour. That's a pig about every three seconds. The "required" speed of the slaughterhouse means that if the initial attempt (or attempts) to kill the pig (or stun it unconscious) fails, they won't stop the "disassembly" line to make sure the pig is dead before they start cutting it open, or before they dip it into a tank of boiling water, which is intended to soften its skin and remove its hair. For instance, the US Department of Agriculture (USDA) documented fourteen humane slaughter violations at one slaughterhouse, where the USDA inspectors found pigs who were "squealing after being stunned [with a stun gun] as many as four times."[8] And as one slaughterhouse worker put it, "There's no way these animals can bleed out in the few minutes it takes to get up the ramp. By the time they hit the scalding tank, they're still fully conscious and squealing. Happens all the time."[9]

While there may well be farming operations or slaughterhouses in North America where these kinds of violations are rare, the cruel treatment of animals described above is not unusual, extreme, or technically criminal. Unlike dog fighting, where a relatively small number of people at the margins of society become addicted to this perverse form of entertainment, factory farming is not the result of a few nasty guys having "fun." Rather, it is mainstream corporate America employing torture and cruelty as means of making money—lots and lots of money for those who mastermind the factory slaughterhouses.[10] For the unfortunate individuals—increasingly, new immigrants and migrant farmworkers—who have to work on these "farms" and in these slaughterhouses for a paltry hourly wage, it is cruelty as a means to an end. This is the business of torture.

8. US Congress, Congressional Record, V. 147, Pt. 7, May 22, 2001 to June 11, 2001, 9879.

9. Eisnitz, *Slaughterhouse*, 71.

10. In 2005, his last year before retirement, Joe Luter made almost eleven million dollars, with another nineteen million dollars in unexercised stock options. See Tietz, "Boss Hog," 114.

When Did This System Come About?

Although crop farming was mechanized in the nineteenth century, industrialized animal farming began with the large industrial slaughterhouses, especially for pigs, in the early part of the twentieth century. According to the 2008 Pew Commission on Industrial Farm Animal Production, Henry Ford got his idea for assembling automobiles from watching how industrialized slaughterhouses "disassembled" pigs.[11] However, it was only after World War II—when people still remembered the dust bowl and food shortages— that the push for a "green revolution" to feed a rising population, a huge availability of inexpensive farmland, a strong futurist mentality, and the desire to apply the factory model to the production of all consumer goods gave rise to factory farming.

The first serious analysis of this phenomenon was in the 1964 book *Animal Machines: The New Factory Farming Industry*, by Ruth Harrison. In the book, Harrison notes "a new type of farming, of production line methods applied to the rearing of animals, of animals living out their lives in darkness and immobility without the sight of the sun, of a generation of men who see in the animal they rear only its conversion factor into human food."[12] Harrison saw not only the fundamental transformation of an "animal husbandry" model to a corporate factory model, she also saw a rapid and fundamental change of culture. As she duly noted: "The factory farmer cannot rely, as did his forebears, on generations of experience gained from the animals themselves and handed down from father to son; he relies on a vast array of backroom boys with computing machines working to discover the breeds, feeds and environment most suited to convert food into flesh at the greatest possible speed, and every batch of animals reaching market is a sequel to another experiment."[13]

Although Harrison adeptly characterized the nature and logic of the factory farm system, and although her work encouraged animal welfare legislation in her home country of England, the animal welfare movement historically got little traction in America; things would get much worse in the thirty-five years after the publication of Harrison's book. This has

11. Pew Commission on Industrial Farm Animal Production, *Putting Meat on the Table*, 5.

12. Harrison, *Animal Machines*, 15.

13. Ibid., 18.

changed slightly in the last decade; a few states have begun to ban gestation crates for pregnant pigs and battery cages for hens, but these victories are small in the grand scheme.

Why Is Factory Farming Wrong?

In the first half of this essay, I sought to explain what factory farming is, when it originated in America, and how it inflicts wanton suffering on untold numbers of animals, a suffering that is by no means necessary for Americans to eat meat. Sadly, America's history is sullied by man's seemingly boundless inhumanity to man, especially during the industrial revolution: we think of the robber barons who exploited workers by paying them a pittance for working incredibly long hours in extraordinarily dangerous conditions; we think of America's sad legacy of child labor; we think of the scourge of slavery. It is ironic that just as America entered a period in which it ended the worst of these abuses of other human beings, it established a new institution that began to exploit nonhuman animals in ways and on a scale that no one could have imagined.

Turning to the Catholic moral tradition, there are a number of ways in which one can criticize the practice of factory farming. In the last fifty years the Catholic tradition has begun to develop the notion of "social sin," and factory farming fits this notion. However, since I wish to focus not on the wrong done by those who engage in factory farming, but on the wrongfulness of one's buying and/or eating factory-farmed meat, dairy, and eggs, I will draw on what the tradition calls *cooperation with wrongdoing*. I will proceed by first defining cooperation with wrongdoing and then exploring cooperation with wrongdoing and animal cruelty.

What Is Cooperation with Wrongdoing?

The idea of cooperation with wrongdoing is simple enough when we think about a variety of crimes. Procuring a gun for someone who plans to commit a murder is a form of cooperation with wrongdoing; buying stolen goods from someone or laundering stolen money are forms of cooperation with wrongdoing, as is knowingly investing in companies whose purpose is to engage in these kinds of activities. However, a simple definition of cooperation with wrongdoing is when a person intentionally or causally assists another person in unjust or wicked activities. A key distinction in the Catholic tradition when speaking of cooperation with wrongdoing is between formal and material cooperation. Formal cooperation is where one shares the object of the wrongdoer's activity. This is typically understood to be someone who advises or counsels the person principally engaged in the wrongdoing, aids them by helping them escape justice, and/or launders the proceeds of their criminality. So the person who invests in a start-up company that will run a series of Internet scams is formally cooperating in wrongdoing. So is the person who knowingly "fences" stolen paintings or buys goods made by exploited child labor.

On the other hand, material cooperation is where a person clearly has other intentions in their actions when they assist others in wrongdoing. Examples of this include a pharmacist who dispenses medication that someone else (unbeknownst to the pharmacist) uses to poison another person, or a UPS delivery person who unwittingly delivers a package that is booby-trapped to kill the recipient. While they causally assisted someone in wrongdoing, they typically did not intend to do so. In these cases of material cooperation with wrongdoing, the actors are engaged in good and legitimate activities, and the bad effects that flow from their activities are clearly outside of their intentions. In more typical examples of material cooperation, the cooperator is well aware of the way a wrongdoer can or is using the cooperator's otherwise good actions to facilitate wrongdoing. In such cases, the person doing an otherwise good action may treat the wrongdoer's activities as an unwanted bad side effect. Moreover, in addition to not intending the wrong action, if cooperation is to be considered material, we have to weigh the good against the potential bad. So a delivery person might know that he or she could potentially and unknowingly deliver a deadly package, despite all precautions, and still see that the good of delivering mail in general outweighs the possible harms that could be done.

Cooperation with Wrongdoing and Animal Cruelty

So now we come to the question of cooperating with cruelty toward animals, whether it involves participating in dog fighting or in factory farming.

Let us begin with those who set up and run a dog fighting operation. These are people who provide the seed funding to begin the operation; find, buy, or steal the dogs, including dogs that are used as "bait" in the training of the fighting dogs; train them to maim and kill other dogs; and in various other ways mistreat them, for example, starve them or socially isolate them to make them more vicious. These people are all engaged in a practice that our society has defined both socially and legally as wrongdoing.

Then there are those people who aid and abet the operation—by bringing dog food, by selling the operators grandstand equipment and seats, by running the food concessions at the dog fights, by advertising the fights through word of mouth and other underground means, and so on. Such people are likely to be formally cooperating with the operation, though in some cases through lack of knowledge or understanding, or even by duress, may be only materially cooperating with the dog fights.

Then there are those who attend the dog fights. Presumably, attendees purchase tickets and/or place bets with the "house." Thus attendees typically financially support the operation. Even if they don't have to pay for a ticket or bet on the matches, they are there to witness this blood sport.

Presumably, the audience sees nothing wrong with what they are witnessing, or else many of them would not be there. However, that does not justify their participation and support of it. While one could say that the audience is only "taking in entertainment" or "attending a sporting event," those are simply not adequate descriptions of what is going on. We cannot simply choose a morally neutral way of interpreting these actions, but have to take into consideration what is actually happening. The description must match reality. And one of the morally significant true descriptions of what spectators at dog fights are engaged in is morally and financially supporting the institutionalized practice of animal cruelty and torture. This description is much more truthful than "they are just taking in entertainment" because there are no credible mitigating or justifying factors for their support of this blood sport. To say "we all need some entertainment or relaxation," or "this is a good opportunity to spend time with my friends," does not change the fact that attending these dog fights hardly makes sense unless one approves of them. The cruelty to these dogs is not an incidental side effect to dog fighting. It is inherent to the sport of dog fighting as it is practiced.

In short form, a similar argument applies to eating pig meat, 95 percent of which is produced by factory farms, a bureaucratic and institutionalized structure that, again, gives no significance to the welfare or well-being of the animals apart from what maximizes the corporation's profit. Since this cruelty to the pigs is inherent to the production of factory-farmed pig meat—what I have called cruelty meat—does purchasing and eating pig flesh fall under the category of formal cooperation with wrongdoing?

For it to be material cooperation, the cruelty would have to be an unfortunate side effect that was not essential to the production of the meat as it is actually produced today in America.[14] However, in North American factory farming, cruelty is not a mere evil side effect or by-product to some legitimate good of eating pig meat. The cruelty is as an essential and necessary part of the logic of factory farming as is the cruelty to dogs in contemporary dog fighting. For in factory farming, the welfare of the animals is of no accord; it is entirely a matter of raising the animals in a way that maximizes profits. Any care or consideration given to the animals in the logic of factory farming is ordered to future maximization of profit. A proper description of factory farming understands cruelty as an essential element, and thus meat that one knows is from such a source is improperly referred to merely as meat, but is properly and truthfully described as cruelty meat.

Thus, if I were to eat North American factory-farmed bacon or ribs, I would consent to the cruelty that is inherent in the production of that bacon and ribs. It is analogous to buying stolen property. Even if I intend only good and upright uses of a bicycle or a flat-screen television, if I know (or have very good reason to believe) it is stolen property, then I am formally cooperating with wrongdoing. I consent or even contribute to the wrong—both the wrong done to the victim of the theft, and the wrong of supporting and sustaining the thief in his business. So it is if I eat factory-farmed bacon or ribs. I consent and perhaps contribute to the wrong done to the victims of the cruelty, and I support and sustain the

14. Furthermore, for it to be acceptable material cooperation, the good of eating pig meat would have to outweigh the cruelty that factory farming their bodies produces.

wrong done by the factory farm industry. Hence I formally cooperate in the cruelty to pigs when I buy and/or eat the bacon or ribs.

This is especially true since there is no need to eat cruelty pig meat. Millions of Americans don't eat pigs. And if you can afford it and want it, you can search for and pay the premium for pigs raised largely free of the worst cruelty (although this pork is harder to find). There's simply no moral justification (or "duress" in the terminology of moral theology) for continuing to buy and consume cruelty pig meat. Doing so is ignorance, laziness, or gluttony, or perhaps all three.

Final Considerations

In this essay I have argued that wanton animal cruelty is an inherent element of modern American factory farming, and that if we wish to be morally serious human beings, we should refuse to cooperate with this hideous wrongdoing. Noncooperation requires that we refuse to buy or eat cruelty meat. Within the limited argument I have made in this essay, that means not buying any kind of pig meat unless you have very good reason to believe that that meat did not come from factory-farmed animals. Similar arguments can be made regarding other factory-farmed animals.

Factory farming is problematic for reasons beyond those upon which I have focused in this essay. Factory farming contributes more to global warming than all our motor vehicles combined. In a world with so much starvation, the diversion of huge amounts of grain to factory-farmed animals is extremely wasteful. Eating hormone- and antibiotic-stuffed cows, pigs, and chickens harms our endocrine systems and makes us far more susceptible to drug-resistant "superbugs," which kill more people than we'd like to acknowledge. Our meat-heavy diets—diets made possible because of cheap industrial meat—are generally bad for our health. While all significant evils, they are not the point here.

Beyond that, there are also arguments one can make as to why one might not want to eat pigs or other kinds of animals, whether factory farmed or not. Some of these arguments—whether they be about the health or ecological benefits of not eating animals, or about the consideration we should show to other animals as God's creatures—are serious and worthy of consideration.[15] However, the moral argument against eating factory-farmed pigs seems overwhelmingly obvious. If one is not willing to consider and act on that, then these other arguments would seem to have little chance of a fair hearing, though the health argument, with its appeal to blatant self-interest, is certainly successful at times.

Furthermore, Christians have a responsibility not to eat factory-farmed animals because of the potential scandal. By "scandal," the Christian tradition means that when those of us who are exemplars for other Christians—whether as parents, teachers, priests, ministers, or lay leaders—do things that we know are wrong, we may lead others to think that such wrongs are actually morally acceptable. This is the point of Matthew 18:6: "If any of you put a stumbling block before one of these little ones who believe in me, it would be better for you if a great millstone were fastened around your neck and you were drowned in the depth of the sea." Once we understand the evil of cruelty meat, we have a particular obligation to witness to those who do not yet understand this form of cruelty.

There has not been enough leadership on this issue by Catholic theologians. One, however, has spoken out on one aspect of the issue, and his words are worth quoting: "Certainly, a sort of industrial use of creatures, so that geese are fed in such a way as to produce as large a liver as possible, or hens live so packed together that they become just caricatures of birds, this degrading of living creatures to a commodity seems to me in fact to contradict the relationship of mutuality that comes across in the Bible."[16]

---

15. I have argued elsewhere that we should consider vegetarianism based on our Christian witness to the eschatological peaceable kingdom. See Berkman and Hauerwas, "Trinitarian Theology of the 'Chief End of All Flesh,'" and Berkman, "Consumption of Animals and the Catholic Tradition."

16. Ratzinger, *God and the World*, 78–79.

12

Does "Made in the Image of God" Mean Humans Are More Special than Animals?

Stephen R. L. Clark

RECEIVED OPINION IN ALL civilized societies is that human beings are special. Only "primitives," it is supposed, can think of themselves as only one tribe amongst many, hunting and being hunted alongside their non-human cousins. Even Hindus, who honor the gods in animal form and who conceive that God could be incarnate as a turtle as easily as a human, acknowledge that being born human is a privilege and rare opportunity. Stoic philosophers were confident that only human beings (and only a few of them) could be God's "friends," and that the whole world was created for the use of such "rational" beings as us. The Hebrew Scriptures testify that humanity was made "in God's image," and granted dominion over all other living things, "the fish of the sea, and over the birds of the air, and over the cattle, and over all the wild animals of the earth, and over every creeping thing that creeps upon the earth" (Gen 1:26). In a later chapter we were even given them as meat, and told that "the fear and dread of you" shall be upon them all (Gen 9:2–4).[1] According to the *Catechism of the Catholic Church*:

1. See the chapters by Carol J. Adams and Judith Barad in this book for different ways of reading these passages.

> Of all visible creatures only man is "able to know and love his creator." He is "the only creature on earth that God has willed for its own sake," and he alone is called to share, by knowledge and love, in God's own life. It was for this end that he was created, and this is the fundamental reason for his dignity. Being in the image of God the human individual possesses the dignity of a person, who is not just something, but someone. He is capable of self-knowledge, of self-possession and of freely giving himself and entering into communion with other persons. And he is called by grace to a covenant with his Creator, to offer him a response of faith and love that no other creature can give in his stead.[2]

Quite where we get such exact information about the abilities of other creatures, and the purposes of their Creator, is unclear: the passages in Genesis at any rate are less explicit. Nevertheless, the *Catechism* goes on to insist, on John Chrysostom's word, that "man [is] more precious in the eyes of God than all other creatures! For him the heavens and the earth, the sea and all the rest of creation exist"[3] (even though, as the *Catechism* also notes, that God creates others in creation and calls them good before God gets around to "making man"). Some commentators have gone further, insisting that all other created things are useful only during this earthly life, and will have no share in the coming or eternal kingdom. This claim, like the others, seems not to be supported by any relevant revelation.[4]

---

2. *Catechism*, 356–57. That theologians and philosophers speak of Man, and also use the masculine pronoun to refer to God, is a fact with some connections to the topic of this paper: typically, the masculine is taken to be the active, "rational," commanding form. "Nature" has to put up with things—and so is considered feminine. It does not follow that we would have different attitudes if we were consistently gender neutral in our language, but the masculinist bias is indeed one to be noted, and as far as possible disowned. I have not struggled to revise the language of the *Catechism*, but sought a better balance in my own words hereafter.

3. John Chrysostom, *In Gen. sermo* 2, 1: PG 54, 587D–588A, cited in *Catechism*, 358.

4. So Aquinas *Summa Theologiae*, Suppl. 91.5: "If the end cease, those things which are directed to the end should cease. Now animals and plants were made for the upkeep of human life; wherefore it is written (Genesis 9:3): 'Even as the green herbs have I delivered all flesh to you.' Therefore when man's animal life ceases, animals and plants should cease. But after [the renewal of the world] animal life will cease in man. Therefore

Even those would-be-modern thinkers who wish to disown any pre-Darwinian influence on their thinking often insist that human beings must matter more than any other creature. At least they must matter more *to us* (who are, presumably, human beings ourselves), but this is reckoned more than just species solidarity. It is supposed that "really" human beings are "rational" or "personal" beings, though those of our own species who do not quite meet the grade should still be counted along with the rest of us, rather than being ranked as "only animals." We take this latter step mostly for fear of what could be done if our masters were allowed to decide who counted as "really human": better to insist that everyone biologically human should have the same respect as those whose nature "really" demands it. Everyone who is anyone seems to agree, in practice, with the *Catechism*. Man alone is "capable of self-knowledge, of self-possession and of freely giving himself and entering into communion with other persons." Moderns, abandoning a belief in God or the gods, and reckoning that all earthly life is evolved solely by Darwinian selection, from a common stock, and without any guiding hand, have less metaphysical reason to be confident that human beings are special,[5] but somehow the thought remains.

Treating Humans as if They Were Special

Radical moralists with a greater respect for evolutionary theory and for the products of evolution may be tempted to insist, on the contrary, that a

---

neither plants nor animals ought to remain." Hans Urs von Balthasar disagrees, saying that Aquinas and other Catholics have in this regard pronounced a "cruel verdict" that "contradicts the Old Testament sense of the solidarity between the living, subhuman cosmos and the world of men . . . the prophetic and Jewish ideas of divine salvation in images of peace among animals . . . and it also goes against a deep Christian sense . . ." Balthasar, *Theo-Drama*, 5:421. My thanks to Andy Alexis-Baker for this apposite and very welcome quotation.

5. To avoid an easy misunderstanding: that all earthly life is related, that new sorts of creature are constantly emerging, that novel traits can spread through a population when they offer a slight reproductive advantage, and that multicellular creatures, especially animals, are likely to form new "species" (reproductively isolated populations), are all very well supported claims that no theist need deny. That this process is never influenced by standing patterns, ethical ideals, or the Word of God is not a scientific but an ideological claim, at odds with theism. See my *Biology and Christian Ethics*.

species is no more than a set of interbreeding populations. Our own species is—genetically speaking—relatively homogeneous (more so, indeed, than chimpanzees or other primate groups), since we are all descended from a small, remnant population existing less than a hundred thousand years ago. This may not be true forever: species, including ours, may grow more varied, and may even break up into distinct descendant species.[6] Even now there is no biological reason to insist that all and only members of our species have some special character that warrants special treatment: we are not all very rational, nor can we all speak or reminisce or plan our lives any better than members of other species. We are not all self-possessed, and hardly any of us can truly claim to "know ourselves." Nor is it obvious that just those characters or even potential characters *should* grant us a special status. We do not ordinarily think that rational adult human beings should be given priority over human infants, nor do we value the latter solely in the hope that they will grow up.

> Suppose he [that is, a particular "backward" child] did remain more like a child than the rest of us. Is there anything particularly horrible about a child? Do you shudder when you think of your dog, merely because he's happy and fond of you and yet can't do the forty-eighth proposition of Euclid? Being a dog is not a disease. Being a child is not a disease. Even remaining a child is not a disease.[7]

By what right do we insist that dogs and children and not-very-clever people matter less to their Creator or to sensible people? If there is no guiding purpose in "creation" (that is, if there is no God), why exactly should "we" here and now insist that only members of an accidentally isolated, and transient, biological group "matter"? If there is a guiding purpose, why should we suppose that God hates anything that God has made? Why then should God have made it?[8] If we take the modern biological synthesis as our only guide, it is hard to see that there are any

6. I have examined this possible future in "Elves, Hobbits, Trolls and Talking Beasts," 151–67 (a revised version appeared in my *Philosophical Futures*).

7. Chesterton, *Four Faultless Felons*, 39.

8. See, for example, the *Wisdom of Solomon* 11:24: "For you love all things that you have made, for you would not have made anything if you had hated it."

"moral facts" to guide us, beyond whatever sentiments and repugnances we happen to have inherited. Whether our species will survive at all, and whether—if it does—our descendants will be recognizably "human," are both uncertain. Why not rather give our loyalty and affection to all *primates,* or all *mammals,* or all *vertebrates*? Isn't "speciesism" as irrational as racism? This would not be to say that it is wrong (if there are no actual, factual wrongs), but at least it would have no greater standing than the sympathy we mostly feel for other creatures. How can it be true both that there are no "moral facts" binding on all "rational minds," and that we would be wrong and irrational to value porpoises or dogs or apes as well as people?

Atheistic humanism, which somehow still gives priority to the *human* over the nonhuman, is perhaps pragmatically defensible. It may be true, as Cicero suggested, that we all (or almost all) have friendly feelings toward the human form wherever we may find it, and should trust those feelings rather than the dislike, fear, or envy that we also feel. Most peoples, anyway, no longer wish to obliterate or enslave their human cousins—and this is just as well, if those cousins now could do the same to us. Civilized peoples will no longer imprison and experiment on "savages" or even "criminals" because we are uneasily conscious that we might ourselves be seized upon when fortune changes. But neither civility nor civilization are as secure as we might wish: civilized people in fact have done these things in living memory, and may yet again. Atheistic moralists even now may sometimes be heard defending the killing of infants, imbeciles, the insane or senile or terminally depressed. "Humanity," as such, is no longer an absolute bar against such acts (if it ever was), and "human beings" are no different in kind than cattle (whom some radical moralists may wish to treat much better than in fact we do, while still suggesting that neither cattle nor "marginal humans" can have any personal vote in what is done to them).

If we should treat nonhuman and human beings alike when they are alike, one conclusion, indeed, is that we should treat nonhuman beings much better: we should consider their feelings, and their interests, as having the same weight as ours. Unfortunately, it is at least as likely that we shall treat *human* beings much worse: we shall reckon up their feelings and interests in a totalizing calculation that denies the human individuals any real say. We shall treat human beings like animals more eagerly than we ever treat animals like human beings—even when we do, in a way, intend to do them good.

> The practical weakness of the vast mass of modern pity for the poor and the oppressed is precisely that it is merely pity; the pity is pitiful, but not respectful. Men feel that the cruelty to the poor is a kind of cruelty to animals. They never feel that it is justice to equals; nay, it is treachery to comrades. . . . All the despair about the poor, and the cold and repugnant pity for them, has been largely due to the vague sense that they have literally relapsed into the state of the lower animals.[9]

It is unsurprising, accordingly, that more traditional moralists, whether they draw their inspiration from the Hebrew Scriptures or the classical philosophers, are likely to wish to reinstate the special status of humanity. Being "rational" cannot be quite what matters most, since many human beings are not rational (being infantile, deranged, senile, or merely rather stupid), hardly any are rational all the time (being ignorant, deluded, self-centered, and impulsive), and some nonhuman beings, by any objective standard, are at least as "rational" as most of us, even if they cannot speak. Traditional moralists may rather prefer to insist on the less tangible factor of being "in God's image" (which at least has more metaphysical and poetic resonance than Francis Fukuyama's "Factor X").[10]

Acting as if We Were Special

So what does it mean to be made "in God's image," and what are its implications, not for how we should be treated, but for how we should ourselves behave? The question is significant not only for those inspired by the Hebrew Scriptures, but also for other moralists, as it addresses issues now generally neglected. Whereas atheistic humanists and anti-speciesists

9. Chesterton, *Charles Dickens*, 197.

10. Fukuyama, *Our Posthuman Future*, 150: "You can cook, eat, torture, enslave or render the carcass of any creature lacking Factor X." What that factor is, however, he does not say.

alike have focused their attention on the particular properties of individuals, human or nonhuman, an older tradition suggests that individuals are members one of another, that none are self-sufficient. Whereas modern moralists, once they have decided what it is that is of value, are likely to rank individuals by how much they have of what is valued, the older tradition may be content to notice that no one actually has very much of what is valued—but that all, somehow, are to be valued for their *connection* with true value. I shall return to these suggestions. But first, what does it mean to be "made in God's image"?

Greek philosophers, as I have indicated, could interpret such a claim quite simply: God is a rational being, having reasons for what "He" does, and knowing enough to act on them. Other creatures in the world do not strictly *act* at all, since they do not have reasons. They do not have reasons, because they cannot investigate to see whether they have *good* reasons, nor can they modify their behavior to serve those reasons. They may be moved by fear or by desire, and to that extent do feel some things to be "bad" or "good," but cannot reevaluate those judgments in the light of a larger knowledge, nor judge themselves to be failing. Strictly, it may then come to seem, *God* does not have such reasons either, since there is no possibility in God of error, nor does God ever need to work things out as we do! So God, after all, is not one of us. A more sophisticated philosophy may suggest instead that human beings can have a relation with God that other creatures do not have, not because God is *like* us (since that is not true), but because our "rationality" offers a glimpse of things through God's eyes. All finite creatures are limited by their particular view of things: only the Infinite God contains all views. Human beings—or at least so the philosophers thought—can get a glimpse of the world-that-is, not just the world-for-us.

Will this serve to explain the idea that we are "in God's image"? Not that we are remotely like God, nor members of any class that equally contains both God and us, but that we sometimes and in some measure "reflect" God's being: the world-that-is can flicker across our consciousness, and we (sometimes, and very feebly) recognize that we are not ourselves the only center of the world. Sometimes we see a divine glory in the world and are reminded of a glory beyond it. But that is a very strange reason from which to conclude that everything is made and done "for us"! Even the *Catechism of the Catholic Church*, which asserts so bluntly that "man is the only creature on earth that God has willed for its own sake," and that "man" is more precious to God than any other creature, also declares that everything is given to us so that we may present it back to God.[11] We are not, after all, the only creatures that God loves. The *Catechism* also admits:

> Each creature possesses its own particular goodness and perfection. . . . By the very nature of creation, material being is endowed with its own stability, truth and excellence, its own order and laws. Each of the various creatures, willed in its own being, reflects in its own way a ray of God's infinite wisdom and goodness. Man must therefore respect the particular goodness of every creature, to avoid any disordered use of things which would be in contempt of the Creator and would bring disastrous consequences for human beings and their environment.[12]

Though in *Evangelium Vitae* John Paul II insisted that human beings were to be considered special, he also declared that

> The dominion granted to man by the Creator is not an absolute power, nor can one speak of a freedom to "use and misuse," or to dispose of things as one pleases. The limitation imposed from the beginning by the Creator himself and expressed symbolically by the prohibition not to "eat of the fruit of the tree" (cf. Gen. 2:16–17) shows clearly enough that, when it comes to the natural world, we are subject not only to biological laws but also to moral ones, which cannot be violated with impunity.[13]

Even if all things are created for our good, it does not follow (how could it?) that we may lawfully use them for bad ends or indeed for any end but God's greater glory (which is, to let them be what God would wish).

This much can be generally agreed: not all the purposes for which we have used nonhuman creatures are good. Even if they are given to us

11. *Catechism,* 358

12. Ibid., 339.

13. John Paul II, *Evangelium Vitae*, par. 42. John Paul II was citing his previous encyclical letter, *Sollicitudo Rei Socialis*, par. 34.

as food, it does not follow that we should make them suffer merely to add a relish to the meal. Even if we may use them to discover remedies for earthly diseases or disabilities, we must then seek to live in some way worthy of their sacrifice. Decent farmers traditionally acknowledge that they have duties of care toward their animals, and moralists in both the Greek and the Hebrew tradition have wished that our rulers be "good shepherds" (and not just exploitative shepherds).

> Prophesy, and say to them—to the shepherds: Thus says the Lord God: Ah, you shepherds of Israel who have been feeding yourselves! Should not shepherds feed the sheep? You eat the fat, you clothe yourselves with the wool, you slaughter the fatlings; but you do not feed the sheep. You have not strengthened the weak, you have not healed the sick, you have not bound up the injured, you have not brought back the strayed, you have not sought the lost, but with force and harshness you have ruled them. . . . I am against the shepherds; and I will demand my sheep at their hand, and put a stop to their feeding the sheep; no longer shall the shepherds feed themselves. I will rescue my sheep from their mouths, so that they may not be food for them. (Ezek 34:2–4, 10)[14]

Decent experimentalists may also honestly seek to minimize the trouble they cause their victims in their pursuit of knowledge (whether or not that knowledge is directly helpful to humanity). In doing this, after all, human beings may actually be doing a little better than other predator species: cats generally show no compunction in their play; wild dogs rip the bellies of their prey; ichneumon wasps plant eggs in living caterpillars (and Darwin felt—not quite absurdly—that this was enough to show that the Creator was not a loving God[15]).

14. See also Plato, *Republic* 1.345b.

15. Darwin, *Life and Letters of Charles Darwin*, 2:105: "I cannot persuade myself that a beneficent and omnipotent God would have designedly created the Ichneumonidae with the express intention of their feeding within the living bodies of Caterpillars, or that a cat should play with mice." The theme, as it occurs in assorted Victorians, is discussed by Gould, *Hen's Teeth and Horse's Toes*, 32–44. It is odd, perhaps, that few of those who are moved by the caterpillar's fate take much notice of animal suffering in their own lives and practice; see my "God, Good and Evil," 247–64.

But the very claim that human beings are made to remind us of God and that it is in Christ that God's true image and God's purposes for us are seen, perhaps suggests that even more is expected. Even pagan theologians thought as much: "for the son of Cronos has ordained this law for men, that fishes and beasts and winged fowls should devour one another, for right [*dike*] is not in them; but to mankind he gave right which proves far the best."[16] If we have been made "in God's image," may we not be expected to live by the law God gave us, rather than pursue the cannibalistic pattern loose in Nature? The *Catechism* insists that "in reality it is only in the mystery of the Word made flesh that the mystery of man truly becomes clear."[17] It is there that the true image is to be found, in one who "being in the form of God did not think to snatch at equality with God, but taking the form of a servant, became obedient to death, even the death of the cross" (Phil 2:6–8). How can that be made an excuse for crucifying others?

> Ask it for once without presupposing the answer of the egotism of our species, as God might ask it about his creatures: Why should a dog or a guinea pig die an agonizing death in a laboratory experiment so that some human need not suffer just that fate?[18]

But are we not worth more than many sparrows or than sheep (Luke 12:6–7; Matt 6:26; 12:12.)? The first question was posed to suggest to Jesus's disciples that they need not worry so much about the future, since God knew their necessities. The second was a reminder to his critics that it was lawful to do good on the Sabbath (precisely by rescuing a sheep fallen into a well). Neither can be used to suggest that God does *not* care for sparrows or for sheep, since the central point is, clearly, that God does—and that those who think that they are worth more than the nonhuman are called to *behave* as if they were![19] "Does God care for oxen?" (1 Cor 9:9). Obviously, yes, since "every wild animal of the forest" and "the cattle on a thousand hills" are God's (Ps 50:10). Till the early nineteenth century, the

16. Hesiod, *Works and Days* 1.275.

17. *Catechism*, 224, citing Paul VI, *Guadium et Spes*, par. 22.1.

18. Kohák, *Embers and the Stars*, 92.

19. See Nekeisha Alexis-Baker's essay in this book for an extended reflection on this passage.

only general laws protecting nonhuman welfare were to be found in the Torah (though this is not to say that other human societies did not care for animals, nor that Hebrew practice was consistent). Neither the Torah nor the growing body of Western law on the subject has done much to improve the condition of the creatures who live at our mercy. But they do signify at least a little recognition that we need to show them mercy.

Chesterton, speaking within a Catholic tradition (though years before his formal conversion), insisted that "cruelty to animals is cruelty and a vile thing; but cruelty to a man is not cruelty, it is treason. Tyranny over a man is not tyranny, it is rebellion, for man is royal."[20] But much is expected of royalty. Real kings, we are told, are servants, and not despots. "Whoever wants to be first must be last of all and servant of all" (Mark 9:35).

Atheistic naturalists may be mistaken in supposing that human beings are not special: indeed, they are probably living proof that after all we are. If we were not in some sense "special," what reason could we have for thinking that the capacities and talents bred into us by aeons of Darwinian evolution were sufficient to let us learn about the world at large or about our evolutionary past? "The fish does not trace the fish-bone pattern in the fowls of the air; or the elephant and the emu compare skeletons."[21] Theists may well be right to believe, or hope, that we have a chance, as human beings, to catch glimpses of the divine, and "live in unity and godly love." That dream may be a distant one:

> The wolf shall live with the lamb, the leopard shall lie down with the kid, the calf and the lion and the fatling together, and a little child shall lead them. The cow and the bear shall graze, their young shall lie down together; and the lion shall eat straw like the ox. The nursing child shall play over the hole of the asp, and the weaned child shall put its hand on the adder's den. They will not hurt or destroy on all my holy mountain; for the earth will be full of the knowledge

---

20. Chesterton, *Dickens*, 197; see also Chesterton, *All Things Considered*, 215. Chesterton, I should add, though he mocked vegetarians (such as his friend Shaw), was opposed to vivisection, and frequently acknowledged the claims of the nonhuman on our sympathy and respect. See further my *G. K. Chesterton*.

21. Chesterton, *Everlasting Man*, 307.

of the Lord as the waters cover the sea. (Isa 11:6–9; see also
65:17–25)

We live in a fallen world, and the glimpses we get of that better world
are rarely enough to distract us from our immediate profit. We are also
very much inclined always to favor our own family, our tribe, our species,
and give far more credit than is rational to the capacities and talents our
Creator gave us. The likeliest meaning of the verse in Genesis, as it was
first intended, was only that Adam was to be God's viceroy here on Earth,
and given talents to understand and guide all other earthly things. Maybe,
as later tradition says, he was also to rule angels, and intended as the focus
of earthly and heavenly kingdoms. How can it follow that he was to kill
and oppress his subjects? If we are intended, as the *Catechism* suggests, to
share God's life, had we not better remember that God is love? And if this
story is entirely false, and atheistic naturalists have somehow caught the
truth, maybe it would still be better to learn how to love the creatures with
whom we share mortality.

13

Can the Wolf Lie Down with the Lamb without Killing It? Confronting the Not-So-Practical Politics of the Peaceable Kingdom

Tripp York

The obsession with putting ourselves at the centre of everything is the bane not only of theologians but also of zoologists.

—YANN MARTEL, *LIFE OF PI*[1]

I'M NOT QUITE SURE whether it was fortuitous or providential, perhaps both, but as I was writing this chapter my fiancée, Carly, and I were watching a documentary on wolves. Carly is a doctoral student in the field of zoology with a fervent commitment to wildlife conservation. So what little time we spend watching television is in the company of the Discovery Channel, the Science Channel, and National Geographic.[2] It is far more

1. Martel, *Life of Pi*, 31.

2. *Animal Planet* was, at one time, one of our primary choices in television programming. Over the last few years, however, the channel has radically altered its direction and has opted for shows that promulgate the notion that most animals primarily seek to

informative than *Two and a Half Men*, and hardly as saccharine. Indeed, as much violence as we have witnessed in the animal kingdom, intra- and interspecies-wise, we had to turn our heads at one particularly vicious moment. The documentary was narrating a territory battle between two families of wolves (typically, wolf packs are comprised of blood relatives). As the older pack was forced out by a younger, stronger, and more numerous family of wolves, other creatures in the vicinity had to adapt to the new regime. Two coyotes, a male and a female, which had learned the territorial rules with the previous pack, stumbled upon the new group just as it took over. The wolves quickly descended upon the pair of coyotes. Though the female coyote escaped, her male mate was not so fortunate. At least a half dozen wolves captured the coyote and viciously ripped into its neck, face, and belly, consuming the coyote's entrails while tearing off its face. They showed no mercy. There was no simple nick on the tail given as a warning. The ferocity of the wolves, in light of the coyote's inability to defend itself, was terrifying. As we watched six or seven of them thrash the much smaller coyote, we averted our gaze. We were not surprised so much as we were horrified at the spectacle called "survival."

This is, of course, standard fare in the world. Creatures prey on one another. It is how they survive and provide for their young. What caught us so off guard was not this reality, but its momentary raw brutality. Their attack on the coyote did not occur simply for food, though the wolves did eat him; rather, it occurred as a show of strength, intimidation, and dominance. It was a bloody and violent explanation of the way things were going to be within the territory of this new wolf pack. This was simply their way of asserting themselves so that they could survive. Their behavior was not unforeseen or rare. It's just the way of the world.

As we mourned the loss of the coyote, the female who escaped had to continue living. Though she, too, was in a state of mourning, the next image revealed her in pursuit of a fox. She had immediately changed from prey to predator. In this case, the fox escaped. We were thrilled for the fox. It seemed as if some small victory had occurred in this conflict-torn arena

---

cause harm to humans. They have increasingly played up the violent tendencies within a number of species. This occurred, interestingly enough, around the same time that *Animal Planet*'s slogan became "Surprisingly Human."

called "nature." Granted, we know that this was probably not much of a victory for the hungry coyote.[3]

The next scene followed the same fox that had previously escaped its slightly larger foe. Though we found ourselves hoping the fox would out-fox the coyote, our cheer for her escape dissipated as she soon began prey-ing on a number of moles. Though we felt sorrow for the moles caught and consumed, would we not feel just as much sorrow for a starving fox? What about creatures that became food for the moles that escaped be-coming food for the fox? The moles escaped their predator only to kill and eat as many invertebrates as they could find. What about their lives? Or, what about the lives of the smaller invertebrates that fed the larger invertebrates that fed the moles that fed the foxes that fed the coyotes that fed the wolves? At this point, we had no idea who to "pull for." In pulling for one individual we were inherently pulling against another, and who are we to determine which creature is of more significance? Do we just base it on the cuteness of the creature? I fear such a response would reveal that we, too, have not escaped the indoctrination of something like *Two and a Half Men*.

Some may be tempted to refer to this cycle of life as vicious and cruel, though many will refer to it as only natural. In the latter sense, it is nei-ther good nor bad. Some naturalists suggest that we must simply come to terms with the fact that nature is indifferent to the pain and suffering each creature endures during its brief lifespan. Yet, despite such an outlook, the natural world remains, for some, incredibly beautiful. Whether it is the mountains with their rivers, forests, and abundant wildlife, or the ocean that hosts incredibly diverse and complex ecosystems in even the shallow-est of waters, the planet remains a marvel that boasts of God's goodness and creativity. That such an awareness is often an occasion for arguments for God's existence belies, unfortunately, a very rudimentary and surface-level glance. Such God-ordained beauty often dissipates upon closer examina-tion. The Pisgah National Forest in western North Carolina, for instance,

3. The coyote was, in this case, attempting to kill the fox more for territorial reasons and food scarcity than as a meal. Coyotes are, nevertheless, opportunistic eaters and will certainly eat a fox. For an in-depth examination into the coyote's ability to perse-vere, especially in light of our perennial efforts to eliminate them from existence, see DeStefano, *Coyote at the Kitchen Door*.

is a beautiful landscape teeming with incredible biodiversity. Upon closer look, however, one must take into consideration the vast amount of pain and suffering occurring within it. The forest contains emaciated creatures trying to feed off other emaciated creatures, animals searching for food to give to their offspring (many of which will not survive infancy), and many other creatures just trying to avoid becoming someone else's meal. Even the trees are in a slow, precarious march to death. As beautiful as the oaks, pines, cedars, and firs may be, they are infested with parasites that can only survive by slowly destroying their scenic hosts. Those parasites are being consumed by other parasites, and those parasites are being destroyed by bacterial parasites. This is called a thriving ecosystem. Nature, we might say in a rather hyperbolic tone, is one big parasite. Even no less a biologist as Charles Darwin remarked, "What a book a devil's chaplain might write on the clumsy, wasteful, blundering low and horridly cruel works of nature."[4]

Perhaps this is a cynical way of approaching nature; then again, perhaps not. Even the biblical writers speak of a time when creation will no longer have to endure the bondage of decay.

> For the creation waits with eager longing for the revealing of the children of God; for the creation was subjected to futility, not of its own will but by the will of the one who subjected it, in hope that creation itself will be set free from its bondage to decay and will obtain the freedom of the glory of the children of God. We know that the whole creation has been groaning in labor pains until now. (Rom 8:19–22)

This is a creation that, while created good, now anxiously awaits its redemption from death, pain, and sorrow. This is especially clear when we juxtapose this reality with the vision of God's holy mountain in Isaiah 11.

---

4. How interesting that Darwin referred to nature as cruel. As if, for a naturalist, there can be some point of reference for the meaning of such a word outside of the very thing (nature) he is referencing. Nevertheless, such a quote has been utilized in service of arguments against the existence of God by, in particular, Richard Dawkins. See, for instance, Dawkins's *A Devil's Chaplain.* Such arguments are only persuasive if one has first bought into the idea that God is an agent discoverable in the universe. Surely, orthodoxy protests such a notion, and, ironically, must agree with many of the arguments against the existence of God.

Despite all of the violence and wastefulness that occurs in nature, Isaiah depicts a time when

> The wolf shall live with the lamb, the leopard shall lie down with the kid, the calf and the lion and the fattling together, and a little child shall lead them. The cow and the bear shall graze, their young shall lie down together; and the lion shall eat straw like the ox. The nursing child shall play over the hole of the asp, and the weaned child shall put its hand on the adder's den. They will not hurt or destroy on all my holy mountain; for the earth will be full of the knowledge of the Lord as the waters cover the sea. (Isa 11:6–9)

While this could be read as a lovely metaphor of how we want things to be, or as a literal interpretation of which Christian hope is predicated, we have to ask certain questions: How practical is this? Can it be lived? Is it not a depiction of a reality completely beyond our control? If this vision is purely impractical, unrealistic, and unlivable, why bother? After all, isn't it the case that carnivores and omnivores require the death of others for their very existence? If so, how realistic is it for Christians to attempt to embody the vision as given in Isaiah? How are we supposed to live in a peaceable-kingdom-world that does not match up with the so-called real world?

A Boy and His (Eschatological) Wolf

For that original goodness that will be one day all things in all already shown forth in this saint all things in all.

—THOMAS OF CELANO

The above quote refers to Francis Bernardone, popularly known as St. Francis of Assisi. As is well known, Francis is the patron saint of animals. It would probably be safe to say that he is *the* patron saint of animals.[5] The

5. Francis is also the patron saint of the environment. I have never understood the separation of animals, human or nonhuman, from something called "the environment." For more literature on various saints and animals, see Waddell's *Beasts and Saints*.

quote follows a section in which his first biographer, Brother Thomas of Celano, discusses Francis's interactions with animals. Francis is known for his persistent preaching to any creature that would listen. If all animals belong to God (Ps 24:1), if God cares for all animals (1 John 4:16), if God is concerned with the salvation of animals (Jonah 4:11), and if Jesus commands us to preach to all creation (Mark 16:15), then this meant, for Francis, that he too must care for, save, and preach to all creation. He cared for creatures by demanding that we not carelessly wound or hurt any animal, and that we always show compassion for any creature in need. He preached to animals and even demanded that birds and crickets sing songs to their Creator.[6] In one particular case, he even negotiated a tense situation between a wolf and a small community of people. He asked the wolf to cease frightening the people in trade for the very reason the wolf was a so-called problem: food. The hungry wolf was only trying to survive. Due to the people's fears, a tense situation erupted between the two species, causing constant animosity and anxiety. Francis negotiated between the two, discovered the problem's root, and created a solution. After asking both parties to repent of their sins, he commanded the wolf to cease terrorizing the people, as they are made in the image of God, and the people to do their part—practice hospitality to the stranger. This arrangement worked for several years, with the wolf going door to door for food and with each person caring for the creature, until the wolf died. By this time, the small community had grown attached and lamented the wolf's death.

Though this story may very well be the product of exaggeration, what is significant is that Francis's biographers viewed him as the paradigmatic example for how to deal with human-wildlife conflict. Though there are now an abundance of PhD programs rooted in this very discipline, most of human history's resolution has often been to kill or destroy the offending nonhuman.[7] Yet Francis's sainthood is interwoven with his un-

---

Despite its unfortunate name, the book includes a number of interactions between Christianity's most devout and various individuals from the animal kingdom. It also contains lovely woodcuts by Robert Gibbings.

6. Thomas of Celano, *St. Francis of Assisi*, 269–74. For more on how Francis understood all creation in terms of salvation, see my chapter "Christianity Is for the Birds," in *Third Way Allegiance*, 25–27.

7. However, medieval law applied to animals and humans in which serious trials and

derstanding of how all creation participates in the salvific economy of the triune God. Creation is not inconsequential to salvation. If matter does not matter then salvation, the redemption of all things, is meaningless. Because the medieval church was very well guarded against gnosticism—specifically its refusal to see creation as a direct good from God with its concomitant desire to seek salvation from the material world—they at least had the resources to understand that redemption is not something meant for intangible souls. The redemption of creation is material, and includes all creation. Otherwise, if salvation is not deliverance of the very "thing" God pronounced good, then we might as well eat, drink, and be merry, for tomorrow we die.

I introduce Francis into this chapter because he disrupts the poverty of our imaginations. He does so by thinking it crucial, for faithful Christian existence, to live a resurrected life in light of Christianity's eschatological nature (eschatological meaning that we live with the "end" in view). His life is a crowning example of what it means to live in a particular kind of world that only some people can see. Christianity (as with any religion or culture) provides a particular lens for how its adherents can navigate the world. A vital part of Christianity's lens, or grammatical framework, revolves around time—specifically, that being a beginning, middle, and an end. Prior to the primordial fall, Christianity asserts that creation was at peace with itself. How such peace was originally undone

---

lawsuits were argued with canon lawyers appointed to argue on behalf of the animals and on the prosecution side. These trials were expensive, time-consuming affairs that showed just how serious they were taken. Sometimes the animals won. For example, a French jurist named Bartholomé Chassenée (1480–1542) successfully defended a community of rats against a lawsuit by arguing that the rats failed to appear in court because they had been threatened by too many cats! And when an ecclesial court excommunicated field mice in Glurns for destroying crops in 1520, the court also granted a pardon to all pregnant and adolescent mice. Thus communication between humans and animals was not the province of exceptional saints or superstitious peasants, but educated, "serious" people as well. Even great Enlightenment thinkers like Gottfried Wilhelm Leibniz wrote about animal trials in all seriousness (see Leibniz, *Theodicée*, 1:314). In this way, nonhuman animals were placed within the community of justice and not outside of it as they are in our modern, rationalized technological society. For more on this, see Dinzelbacher, "Animal Trials," as well as Jeffrey St. Clair's "Let Us Praise Infamous Animals," in Hribal, *Fear of the Animal Planet*, 1–8. I am grateful to Andy Alexis-Baker for reminding me of this much neglected aspect of medieval history.

is something of a mystery, but many within Christianity have suggested that it was undone through human disobedience, and this placed creation at odds with its creator.[8] This, too, was an act of creation. It created the secular, not as a domain but as a time. The secular is the time between times, ripe with violence, sickness, death, war, famine, and destruction. Once this time is no more, the end will resemble the beginning inasmuch as all will be subsumed into its original purpose.[9]

This way in which Christians see the world renders Christianity eschatological. James McClendon argues that Christian faith "sees the present in correct perspective only when it construes the present by means of the prefiguring past (God's past) while at the same time construing it by means of the prophetic future (God's future). 'This is that' declares the present relevance of what God has previously done, while 'then is now' does not abolish the future but declares the present relevance of what God will assuredly do."[10]

McClendon is arguing that inasmuch as Christianity is eschatological, it refuses any sort of depiction of the world as, "that's just the way it is." By its very eschatological nature, Christianity resists the inherent violence assumed in accounts of nature that tempt us to imagine death as a prerequisite to life, and it protests the sort of pragmatic realism that tempts Christians to lead lives of practical atheism. What this demands is a proper understanding of the purpose of creation—which Christianity claims is to glorify the triune God. All of creation, from red howler monkeys to Indonesian mimic octopi, exists to glorify God. Of course, there is very little to suggest that these creatures recognize this as their purpose, as they are, along with humans, doing everything they can just to

---

8. Such an understanding of the fall is problematic for a number of reasons. First, it does not accurately reflect what is going on in the text. The serpent is already at odds with the purpose of creation prior to the story of Adam and Eve. Also, scientific evidence clearly reveals a violent world prior to the introduction of humans—that is, the Tyrannosaurus rex was not a vegetarian. How the fall could ever occur is a more interesting theological debacle. For a discussion of the impossibility of the fall, see Milbank's *Being Reconciled*, 1–25.

9. The word *end* is not just understood as "the end," but as "an end." Creation is not an act in and for itself, but it has a purpose that is known by how Christ illuminates what it means to be a part of a new creation.

10. McClendon, *Systematic Theology*, 69.

survive.[11] Nevertheless, one of the central claims of Christianity is that creation is ongoing, and that it is, ultimately, a narrative of fulfillment. Stanley Hauerwas and John Berkman argue that it is from "our conviction that God redeems all of creation we learn that God, having created all things, wills that all things enjoy their status as God's creatures."[12] A Christian account of creation, therefore, does not end with the first two chapters of Genesis but must include passages such as Isaiah 11, Romans 8, and Revelation 21. Creation can only be properly understood in light of its original purpose, its ongoing struggle with fulfilling that purpose, and its ultimate completion.

This is why the witness of someone like St. Francis is so vital to how Christianity tells its own story. Francis's very life was a gospel. By that I mean it was good news to all creatures because he attempted to reflect the gospel that is Jesus for all of creation—not just one species. He understood that all animals, insomuch as they have a common Creator, were both his covenant partners and his kin (and this is centuries prior to Darwin!). What made Francis, for example, avoid stepping on worms or habitually set food out for insects in the winter was not that he was an "obsessed animal lover." Rather, he understood the purpose/end of creation. Because he lived an eschatological life, he could not imagine behaving otherwise to that which God declares "good." Francis imagined that humans were in the privileged and burdened position to name and care for all animals in the manner in which Jesus names and cares for all of us. Thus he was able to resist seeing animals as mere objects for our own use. It is precisely on this point that Christians name other animals well when we name them eschatologically. In order to do this faithfully, we have to be able to name animals in such a way that our treatment of these creatures tells them, and others, who we think they are in light of the purpose of creation. This is no easy task, as the principalities and powers have tempted many of us to forfeit any rich eschatological understanding of our own narrative. For instance, by imagining that pigs should be named "bacon," or snakes

11. Most creatures, if not all, only need to survive long enough to reproduce—which is what many biologists and zoologists will say is a creature's only real (or at least empirical) purpose.

12. Hauerwas and Berkman, "Trinitarian Theology of the 'Chief End of All Flesh,'" 69.

"belts," or crocodiles "boots," or elephants "circus entertainment," or cows "milk machines," or rabbits "safe cosmetics," we make it difficult to recover adequate theological language. Is it not the case that the story of creation, as found in Genesis, Romans, and Isaiah, provides us with resources for naming animals differently than the above designations?

If so, I imagine that the first eschatological act we must perform, as intimated above, is getting our language right. If we are to be faithful to our own narrative, and that which we purport to be true, then the naming of animals must correlate with our habits and practices as informed by God's peaceable kingdom. If Christians and non-Christians are to see a world that is intelligible in light of our claims, then we must speak, and perform, a very particular kind of language. For instance, as a thought experiment, what if we ceased using descriptions that label animals as products, cosmetics, food, clothing, entertainment, and pets[13] and decided to call them, first and foremost, *"our covenant partners"*? Wouldn't that be profoundly more biblical than the previous alternatives? What difference, if any, would that make? Or, what if we resisted the story that the biomedical sciences have imposed upon us and renamed "lab rats" our "kin"? How could a Christian ever faithfully call a creature of God a lab rat? From what story does that originate? Is that labeling a truthful account of those who think that God created, ordered, and redeemed the world, or is that a description of a world in rebellion against that which God called good?

So, instead of calling animals food, cosmetics, medicine, clothing, and entertainment, I wonder what difference it would make if we referred to them as manifestations of God's creative wisdom who are our covenant partners participating in God's redemptive history. This does not romanticize nature or the animal kingdom; it simply names the world biblically rather than naming it using the common conception that animals are here for no other reason than our species-centric benefit. What are Christians saying about creation's purpose when we name it based on how we, only one of a myriad of species, can plunder it for whatever uses our greed leads us to discover? Is this not a poor witness to the way the world was

---

13 Stephen Webb offers the most persuasive argument I have encountered for the retaining of the word *pet*. I remain, however, unconvinced that such language can fully bring about the kind of mutuality Webb desires. For a thorough discussion on the use of this language, see his *On God and Dogs*, 69–84.

created, was meant to be, and will one day be again? Is it not both our burden and privilege to embody Isaiah's vision so that others may catch a glimpse of that which we claim to be true? While it is true that the kingdom is not yet fully realized, it is up to Christians to be faithful to their understanding of creation, so that others will know there is an alternative to this vision of a world at war with itself. Otherwise, how can anyone know that there is a different way of interpreting creation than what seems to be the senseless, wasteful, and cruel practices of the cold and indifferent cycle called nature?[14]

A Boy and His (Eschatological) Crocodile

It is we who have to change, not they . . . If Virgil and Beatrice have to change according to someone else's standards, they might as well give up and be extinct.

—YANN MARTEL, *BEATRICE AND VIRGIL*

On September 4th, 2006, Steve Irwin, also known as the "Crocodile Hunter," was killed by a stingray.[15] Although many of his admirers and critics had expressed concern about the risk of his hands-on approach with creatures, his death still came as a shock. Perhaps part of the shock stems from our celebrity-obsessed culture's tendency to attach immortality to celebrities. While I think this may be partially true, I also think it may have had more to do with the manner in which he was killed: impaled through the chest by a nonaggressive creature that has claimed, barely, a handful of people in the Australian waters. Indeed, stingrays are sort of

---

14. I am not suggesting that only Christians can provide this alternative. If this were the case, I fear that the world would be without much hope at all! Clearly, other religions, cultures, and naturalists produce groups and individuals that embody an alternative to our participation in an assumed ontologically-ridden violent world. As the last section of this essay will show, I think Christians have much to learn from those of no clear religious affiliation whatsoever.

15. This latter section leans heavily on a previously published article of mine titled, "Crocodile Lover: Learning from Steve Irwin," 9–10. It was later republished with the title, "The Theological Significance of One Strange Australian," in *Third Way Allegiance*, 28–32.

the "petting-zoo" creature of the waters. There is even a tank where you can touch and feed stingrays in the Opry Mills Outlet Mall in Nashville, Tennessee (as well as in countless aquariums). That Irwin was killed by such a passive creature is surely ironic and difficult to believe.[16]

On this point, I find Irwin's life to be of significance for Christian reflection. His life was, in many ways (intentionally or not), an eschatological witness to the way the world was created, its intention and purpose, and to the manner in which it will be redeemed. He did not treat nonhuman animals the way many animal rights advocates desire: leaving them to their own devices. He did not think it was responsible to adhere to the complaints of groups like PETA that wanted him to stop touching nonhuman animals and interfering with their lives. As we already know, it's way too late for that. We have already touched them and interfered in their lives—and in the most damaging ways. Irwin acknowledged criticisms about his approach, yet argued that if there is any hope for animal conservation, then we have to be as physically involved as possible.[17] He took, I believe, a more biblical approach in that he recognized nonhuman animals as our kin. He did not simply let creatures be; rather, he intervened on their behalf because he recognized the beauty, the goodness,

16. In an interview about Irwin's death, popular conservationist Jack Hanna said, "I never pictured a croc doing it, but I never pictured a stingray doing it, either. It's like me being killed by a poodle."

17. There is legitimacy to many of the complaints against Irwin's approach to conservation. Chasing, grabbing, and jumping on animals certainly causes undue stress to each individual. It can also, unwittingly, teach others that this is the appropriate way to handle animals (if they should be handled at all). Irwin argued that proper handling, especially in a land like Australia (where many of the animals are venomous), is responsible in terms of knowing how to negotiate human/nonhuman conflict. He also found it important in terms of teaching people how to love that which they may otherwise deem unlovable. He would often say that people want to save that which they love, and so he wanted to present as intimate a picture of animals as possible. Prior to Irwin becoming an international success, there were two ongoing television shows preaching the importance of animal conservation. There are now more than thirty. I find that to be a far more compelling and successful approach than the throwing of fake blood on people wearing fur (as tempting as that may be). Nevertheless, for a helpful conversation arguing for and against celebrity conservationists, their tactics, and how Irwin was often not always consistent in regard to understanding a number of ecological issues in his homeland, see Paquette, "Importance of the 'Crocodile Hunter' Phenomenon," and Bradshaw, Brook, and McMahon, "Dangers of Sensationalizing Conservation Biology."

and the mystery that is found within all of creation. He saw these animals as fellow creatures that desperately require our care. As with Francis, he understood that there was a commonality that linked all creatures, regardless of species. Neither Irwin nor Francis was able to understand how anyone could be indifferent to the plight of creation. For either creation is good or it is not good—and if it is good then it cannot be good for it to be destroyed.

At the same time, I want to be careful not to underwrite any kind of mawkish idealism. Irwin never romanticized wildlife, and neither should we. He never imagined that if one simply spent enough time caring for a crocodile that it would become his friend.[18] That was, of course, neither his task nor his calling. His job was to help spread the good word of wildlife conservation. Though acting on their behalf, he never assumed that such creatures would ever thank or love him for it. Yet, this is what makes his witness all the more interesting. His love for these creatures is all the more impressive as it was, generally speaking, nonreciprocal. He did not love a creature because of the possibility of a mutual love affair; rather, he loved these creatures simply because they were creatures. He loved them

18. At his memorial service, Steve's father, Bob Irwin, said, "Please do not grieve for Steve, he's at peace now. Grieve for the animals. They have lost the best friend they ever had, and so have I." I take this as recognition that Steve was the best advocate a crocodile, Komodo dragon, banded sea snake, or any other animal, for that matter, could find. Of course, some animal advocates would disagree. See, for instance, Hribal, *Fear of the Animal Planet*. Hribal protests, in particular, the kind of animal handling found in circuses and zoos. While this book is an indispensable collection of stories displaying various animals' refusal to act according to human desires, it is, unfortunately, egregiously unsophisticated in its understanding of both animal behavior and the work of zoos. Every example used to buttress Hribal's case actually finds agreement with the very people (zookeepers, in particular) he thinks he is condemning. It's part of the reason why, at least in the case of zoos (and due to the good work of people like Hribal and other animal activists), so many of them, under the direction of the Association of Zoos and Aquariums, are altering their purpose to focus primarily on conservation, habitat rehabilitation, and breeding and release programs. Much of animal keeping is moving to a protected or no-contact policy that, unfortunately, has to continue displaying animals that cannot be rereleased into the wild so that these conservation centers can help ensure that other creatures will not need to end up in zoos. Many zoos, conservation centers, and wildlife parks actually function as a safe place *from* humans. If anything, that is certainly a stronger condemnation of human/animal interactions than is the relatively minute number of careless animal keepers.

because they reflect creation's mystery. He loved them because he loved the world. He called snakes, crocs, spiders, and many other dangerous creatures "beauts." That is, I imagine, part of what it means to name creatures well. He looked at animals with an entirely different lens than that which many of us are accustomed to wearing. Despite creation's present parasitical nature, despite those things we might see as wasteful, cruel, or ugly, he was able to see something much deeper. He practiced a vision of how things could and/or should be, and for that, he lived a kind of incarnational theology that puts many of us to shame.

Many times, as I watched *The Crocodile Hunter Diaries*, I would reflect on Isaiah 11:6: "The wolf shall live with the lamb, the leopard shall lie down with the kid, the calf and the lion and the fatling together, and a little child shall lead them." When one watched the crocodile hunter in action, it was easy to compare him to the kind of child referenced in Isaiah. He never seemed to see a world that most "responsible" people demand we embody; instead, he looked upon creation with the eyes of a child—one that could play over the "hole of the asp" and put his "hand on the adder's den" (Isa 11:8).[19]

19. Irwin was not a vegetarian. Given his harsh comments about Australians' eating kangaroos and other cultures consuming snakes or dolphins, it's hypocritical that he ate cows. Were they not "beauts"? Irwin considered being a vegetarian but thought it better for a larger body of wildlife that he eat some flesh. In an interview with *Scientific American* in 2001, he said, "I went through a big stage of my life where I thought, you know, maybe it would be better to be a vegetarian, so I researched it. In no uncertain terms did I research it. Let's say this represents one cow, which will keep me in food for, let's say, a month. Now that cow needs this much land and food. Well, you can imagine, that cow needs x by x amount of land, and you can grow trees in it. Around that cow, you can have goannas, kangaroos, wallabies. You can have every other single Australian animal in and around that cow. If I was a vegetarian, to feed me for that month, I need this much land, and nothing else can grow there. Herein lies our problem. If we level that much land to grow rice and whatever, then no other animal could live there except for some insect pest species. Which is very unfortunate." Irwin, "Protecting Wildlife in His Own Backyard." What is most unfortunate is his incredibly naïve understanding of how damaging to the environment is the breeding of cattle for food. Also, cows, too, must eat. They require a whole lot of land, as Irwin argued, in which nothing else can grow. His defense is just baffling. The amount of land required to grow food for vegetarians/vegans is a fraction of what is required to breed and sustain animals for our consumption.

Nevertheless, Steve Irwin was killed by one of the very creatures he loved so dearly. The fact that a stingray plunged its spine into his chest while he was filming a documentary on the deadliest creatures in the ocean should not be lost on us. We live in a world at odds with itself, and no one understood this better than Irwin. Creation awaits redemption, and it is only in light of this redemption that we can appropriately understand something called "creation." We pine for that moment when "nothing harmful will take place on the Lord's holy mountain" (Isa 11:9), but until then, all we have are glimpses of God's peaceable kingdom. A few saints and a handful of popular conservationists such as Steve Irwin, Jane Goodall, Jeff Corwin, Richard O'Barry, and Jean-Michel and Philippe Cousteau provide us with such glimpses. Though these conservationists differ radically in their approach (and it is in their differences that I think we have the best chance for improving our approach at habitat and species conservation), they provide us with an intelligible means of participating in this ongoing narrative called creation. In this time between times, they are curiously faithful practitioners of the eschatological vision we find in Isaiah. I say "curiously" because, in the case of the above-mentioned conservationists, it is by no means clear that any of these people utilize biblical resources for doing what they do. In this sense, as in so many others, Christians are being out-narrated by individuals who appear to have a more faithful understanding of what it means to live peaceably than those within our own tradition.[20] It is the experimental witness of such people that provides hope that there is some alternative to simply biding our time, waiting for an intervention, and just embodying the fallen nature of this world. It's simply not good enough for us to say, "Well, wolves eat lambs, therefore I can, too." To be ensnared in such an argument is to

20. This should not, for two reasons, be interpreted as an argument for anonymous Christianity. First, I wish to avoid such imperialism, and second, this would assume that there is something in Christianity for these people to gain in their approach to animal conservation. I'm not sure, at least within the parameters of North American contemporary Christianity, there is anything for anyone outside of Christianity to learn that would be beneficial to animal conservation. Christians are the ones who need to be on the learning side of what it might mean to envision the wolf lying down with the lamb, and it starts by studying the lives of the aforementioned conservationists as well as reading the works of people like Frans de Waal, Jeffrey Masson, Marc Bekoff, Sue Coe, Mark Rowlands, Amy Hatkoff, Cleveland Amory, and Ruby Roth, among others.

concede our most important resource for that which we claim to be true: our witness. The point is not what are we going to do to keep the wolf from killing the lamb, but how are we going to live lives that reflect our tradition's best claims as to the *purpose* of all creation. Doesn't the refusal to eat or wear animal flesh point to this ordained end? Or, what about those people who dedicate their lives to healing sick creatures, caring for them, binding their wounds and raising the orphaned so that they can live lives that reflect the beauty and mystery of creation? Is this not a witness to that for which we were created? For a faith that is eschatological in nature, what are we waiting for? To be sure, it may be the case that what we, undoubtedly, are waiting for (to paraphrase a famous philosopher) is another—doubtless very different—St. Francis . . . or Steve Irwin.[21]

21. I am indebted to Claire Priddy, Carly Sinderbrand, and David MacDougall for their invaluable suggestions on an earlier draft of this essay.

14

Vegetarianism: A Christian Spiritual Practice Both Old and New

By Danielle Nussberger

THERE WAS AN ANCHORITE [a hermit] who was grazing with the antelopes and who prayed to God, saying, "Lord, teach me something more . . ."[1]

As grateful companions to all the earth's inhabitants, we are like this early Christian hermit who fervently wished to know firsthand how to meaningfully exist in careful harmony with the living beings of God's exquisite creation. This time-honored pursuit for an all-inclusive solidarity amongst God's creatures (Isa 11:6–8) signals our supreme yearning for union with the triune God, who is the providential designer of creation's "unity in difference." As Isaiah indicated, ultimate union with God will mean living in the peaceable kingdom: "There shall be no harm or ruin on all my holy mountain; for the earth shall be filled with knowledge of the LORD, as water covers the sea" (Isa 11:9). When we, like the Christian hermit, ask to "learn more," we are pining for this "knowledge of the LORD" to overwhelm us and to heal our wounded lives and our fractured attachments to other living beings. This knowledge of God or union with God

---

1. Passage quoted from *World of the Desert Fathers*, 20.

causes the cessation of human domination whose false power tears apart the life-giving bonds of creation. Peace on the earthly plain, then, is a sign of divinely graced communion with God. Practices of nonviolence result from knowledge of God and also generate a more radical entrance into the divine mystery that is their source. Vegetarianism—a specific practice of nonviolence—can thus be a respected component of an authentic Christian spirituality whose uppermost goal is union with God and whose organic expression is a substantial moral character that proclaims Christ to be King of the peaceable kingdom.

In order for vegetarianism to be a sound element of a healthy *Christian* spirituality that convincingly conveys itself in a robust moral existence, it must radiate from a comprehensive spiritual program rooted in Christ, the sustaining vine of the Christian moral life. In the pages that follow, I offer an ancient example of just such a vegetarianism, one that was rooted in a broader spiritual base that blossomed forth from imitation of Christ through receptivity to his presence in the Scriptures. Many of the Christian ascetics (men and women of self-denial) who withdrew to the Egyptian desert in the fourth and fifth centuries practiced this spiritually germinated vegetarianism. These desert *ammas* (mothers) and *abbas* (fathers) journeyed into the literal wilderness and the metaphorical wasteland of inner solitude in order to imitate Christ's archetypal self-denial and its climax on the cross.[2] When we appreciate and learn from this early spiritual program of self-emptying, we gain resources to embark on a contemporary spiritual regimen that includes the discipline of vegetarianism. Abstaining from meat and other animal products becomes a means of controlling selfish human appetites that wage violence against the peaceable kingdom by halting its all-inclusive solidarity and thereby impeding union with God in Christ. A vegetarianism that is situated within an ascetical spirituality oriented toward intimacy with God in Christ can help fashion a peace-making human being who is faithful to her primary relationship with God and to her moral obligation to protect and enhance her relationships with other human beings.

---

2. To sample some of this desert wisdom, see *Sayings of the Desert Fathers.*

The Example of Desert Asceticism

The desert fathers and mothers of the fourth and fifth centuries will be our precedent for the claim that a Christian-based vegetarianism and its regard for animal welfare reinforces (rather than weakens) the Christian's quest for union with God as seen in the moral obligation to love one's neighbor. Their spiritual vision saw that every choice *for* another living being steadily strengthens one's communion with God and other human beings, and that every choice *against* another living being progressively erodes one's friendship with God and others. To find out how they arrived at this particular insight through a thoroughgoing adoption of Christ's disposition of self-abandonment, we will immerse ourselves in their worldview by closely following one of their most notable exemplars, Antony the Great (251–356 CE).[3]

Athanasius's *Life of Antony* (350 CE) lays bare the following chief characteristics of Antony's spiritual process of self-abnegation: 1) an attentiveness to Christ's call to obediently part with his home and community and to progressively secure inner solitude for the emptying of self-motivated desires that had taken God's place; 2) periods of temptation wherein the inner demons of possessive desire gained strength and then subsided because of Antony's growing faith in the power of Christ's humility; and 3) the gradual shift from self-oriented passions to godly ordained desires that initiated a healing ministry in the heart of the community. These periods of service to the villagers reinforced Antony's devotion to a perpetual, rigorous *ascesis* (discipline) that would further redirect the self to God for the selfless benefit of others.[4]

As he matured in the ascetic life, Antony learned to keep a watchful eye on the quality of every desire (and its corresponding act), because he now knew that each one worked to shape him into the kind of human being that he would become. A longing and its realization that saw the other as belonging to God and as beautiful in God's eyes would form him into one who was united to God and others, whereas a desire and its

3. I chose to focus on Athanasius's *Life of Antony* because of its almost immediate, widespread influence on the future of desert monasticism. For a comparable tale about a prominent desert mother, see Pseudo-Athanasius, *Life of Blessed Syncletica*.

4. Athanasius, *Life of Antony*.

fulfillment that saw the other as belonging to Antony would de-form him into one who was lost from God and others in the death of sin. Were he to satisfy the appetite to own the other, he would do violence to the other, to himself, and to his relationship with God. He would deny Christ's gift of salvation that freed him from selfish desire and that brought him into glorious union with God through the Holy Spirit. Christ was the source of unity with God and others, and he therefore had to be Antony's stronghold in the arduous journey of transforming his desires.[5]

Let Antony be our guide, then, through the elements of his ascetical imitation of Christ. Here, we can discern the intricately woven spiritual tapestry that contains the thread of vegetarianism. This ascetic vegetarianism is a spiritual praxis of nonviolence connected to other ascetic disciplines that foster union with God and others.

1) Attending to Christ's Call

Antony began his lifelong pilgrimage in the desert when he heard the Jesus of Matthew's Gospel addressing him directly: "Go, sell all you have and follow me" (Matt 4:20).[6] Without hesitation, Antony obeyed; he gave everything away and moved to the edge of town to become an ascetic— one who loses his false ego by prudently controlling his passions so as to find his genuine self in the unparalleled hunger for God. From this point on, Antony underwent increasingly more intense stages of detachment by simultaneously progressing further and further outward into the wilderness (from the edge of town, to the tombs, to the outer mountainous regions) and further and further inward into the depths of his being.[7] By giving up his home and all personal and physical attachments, Antony had embarked on a laborious journey of introspection, one that brought him closer to himself by bringing him closer to God. He learned a criti-

5. Paul van Geest argues that Athanasius portrays five stages of monastic formation in his *Life of Antony*, the last of which demonstrates how *ascesis* is sustained by love for Christ. See "Anthanasius as Mystagogue," 199–221.

6. Athanasius, *Life of Antony*, 31.

7. For an expert interpretation of the role of space—both internal and external—in Antony's spiritual journey, see Burton-Christie, "Place of the Heart," 45–65. Burton-Christie writes, "Antony not only moves further *out*; he also moves further *in*—into solitude, into himself," 52–53.

cal spiritual lesson: the God of salvation came startlingly closer when the ascetic made room for God through persistent practices of self-emptying. Moreover, he learned that one could finally see one's godlike image (Gen 1:27) after having removed the narcissistic impediments that had once concealed it.[8]

Antony became a renowned desert *abba* by understanding the necessity of detaching himself from self-oriented passions that did not respect the other as other and as having a singular part in God's creation. He knew he had to vigorously resist and redirect misguided desires for self because more often than not they used and manipulated others for individual interest and pleasure. In order to demolish the idol of the ego, he had to acknowledge and pledge not to repeat a history of abuse that resulted from blind fixation on distorted yearnings and allegiances. Antony's ascetic outlook reasoned that the others to whom our desires are directed are not the sinful ones; they do not lead us away from God. The sin lies in a self-interested fastening on to others that is the converse of loving relationship; this draws one away from others and away from the Lord of life. When Antony emptied himself completely of all such injurious associations, he made space for God to dwell in him—the redeemer God who would heal his relationships with others and restore his rightful unity with God and all beings within God's creation. He discovered that God intended him to embrace self-denial so that he might become fertile soil for a new life of graced "being in relation."

Antony's biographer, Athanasius, found in Antony a flesh-and-blood testament to Christ, the divine Savior who was "one in being with the Father."[9] As Athanasius had taught and as the Council of Nicaea (325 CE)

---

8. Columba Stewart, OSB, explains this spiritual lesson that was inherited by St. Benedict of Nursia in the sixth century and passed down in his Rule: "Every practice and discipline of the monastery should heighten awareness: this is the meaning of self-renunciation, the lessening of me for the increasing of God. . . . The external and physical disciplines of the monastic life establish parameters and space for the transformation of mind and heart that Benedict calls *conversatio morum*," *Prayer and Community*, 88–89.

9. In his introduction to Athanasius's *Life of Antony*, Gregg writes, "Advocacy of the Christian beliefs articulated by the Council of Nicaea in 325 . . . was Athanasius's consuming vocation . . . Although the works published here do not purport to be polemical writings, they too provide evidence of Anthanasius's vigilance against unorthodox ideas and doctrines," 1.

had confirmed, our salvation in Christ meant that he was God-made-human. This was the Son who abandoned himself to the Father's will and descended to earth from heaven to become human. Through the Son's self-emptying—which theologians call "kenosis"—God's very being was united with all humanity for their redemption.[10] When he contemplated Antony as Christ's disciple, Athanasius realized that the person seeking union with God was called to imitate Christ's kenosis. Just as the Son had emptied himself in "descending" to become one with human beings, in a similar way the human person had to empty himself in "ascending" to become one with God. Antony was clearly "ascending" in his spiritual journey to union with God. He struggled daily to relinquish himself and to open himself up to be filled with the Spirit. Athanasius saw that instead of losing his human identity by sacrificing his desires, Antony had entered more deeply into his own heart where he found himself in finding God. He no longer used others as fulfillers of his wants. In turn, those others could take their proper place as others in relationship with God. Just as the Son's devotion to the Father in his incarnational kenosis revealed God's "being in relation," in a similar way Antony's ascetical obedience to Christ manifested our graced relation to others in and through God's love for creation. Antony's committed vegetarianism was one of the central ways in which he enacted this divinely gifted fellowship with all God's creatures, human and nonhuman animals alike. For striving for unity with nonhuman animals was requisite for establishing a community of just and merciful human beings who imaged Christ.

2) The Temptation of Autonomy

The road to union with God through a selfless reorientation to others was a complicated one. Antony's intensified isolation could be dangerous, because when alone illusions could multiply. All by himself in the darkness of a tomb, his imagination ran wild and the demons of his old desires appeared to him. They tried to convince him that they were his faithful friends and that they only wanted to see him strong and contented. It

---

10. Kenosis means an "emptying" and is christologically defined in terms of the Son's self-emptying that Paul describes in Philippians 2:7: He "emptied himself, taking the form of a slave, being born in human likeness."

could never be wrong for him to satisfy his hunger with life's pleasures, or else he would die. Others existed for his satisfaction, and knowing what they could do for him did not necessarily entail hurting them. These demons terrorized him. Their relentless violence exposed the lie of the masterful, atomized self. The Savior had taught Antony that there could be no strength in destruction; the only power worthy of the name was that of communion in love, and this could only be realized through giving oneself away. Confronted by his selfish desires, Antony faced the ugly reality of sin and ran to safety in the humble Christ. Shouting louder than the demons, all he had to do was invoke Christ's name and they fled. Again, Athanasius found the Antony who clung to Christ in his steadfast struggle against sin. There, in Antony's experience, Athanasius could see the truth of Christ, who never ceased to empty himself in order to carry our burden and bring us back to right relationship with God and with all others in God's creation. By the simple, grace-filled act of uttering Christ's name, Antony united himself to Jesus; he gave all of his desires, dreams, and imaginings over to the Christ who would recast them into the shape of sacrificial kenosis. Alone in the silence of a dark, empty tomb, Antony was one with the whole world.[11]

3) The "Passionlessness" of Compassion

Alone with Christ, Antony's solitude re-formed his once self-motivated passions into godly ordained desires that recognized who others truly were in God's grace rather than misunderstanding them as objects of his ego-centric expectations. The precise point of self-transformation from ego to graced "being in relation" was known as *apatheia*, which means "absence of passion" or "passionlessness."[12] Having watched Antony's temptations in the tomb, we know that this term could not have meant that the ascetic was supposed to be aloof and uncaring, oblivious to the needs of others. Such disinterestedness in the community would have been the result only if Antony had given in to the demons. Rejecting the demons by calling for

11. For passages dealing with Antony's struggles with the demons, see *Life of Antony*, 37–39. See also Burton-Christie, "Place of the Heart," 51–55.

12. For important background to the origins of *apatheia* and its meaning, see Driscoll, "*Apatheia* and Purity of Heart in Evagrius Ponticus," 141–59.

Christ meant that Antony had escaped the chains of a cruel autonomy and embraced his innate bond to the rest of humanity in Christ.

The advancement to "passionlessness" entailed letting go of selfish desires so that God's yearnings for the human soul could replace these desires. As a result, Antony and others like him could see all others as they are—cherished beings of God's creation—instead of seeing them as their possessions. *Apatheia* referred to the momentous transition from the blindness of sin and selfishness to the sight of grace and godliness. Outside of *apatheia* one's unruly desires impaired one's vision of God and others and disconnected one from God's love. Within the horizon of *apatheia*, one could truly love because there one could see the other as other and God as God. In his *Life of Antony*, Athanasius portrayed how *apatheia* enabled compassion by presenting the self-denying, "passionless" Antony whose self-giving took root in Christ's passion. His separation from others prepared him to return to the community with Christ's healing love by ministering to his neighbors when they came to him for spiritual guidance. He attended to their needs with the sincerest form of compassion that had been forged by his honest confrontations with the suffocating grasp of a godforsaken, autonomous self.[13]

Antony was simultaneously in community with human beings and other animals by consciously deciding that a vegetarian diet would be a chief aspect of his spiritual discipline. He lived on bread and salt with "no reason even to speak of meat and wine, when indeed such a thing was not found among the other zealous men."[14] Worried that others had gone out of their way to bring him bread, he found a spot of land near a mountain and planted grain for himself and vegetables for those who would come to seek his companionship. When the wild animals tampered with his garden, he spoke to them with the same gentle voice he used to address the weary travelers coming to meet him; he asked them not to hurt him, just as he had not done them any harm.[15] Exercising *apatheia* enabled Antony to relate to the animals as fellow beings, valued creatures in their

---

13. Athanasius, *Life of Antony*, 42–43. For a commentary on the connection between inner solitude and love of neighbor in the lives of the other desert fathers and mothers, see Chryssavgis, *In the Heart of the Desert*, 79–82.

14. Athanasius, *Life of Antony*, 36.

15. Ibid., 68–69.

own right who must not be used and abused as objects for human self-indulgence. His kenotic way of life opened him up to God; and, as a result, he was filled with the grace and wisdom to befriend all God's creatures as treasured kin.

Vegetarianism in the Desert

Antony's ascetical imitation of Christ inspired subsequent desert fathers and mothers to also practice *apatheia* as the means to arriving at love in its purest form: unselfishly loving God and neighbor by participating in the crucified and risen Christ's compassionate communion with creation. In order to dwell within the apathetic home of love—the literal and metaphorical desert—these ascetics trained themselves to unite their desires to God, making sure that even the desire for God was directed by God's grace.[16] In this way, they would avoid the temptation to place the stress upon the "I" who was becoming one with God, rather than appropriately emphasizing the glorious God who was responsible for their reunion. One could lose oneself and God in the desire for *apatheia* if one were not careful to maintain the simplicity and freedom that the desert represented.[17] Take, for example, the following passage from the stories of the desert fathers that introduced this essay:

> There was an anchorite who was grazing with the antelopes
> and who prayed to God, saying, "Lord, teach me something
> more." And a voice came to him, saying, "Go into this ceno-
> bium [monastery] and do whatever they command you." He
> went there and remained in the cenobium but did not know
> the work of the brothers. The young monks began to teach
> him the work of the brothers and would say to him, "Do
> this, you idiot," and "Do that, you old fool." And suffering
> he prayed to God, saying, "Lord, I do not know the work

16. For further thoughts on the role of *apatheia* in the desert, see Keller, *Oasis of Wisdom*, 24–25, 29–30.

17. See Columba Stewart's introduction to the anecdote that follows, titled, "Stories about Simplicity and Humility." Stewart writes, "Foremost among the monastic virtues is humility, which is inseparable from simplicity, and which aims to cultivate a right sense of one's role within God's creation," *World of the Desert Fathers*, 19.

of men, send me back to the antelopes." And having been freed by God, he went back to the country to graze with the antelopes.[18]

In requesting that God "teach him something more," this hermit feared that by naively remaining in the wild with the antelopes he was lamentably missing out on something that would bring him closer to God. God told him to go ahead and experience monastic life where his superiors would tell him what to do. Expecting to receive wisdom from these seasoned monks, the hermit must have been surprised to be greeted solely by words of judgment and reproach. They did not possess extraordinary knowledge that would bring about effortless, instantaneous union with God; unfortunately, they were succumbing to the selfish desire for domination that beleaguers us all. They proved this when they did not welcome their guest with unquestioning acceptance. Having learned his lesson never to take humility for granted, the hermit wished to regain his simplicity and God automatically granted his request.

Returning home, the hermit must have been relieved to find that the antelopes had already been teaching him his "something more" by instinctively remaining intimately connected to each other and the world around them. As herbivores themselves, they already lived the life of the peaceable kingdom, and these compassionate creatures beckoned human beings to model their lives after them. This desert tale maintained that by imitating the antelopes, the ascetic would be following Christ more closely. The hermit was faithful to Christ by imitating the antelopes as antelopes, not as mere literary symbols of human aspirations. The antelopes themselves were good, and they encouraged human beings to avoid the pitfall of defining their humanity in opposition to nonhuman animals. The human person could only become *more* human by interacting with the awesome otherness of the nonhuman animal who had the capacity to critique the human and to call upon her to be "more."[19] We can now

18. Passage quoted from *World of the Desert Fathers*, 20–21.

19. Rachel Muers expertly argues for the real—and not merely symbolic—presence of animals in biblical texts such as the book of Job. As readers of Job, we are challenged to overcome our ill-conceived biases and presuppositions when we are faced with the magnificent existence of animals who far surpass our ability to control or comprehend them. I believe that something similar is happening when we read this ascetical text. See Muers, "Animals We Write On."

imagine our hermit gratefully learning from the antelopes how to live in harmony with all creatures inhabiting God's magnificent earth.

As the desert ascetics developed habits of *apatheia*, they learned truths about themselves that only wild animals could teach them. In their freedom, these wild animals forced the hermit to question once again selfish human desires—this time the appetite for animal flesh as food and entertainment. The ancient Greco-Roman culture's ghoulish fascination with animal torture in the colosseum was yet another example of how the distorted human desire to possess others resulted in their annihilation and in the dehumanization of the persons who destroyed creation's divinely intended peace and harmony. It therefore meant something to the desert ascetics to consume food that had been obtained through the brutal killing of animals; to give in to this form of violent objectification of the other for personal pleasure and gain would make them all the more prone to choosing all manner of things that would severely divide them from God and others.[20] As a spectator in the colosseum, for example, no one could deny that lust for animal blood fueled human carnage.

For many desert ascetics, the decision to be vegetarian was fitting when considered in the context of their spiritual program of self-emptying that we have come to know with Abba Antony as our guide.[21] The ascetic trained him or herself to separate from selfish desires to own another for personal satisfaction. In turn, this letting go of narcissistic passions opened up one's mind and heart to be inspired by God's loving

20. I am indebted to Blake Leyerle for providing us with the sociocultural background and rationale of early monastic vegetarianism. See her "Monks and Other Animals." Leyerle writes, "The avoidance of meat, therefore, is in service of a wider formation in nonviolent behavior. Meat in its origin is connected with violence, and as a foodstuff, it feeds the passions particularly." Leyerle, "Monastic Formation and Christian Practice," 102.

21. This tradition of monastic vegetarianism (at least with regard to red meat) was later inherited by Benedict of Nursia, who included it in his sixth-century monastic rule. See *Rule of St. Benedict*, 62. Chapter 39, verse 11 of the Rule reads, "Let everyone, except the sick who are very weak, abstain entirely from eating the meat of four-footed animals." Over time most Benedictine communities will discontinue this prohibition. But the Cistercians, established in the eleventh century, will recover it when adopting a more literal reading of the Rule. This shows us how remnants of the early desert vegetarianism have remained up until the present day, meriting our attention for a contemporary appropriation of vegetarianism as a Christian spiritual practice.

intentions for oneself and for others. Letting go gave the ascetic the opportunity to love in union with divine mercy and compassion. Some of the ascetic's spiritual practices included repetitive disciplines of prayer, recitation of Scripture, manual labor, and self-denial in living accommodations and foodstuffs. For the many ascetics who exercised their self-restraint through a vegetarian diet, there was a corresponding relationship between the oral recitation of Scripture and the refusal to eat meat.[22] One could not read aloud—and thereby ingest—the word of God while feasting on animal flesh. Violence against animals was the antithesis of professing faith in the Savior of the peaceable kingdom. One became what one ate; and, once God's word had entered the ascetic through the mouth proclaiming Scripture's truth, that word lived within him to mold him into a Christ-like being.

Consuming animal meat would halt one's formation into Christ, because one's narcissistic appetites for control over others would prevail and suppress graced union with God and others. The vegetarian ascetic knew that the moment one made allowances for cruel behavior against any living being, one was developing habits that would slowly erode compassion toward and communion with every other being. Kindness toward other human beings depended upon the graced, habitual performance of every kindness, including grazing with animals rather than killing them or participating in a culture of destruction by consuming them. Furthermore, as we observed in the story of the anchorite who desired to learn something more, the animals were beings to learn from and beings to live with in communion. Their status as others deserving of respect and care was established from the beginning when God created them and deemed them good. Finally, having dominion over them (Gen 1:26) had to be interpreted along the lines of the christological defining of power as self-giving and restorative. To dine on animal flesh was to fall prey to the ego's damaging desire for "power over" others, and it participated in the violent nullification of the animal's significance as companion in the peaceable kingdom.

22. I owe this insight regarding the connection between "eating the word" and consuming food to Blake Leyerle's study of this metaphor's significance for the desert monks in the context of their ascetical diet. See her "Monastic Formation and Christian Practice."

Vegetarianism as a Contemporary Christian Spiritual Practice

Antony and his fellow ascetics knew well that being in right relationship with God and being in right relationship with others go hand in hand. Union with God nurtured through lifelong spiritual practice is lived out in love of neighbor. Reciprocally, the moral life of service perpetually reinforces spiritual praxis and makes way for fuller participation in divine life. As was true for the desert fathers and mothers, our evolving movement from love of God to love of neighbor and from love of neighbor back to its home in the love of God, begins when we stand naked and humble before our Creator and Savior.[23] We imitate Christ, who emptied himself to be one with humanity, by emptying ourselves in order to be united with God in grace. Stripped of the ego's demands, only the desire for God remains. We deny our longings to possess others, because this allows God to restore others to us as they are in their own right—created to reflect God's beauty and goodness. Once we are reunited with others through participation in the Son's "new creation" (Col 1:15), we meet God again, this time clothed in God's own love and compassion. We are now overjoyed to have received the grace to love as Christ loves, to heal as he heals, and to show mercy as he shows mercy.

Our lesson in early Christian ascetical spirituality has taught us that vegetarianism has a place within this symbiosis of spiritual practice and moral activity. Part of our spiritual training involves valuing the place of all others—including nonhuman animals—within God's design rather than fitting them into the chaos of our disordered desires. If we were to control our ungoverned appetites for animal meat, we would find that animals were not created to be ours by feeding our hunger.[24] Our training

23. This core of desert Christianity can be found in future adumbrations of Christian spirituality, for example, in the Ignatian spirituality of the sixteenth century, most notably in the *Spiritual Exercises* of Saint Ignatius of Loyola (1491–1556). See Ignatius's adherence to the practice of "indifference" that is akin to desert *apatheia*, in *Spiritual Exercises*, 32.

24. By so doing, we would be imitating the desert ascetics who, as Blake Leyerle writes, "rejected the categories of their contemporaries (which are also our own). These relegate animals under the heading of essentially other and therefore suitable for our use, indeed exploitation. . . . Such casual exploitation of animals bespeaks a deep acceptance of hierarchy, that the strong are right, simply because of their strength, to make use of the weak however they see fit. In contrast, the desert Christians align themselves

would likely entail periods of temptation similar to Antony's trials with the demons, during which our long habituated desires will insist that we are not responsible for how the animal meat reaches our tables. It must make a difference, the demons will say, that we have not officially acquiesced to animal pain and suffering and even more of a difference that we have not slaughtered the animals ourselves. Once the demons have had their say, however, the inner desert of self-denial will provide the necessary arena to confront the stark reality of our often silent cooperation with socially instituted forms of animal cruelty. Sincerely confessing our sins of omission as well as commission will awaken a heartfelt sorrow that is the first step toward purity of heart in God's presence.[25]

Abstention from meat plays an important part in finding *apatheia*—spiritual freedom from unhealthy reliance upon others that arises from egocentric wants masquerading as needs. We can then transition from adverse dependence to graced interdependence wherein human and non-human animal needs are considered together as we mutually participate in the peaceable kingdom that Christ's kenosis has inaugurated. The non-violent spiritual practice of vegetarianism helps us fashion a divinely ordered inner life of union with Christ that prompts moral action on behalf of social conversion that is equally governed by divine mercy and wisdom. Enthusiastically working toward a reversal of the contemporary culture of violent consumption will repair our bonds with animals and humans alike, because every step toward right relationship with another prepares us to care for all others with the grace of God's love and compassion.

---

voluntarily with the weak: for them, animals are not 'good to eat.'" Leyerle, "Monastic Formation and Christian Practice," 103. Throughout this essay, I am using the term "other" differently than Leyerle uses it here. I invoke it as a positive term that denotes the animal's singularity as one who is not ours and as one with whom we are meant to be in communion.

25. The desert experience of honestly facing up to an ungodly, cultural reality that we have cooperated in can be simulated in this context by watching the award-winning documentary *Earthlings* (2005). Viewing this film and others like it removes our ignorance with regard to animal suffering at human hands and instills an abiding sense of remorse that prompts personal transformation and social action.

Afterword

Brian McLaren

I WAS SURPRISED TO learn recently that Christians who are vegetarian are regularly criticized for their dietary habits. Maybe it goes back to my childhood, when my mother never had to say, "Eat your meat" or "Eat your dessert," but continually had to remind me, "Eat your vegetables!" With her daily dietary exhortation rooted in my memory, eating vegetables has always seemed like the moral high ground, not a reason to be criticized. Who knew that vegetarian Christians needed a theological defense?

Whether or not you are a vegetarian, now that you have read these chapters, you realize that such a theological defense is both substantial and robust. You see that a thoughtful Christian faith makes claims on how and what we harvest, cook, and eat. You understand how our theology forms our attitudes towards cows, swordfish, chickens, and sharks—not to mention broccoli, squash, beans, and tofu.

As I read these chapters, I kept recalling a humorous moment years ago. I had pulled up at a red light behind an old, beat-up Volkswagen Beatle. Its faded blue paint was covered with a motley patchwork of bumper stickers. One bumper sticker in particular grabbed my attention: *I'm a vegetarian—not because I LOVE ANIMALS, but because I HATE PLANTS!* I chuckled, the light changed, and I quickly forgot the bumper sticker . . . until this book once again raised the question for me: In what ways do love and hate—or, short of hate, moral carelessness—characterize my eating habits, my buying habits, and my attitudes toward my fellow creatures? Then I would remember that I am part of the intended audience for the book, that the authors are speaking to me, and that this book might make personal claims on my life.

Back in the early 90s, I was a vegetarian for a few years, not for theological or ethical reasons, but for health reasons. When a vegetarian diet didn't help lower my cholesterol as my doctor and I had hoped it would, I went on medication and started eating meat again, although less than before. In 2006, I began writing a book called *Everything Must Change*. My research convinced me that the typical American diet was ecologically unsustainable, which nudged my eating habits further away from red and towards green.

Then in 2009, for one summer my wife and I ate a very simple diet that included little if any meat—again, more for health than ethical reasons. When that summer ended, we ate even less meat than before. Today, I still have not made an utter commitment to vegetarianism. But I am more convinced—thanks to this book—that making that commitment would be a good choice, one that should be celebrated rather than criticized. I hope you agree.

I hope you also agree that kindness towards our fellow creatures manifests the kingdom of God, while unkindness to any creature manifests its opposite. I hope you agree that in God's peaceable kingdom, all creatures are our neighbors—neighbors to be loved, not exploited, to be known and named, not numbered and utilized. I hope you agree that our corporate food industry is driven to pursue quick profit, not sustained kindness, and for that reason, we cannot simply eat without thinking (and theologizing).

Reading these theological defenses for vegetarianism, I have been moved repeatedly by the beautiful, joyful vision of a life of greater kindness towards all living things. The authors of this volume have presented plant-based eating—contrary to the humorous bumper sticker I once saw—as an expression not of hate for anything but of love for everything. If one sentence in this book stood out in that regard, it was this one, from Danielle Nussberger's chapter:

> Vegetarianism—a specific practice of nonviolence—can thus be a respected component of an authentic Christian spirituality whose uppermost goal is union with God and whose

organic expression is a substantial moral character that proclaims Christ to be the King of the peaceable kingdom.

More and more of us are being convinced that nonviolence—expressed more positively as *kindness*—is essential, not peripheral, to
Christian spirituality. When we apply the rule of kindness to politics, we
find that violence—whether government-sanctioned or not—becomes
increasingly distasteful. When we apply the rule of kindness to communication, we find that all combative rhetoric—language that shames,
dehumanizes, or coerces—becomes distasteful as well.

And when we apply the rule of kindness to our eating, clothing, and
entertainment, we will lose our taste for certain foods and products. We
might find distasteful all foods derived from factory-farmed animals, or
all products that are developed through inhumane animal testing. We
might find distasteful all foods that require killing animals, or all foods
that require causing animals discomfort or pain. Some of us might become
vegan, some vegetarian, some more conscientious omnivores. However
we respond, though, we will hold one thing in common: the desire to
reflect the kindness of God, who, according to Jesus, cares for every bird
of the air and every beast of the field.

Many things in contemporary culture put moral calluses on our
hearts. They desensitize us to unkindness in a thousand ways each week.
Thank God for the authors of these chapters, who seek to heal and re-
sensitize us—to help us feel the joy, beauty, and spirituality of kindness.
And thank God for readers like you, who, by considering their words,
have opened your hearts to being kinder. This message may never be re-
ducible to a bumper sticker, or even a book, but all of us who have felt
the Spirit drawing us towards greater kindness know that nothing leads
us to repentance—to rethinking everything, including what we eat—like
kindness.

Bibliography

Adams, Carol J. *The Sexual Politics of Meat: A Feminist-Vegetarian Critical Theory*. 10th anniversary ed. New York: Continuum, 2000.

Alexis-Baker, Andy. "Violence, Nonviolence and the Temple Incident in John 2:13–15." *Biblical Interpretation* 20 (2012) 73–96.

Anscombe, G. E. M. *Ethics, Religion, and Politics*. Oxford: Blackwell, 1981.

Aquinas, Thomas, Saint. *Summa Theologiae*. Chicago: Benziger, 1947.

Arms, Myron. *Servants of the Fish: A Portrait of Newfoundland after the Great Cod Collapse*. Hinesburg, VT: Upper Access, 2004.

Athanasius, Saint. *The Life of Antony and the Letter to Marcellinus*. Translated by Robert C. Gregg. New York: Paulist, 1980.

Augustine, Saint. *On the Morals of the Catholic Church*. In vol. 4 of Nicene and Post-Nicene Fathers, edited by Philip Schaff. Peabody, MA: Hendrickson, 1994.

Balentine, Samuel. "Ask the animals, and they will teach you." In *"And God Saw That It Was Good": Essays on Creation and God in Honor of Terrence E. Fretheim*. St. Paul, MN: Word and World Theology for Christian Ministry, 2006.

Balthasar, Hans Urs von. *Theo-Drama: Theological Dramatic Theory. Vol. 5, The Last Act*. Translated by Graham Harrison. San Francisco: Ignatius, 1998.

Barad, Judith A. *Aquinas on the Nature and Treatment of Animals*. San Francisco: International Scholars Publications, 1995.

Barr, James. "Man and Nature—The Ecological Controversy and the Old Testament." *Bulletin of the John Rylands Library* 55 (1972) 9–32.

Barth, Karl. *Church Dogmatics*. Vol. 3/1. Edinburgh: T. & T. Clark, 1958.

———. *Church Dogmatics*. Vol. 2/2. Edinburgh: T. & T. Clark, 1957.

Basil, Saint. "On the Hexaemeron." In *Exegetic Homilies*, 3–150. Translated by Agnes Clare Way. Washington, DC: Catholic University of America Press, 1963.

Bauckham, Richard. *The Bible and Ecology: Rediscovering the Community of Creation*. Waco, TX: Baylor University Press, 2010.

———. *Living With Other Creatures: Green Exegesis and Theology*. Waco, TX: Baylor University Press, 2011.

———. *Testimony of the Beloved Disciple: Narrative, History, and Theology in the Gospel of John*. Grand Rapids: Baker Academic, 2007.

Bekoff, Marc. *The Animal Manifesto: Six Reasons for Expanding Our Compassion Footprint*. Novato, CA: New World Library, 2010.

Benedict, Saint. *The Rule of St. Benedict in English*. Edited by Timothy Fry, OSB. Collegeville, MN: Liturgical, 1982.

Berkman, John. "The Consumption of Animals and the Catholic Tradition." *Logos: A Journal of Catholic Thought and Culture* 7 (2004) 174–90.

———. "Towards a Thomistic Theology of Animality." In *Creaturely Theology: On God, Humans and Other Animals*, edited by Celia Deane-Drummond and David Clough, 21–40. London: SCM, 2009.

Bernardi, Giocomo. "The use of tools by wrasses (Labridae)." *Coral Reefs* (2011), DOI: 10.1007/s00338-011-0823-6.

Birch, Charles, and Lukas Vischer. *Living with Animals: The Community of God's Creatures.* Geneva: WCC, 1997.

Bland, Dave. "Homiletical Perspective on Genesis 1:1—2, 4a." In *Feasting on the Word: Year A, Volume 3, Pentecost and Season after Pentecost 1 (Propers 3–16).* Louisville: Westminster John Knox, 2011.

Blevins, John. "Hospitality Is a Queer Thing." *The Journal of Pastoral Theology* 19 (2009) 104–17.

Bradshaw, Corey J. A., Barry W. Brook, and Clive R. McMahon. "Dangers of Sensationalizing Conservation Biology." *Conservation Biology* 21 (2007) 570–71.

Burkert, Walter. *Homo Necans: The Anthropology of Ancient Greek Sacrificial Ritual and Myth.* Translated by Peter Bing. Berkeley: University of California Press, 1983.

Burton-Christie, Douglas. "The Place of the Heart: Geography and Spirituality in the Life of Antony." In *Purity of Heart in Early Ascetic and Monastic Literature*, edited by Harriet A. Luckman and Linda Kulzer, 45–65. Collegeville, MN: Liturgical, 1999.

Calvin, John. *Genesis.* Translated by John King. Edinburgh: Banner of Truth Trust, 1965.

Cassuto, Umberto. *A Commentary on the Book of Genesis.* 2 vols. Jerusalem: Magnes, 1998.

Catechism of the Catholic Church: With Modifications from the Editio Typica. 2nd ed. New York: Doubleday, 1997. Cato. *De Agricultura.* Translated by Andrew Dalby. Blackawton, UK: Prospect, 1998.

Chesterton, G. K. *All Things Considered.* London: Methuen, 1908.

———. *Charles Dickens.* London: Methuen, 1906.

———. *The Everlasting Man.* London: Hodder & Stoughton, 1925.

———. *Four Faultless Felons.* London: Cassell, 1930.

Chilton, Bruce. *Rabbi Jesus: An Intimate Biography.* New York: Doubleday, 2000.

Chrysostom, John, Saint. *Homilies on Genesis.* Translated by Robert C. Hill. Fathers of the Christian Church. Washington, DC: Catholic University of America Press, 1986.

Chryssavgis, John. *In the Heart of the Desert: The Spirituality of the Desert Fathers and Mothers.* Bloomington, IN: World Wisdom, 2003.

Clark, Stephen R. L. *Biology and Christian Ethics.* Cambridge: Cambridge University Press, 2000.

———. "Elves, Hobbits, Trolls and Talking Beasts." In *Creaturely Theology: On God, Humans and Other Animals*, edited by Celia Deane-Drummond and David Clough, 151–67. London: SCM, 2009.

———. *G. K. Chesterton: Thinking Backward, Looking Forward.* West Conshohocken, PA: Templeton Foundation Press, 2006.

———. "God, Good and Evil." *Proceedings of the Aristotelian Society* 77 (1976) 247–64.

———. *Philosophical Futures.* Frankfurt: P. Lang, 2011.

Clement of Alexandria, Saint. *Christ the Educator.* Translated by Simon P. Wood. Fathers of the Church 23. New York: Fathers of the Church, 1954.

Clough, David. "All God's Creatures: Reading Genesis on Human and Non-Human Animals." In *Reading Genesis After Darwin*, edited by Stephen Barton and David Wilkinson, 145–61. Oxford: Oxford University Press, 2009.

———. "The Anxiety of the Human Animal: Martin Luther on Non-Human Animals and Human Animality." In *Creaturely Theology: On God, Humans and Other Animals*, edited by Celia Deane-Drummond and David Clough, 41–60. London: SCM, 2009.

———. *On Animals: I. Systematic Theology*. London: T. & T. Clark, 2012.

———. "Why Do Some People Eat Meat?" *Epworth Review* 32 (2005) 32–40.

Clover, Charles. *The End of the Line: How Overfishing Is Changing the World and What We Eat*. Berkeley: University of California Press, 2008.

Cohen, Abraham. *Everyman's Talmud: The Major Teachings of the Rabbinic Sages*. New York: Dutton, 1949.

Compassion in World Farming. *Global Warning: Climate Change and Farm Animal Welfare*. Godalming, Surrey, UK: Compassion in World Farming, 2008.

Corley, Kathleen. *Women and the Historical Jesus: Feminist Myths of Christian Origins*. Santa Rosa, CA: Polebridge, 2002.

Crossan, John Dominic. *Jesus: A Revolutionary Biography*. San Francisco: HarperSanFrancisco, 1995.

Darwin, Charles. *The Life and Letters of Charles Darwin*. Edited by Francis Darwin. 2 vols. New York: D. Appleton, 1887.

Daugherty, Phyllis M. "Animal Abusers May Be Warming Up for More." *The Daily News of Los Angeles*, February 24, 2005, N15.

Davies, Horton. *Bread of Life and Cup of Joy: Newer Ecumenical Perspectives on the Eucharist*. Grand Rapids: Eerdmans, 1993.

Dawkins, Richard. *A Devil's Chaplain: Reflections on Hope, Lies, Science, and Love*. Boston: Houghton Mifflin, 2004.

Dell, Katherine. "The Significance of the Wisdom Tradition in the Ecological Debate." In *Ecological Hermeneutics: Biblical, Historical and Theological Perspectives*, edited by David Horrell, Cherryl Hunt, Chris Southgate, and Francesca Stavrakopoulou. New York: T. & T. Clark, 2010.

Derrida, Jacques. Of Hospitality. Stanford: Stanford University Press, 2000.

———. "Hospitality." In *Acts of Religion*, edited by Gil Anidjar, 356–57. New York: Routledge, 2002.

DeStefano, Stephen. *Coyote at the Kitchen Door: Living with Wildlife in Suburbia*. Cambridge: Harvard University Press, 2011.

Dinzelbacher, Peter. "Animal Trials: A Multidisciplinary Approach." *Journal of Interdisciplinary History* 32 (2002) 405–21.

Douglas, Mary. *Implicit Meanings: Selected Essays in Anthropology*. 2nd ed. New York: Routledge, 1999.

Douglass, Fredrick. *My Bondage and My Freedom*. New York: Penguin Classics, 2003.

Driscoll, Jeremy, OSB. "*Apatheia* and Purity of Heart in Evagrius Ponticus." In *Purity of Heart in Early Ascetic and Monastic Literature*, edited by Harriet A. Luckman and Linda Kulzer, 141–59. Collegeville, MN: Liturgical, 1999.

Driscoll, Mark, and Gerry Breshears. *Vintage Jesus: Timeless Answers to Timely Questions*. Wheaton, IL: Crossway, 2007.

Eaton, John. *The Circle of Creation: Animals in the Light of the Bible*. London: SCM, 1995.

Eisnitz, Gail. *Slaughterhouse*. Amherst, NY: Prometheus, 1997.

Ellul, Jacques. *Anarchy and Christianity*. Grand Rapids: Eerdmans, 1991.

Eusebius. *Ecclesiastical History*. Vol. 1, Books 1–5. Translated by Roy J. Deferrari. Fathers of the Church 19. New York: Fathers of the Church, 1953.

Feuerbach, Ludwig. *The Essence of Christianity*. Translated by George Eliot. New York: Prometheus, 1989.

Foer, Jonathan Safran. *Eating Animals*. New York: Back Bay, 2009.

Forti, Tova. *Animal Imagery in the Book of Proverbs*. Leiden: Brill, 2008.

Fukuyama, Francis. *Our Posthuman Future: Consequences of the Biotechnology Revolution*. London: Profile Books, 2002.

Fussel, George E. "Farming Systems of the Classical Era." *Technology and Culture* 8 (1967) 16–44.

García-Rivera, Alex. "Come Together." *U.S. Catholic*, February 2008, 47–49.

Geest, Paul van. "'. . . seeing that for monks the life of Antony is a sufficient pattern of discipline.': Anthanasius as Mystagogue in His *Vita Antonii*." *Church History and Religious Culture* 90 (2010) 199–221.

Goihl, John. "Transport Losses of Market Hogs Studied." *Feedstuffs*, January 28, 2008. Online: http://www.highbeam.com/doc/1G1-174281211.html.

Gonyou, Harold W. "Stressful Handling of Pigs." Online: http://www.thepigsite.com/articles/?Display=1246.

Gould, Stephen Jay. *Hen's Teeth and Horse's Toes*. New York: Norton, 1994.

Grandin, Temple, and Catherine Johnson. *Animals Make Us Human: Creating the Best Life for Animals*. Boston: Houghton Mifflin Harcourt, 2009.

Gregory of Nyssa, Saint. *On the Making of Man*. In *A Select Library of Nicene and Post-Nicene Fathers of the Christian Church*, 2nd ser., vol. 5, edited by W. Moore and H. A. Wilson, 387–427. Edinburgh: T. & T. Clark, 1997.

Grumett, David. "Vegetarian or Franciscan? Flexible Dietary Choices Past and Present." *Journal of the Society of Religion, Nature and Culture* 1 (2007) 450–67.

Habel, Norman, editor. *Readings from the Perspective of Earth*. Cleveland: Pilgrim, 2000.

Harris, Michael. *Lament for an Ocean: The Collapse of the Atlantic Cod Fishery*. Toronto: McClelland & Stewart, 1998.

Harrison, Ruth. *Animal Machines: The New Factory Farming Industry*. New York: Ballantine, 1966.

Hatkoff, Amy. *The Inner World of Farm Animals: Their Amazing Social, Emotional, and Intellectual Capacities*. New York: Stewart, Tabori & Chang, 2009.

Hauerwas, Stanley, and John Berkman. "A Trinitarian Theology of the 'Chief End of All Flesh.'" In *Good News for Animals?*, edited by Charles Pinches and Jay McDaniel, 62–74. Maryknoll, NY: Orbis, 1993.

Hesiod. *Works and Days*. Translated by Hugh G. Evelyn-White. Loeb Classical Library. London: Heinemann, 1914.

Hobgood-Oster, Laura. *The Friends We Keep: Unleashing Christianity's Compassion for Animals*. Waco, TX: Baylor University Press, 2010.

———. "'For Out of that Well the Flocks Were Watered': Stories of Wells in Genesis." In *The Earth Story in Genesis*, edited by Norman Habel and Shirley Wurst, 187–99. New York: Sheffield Academic, 2001.

———. *Holy Dogs and Asses: Animals in the Christian Tradition*. Urbana: University of Illinois Press, 2008.

Hochschild, Adam. *Bury the Chains: The British Struggle to Abolish Slavery*. London: Macmillan, 2005.

Hopkins, John Henry. *A Scriptural, Ecclesiastical, and Historical View of Slavery, From the Days of the Patriarch Abraham to the Nineteenth Century. Addressed to the Right Rev. Alonso Potter, D.D., Bishop of the Prot. Episcopal Church, in the Diocese of Pennsylvania.* New York: W. I. Pooley, 1864.

Hribal, Jason. *Fear of the Animal Planet: The Hidden History of Animal Resistance.* Oakland, CA: AK Press, 2010.

Hyland, J. R. *God's Covenant with Animals: A Biblical Basis for the Humane Treatment of All Creatures.* New York: Lantern, 2000.

Ignatius of Loyola, Saint. *The Spiritual Exercises.* Translated by George E. Ganss, SJ. Chicago: Loyola University Press, 1992.

Irenaeus, Saint. *Against Heresies.* In *The Ante-Nicene Fathers,* edited by A. Cleveland Coxe, James Donaldson, and Alexander Roberts, 1:315–567. Edinburgh: T. & T. Clark, 1997.

Irwin, Steve. "Protecting Wildlife in His Own Backyard: Interview with Steve Irwin." By Sarah Simpson. *Scientific American,* March 26, 2001. Online: http://www.scientificamerican.com/article.cfm?id=part-2-protecting-wildlif&page=2.

Janzen, David. *The Social Meanings of Sacrifice in the Hebrew Bible: A Study of Four Writings.* Berlin: Walter de Gruyter, 2004.

John Paul II. *Evangelium Vitae: On the Value and Inviolability of Human Life.* Washington, DC: United States Catholic Conference, 1995.

———. *Sollicitudo Rei Socialis: On Social Concern.* Washington, DC: United States Catholic Conference, 1988.

Jones, C. P. M., and revised by C. J. A. Hickling. "The Study of Liturgy." In *The Study of Liturgy,* edited by Cheslyn Jones, Geoffrey Wainwright, Edward Yarnold, and Paul Bradshaw, 184–209. New York: Oxford University Press, 1992.

Kalechofsky, Roberta. "Hierarchy, Kinship, and Responsibility: The Jewish Relationship to the Animal World." In *A Communion of Subjects: Animals in Religion, Science, and Ethics,* edited by Paul Waldau and Kimberly Patton, 91–99. New York: Columbia University Press, 2006.

Kaminski, J., J. Call, and J. Fischer. "Word Learning in the Domestic Dog: Evidence for 'Fast Mapping.'" *Science* 304 (2004) 1682–83.

Keller, David. *Oasis of Wisdom: The Worlds of the Desert Fathers and Mothers.* Collegeville, MN: Liturgical, 2005.

Kirby, William. *On the Power, Wisdom and Goodness of God as Manifested in the Creation of Animals and in Their History, Habits and Instincts.* Bridgewater Treatises, Treatise 7. London: W. Pickering, 1835.

Klawans, Jonathan. "Sacrifice in Ancient Israel: Pure Bodies, Domesticated Animals, and the Divine Shepherd." In *A Communion of Subjects: Animals in Religion, Science, and Ethics,* edited by Paul Waldau and Kimberly Patton, 65–80. New York: Columbia University Press, 2006.

Klijn, A. F. J., editor. *Jewish-Christian Gospel Tradition.* Leiden: Brill, 1992.

Kohák, Erazim. *The Embers and the Stars: A Philosophical Inquiry into the Moral Sense of Nature.* Chicago: University of Chicago Press, 1984.

Korsak, Mary Phil. ". . . et Genetrix: A five-page poem." In *A Feminist Companion to the Bible,* edited by Athalya Brenner, 22–26. Sheffield: Sheffield Academic, 1998.

———. "Genesis: A New Look." In *A Feminist Companion to the Bible,* edited by Athalya Brenner, 39–52. Sheffield: Sheffield Academic, 1998.

Bibliography

Kraybill, J. Nelson. *Apocalypse and Allegiance: Worship, Politics, and Devotion in the Book of Revelation*. Grand Rapids: Brazos, 2010.

Lactantius. *Divine Institutes*. Translated by Anthony Bowen and Peter Garnsey. Liverpool: Liverpool University Press, 2003.

Lafraniere, Sharon. "Europe Takes Africa's Fish, and Boatloads of Migrants Follow." *The New York Times*, January 14, 2008, A1.

"Last Act for the Bluefin." Editorial, *New York Times*, November 9, 2009, A22.

Lattea, Karen, editor. *"Say to This Mountain": Mark's Story of Discipleship*. Maryknoll, NY: Orbis, 1996.

Leander, Hans. *Discourses of Empire: Mark's Gospel from a Postcolonial Perspective*. Forthcoming.

Leibniz, Gottfried Wilhelm. *Theodicée*. Edited by H. Herring. Frankfurt: Suhrkamp, 1996.

Leibowitz, Nehama. *Studies in the Book of Genesis*. 3rd ed. Jerusalem: World Zionist Organization, Dept. for Torah Education and Culture, 1976.

Leyerle, Blake. "Monastic Formation and Christian Practice: Food in the Desert." In *Educating People of Faith: Exploring the History of Jewish and Christian Communities*, edited by John Van Engen, 85–114. Grand Rapids: Eerdmans, 2004.

———. "Monks and Other Animals." In *The Cultural Turn in Late Ancient Studies: Gender, Asceticism, and Historiography*, edited by Dale Martin and Patricia Miller, 150–71. Durham: Duke University Press, 2005.

Linzey, Andrew. *Animal Gospel*. Louisville: Westminster John Knox, 2000.

———. *Animal Theology*. Urbana: University of Illinois, 1995.

———. *The Link between Animal Abuse and Human Violence*. Portland: Sussex Academic, 2009.

———. "Vegetarianism as a Biblical Ideal." In *Religious Vegetarianism: From Hesiod to the Dalai Lama*, edited by Kerry Walters and Lisa Portmess, 126–39. Albany: State University of New York Press, 2001.

Linzey, Andrew, and Dan Cohn-Sherbok. *After Noah: Animals and the Liberation of Theology*. London: Mowbray, 1997.

Long, Thomas. *Matthew*. Louisville: Westminster John Knox, 1997.

Loyd-Paige, Michelle. "Thinking and Eating at the Same Time: Reflections of a Sistah Vegan." In *Sistah Vegan: Black Female Vegans Speak on Food, Identity, Health, and Society*, edited by A. Breeze Harper, 1–7. New York: Lantern, 2010.

Luther, Martin. *Luther's Works*. Edited by Helmut T. Lehmann and Jaroslav Pelikan. Philadelphia: Muhlenberg Press, 1958.

Marshall, I. Howard. *The Gospel of Luke: A Commentary on the Greek Text*. Grand Rapids: Eerdmans, 1978.

Martel, Yann. *Life of Pi*. New York: Harcourt, 2001.

Masson, J. Moussaieff. *The Pig Who Sang to the Moon: The Emotional World of Farm Animals*. New York: Ballantine, 2003.

May, Gerhard. *Creatio Ex Nihilo: The Doctrine of "Creation Out of Nothing" in Early Christian Thought*. Translated by A. S. Worrall. Edinburgh: T. & T. Clark, 1994.

McClendon, James William. *Systematic Theology: Doctrine, Volume 2*. Nashville: Abingdon, 1994.

Meeks, Wayne. "The 'Haustafeln' and American Slavery: A Hermeneutical Challenge." In *Theology and Ethics in Paul and His Interpreters: Essays in Honor of Victor Paul Furnish*, edited by Eugene H. Lovering and Jerry L. Sumney, 232–53. Nashville: Abingdon, 1996.

Midgley, Mary. *Beast and Man: The Roots of Human Nature.* New York: Routledge, 2002.

Milbank, John. *Being Reconciled: Ontology and Pardon.* New York: Routledge, 2003.

Miller, Chris. "Did Peter's Vision in Acts 10 Pertain to Men or the Menu?" *Bibliotheca Sacra* 159 (2002) 302–17.

Miller, Dale. "Straight Talk from Smithfield's Joe Luter." *National Hog Farmer,* May 1, 2000. Online: http://nationalhogfarmer.com/mag/farming_straight_talk_smithfields.

Molyneaux, Paul. *Swimming in Circles: Aquaculture and the End of Wild Oceans.* New York: Thunder's Mouth, 2007.

Moritz, Joshua M. "Animals and the Image of God in the Bible and Beyond." *Dialog: A Journal of Theology* 48 (2009) 134–46.

Muers, Rachel. "The Animals We Write On: Encountering Animals in Texts." In *Creaturely Theology,* edited by Celia Deane-Drummond and David Clough, 138–50. London: SCM, 2009.

Myers, Ched. "The Cedar Has Fallen! The Prophetic Word versus Imperial Clear-Cutting." In *Earth and Word: Classic Sermons on Saving the Planet,* edited by David Rhoads, 211–22. New York: Continuum, 2007.

Norwegian School of Veterinary Science. "Do Fish Feel Pain? Norwegian Research Suggests They Can." *ScienceDaily,* January 12, 2010. Online: http://www.sciencedaily.com/releases/2010/01/100112090126.htm.

O'Collins, Gerald. "Did Jesus Eat the Fish (Luke 24:42–43)?" *Gregorianum* 69 (1988) 65–76.

Oden, Amy. *And You Welcomed Me: A Sourcebook on Hospitality in Early Christianity.* Nashville: Abingdon, 2001.

Origen. *Contra Celsum.* Translated by Henry Chadwick. Cambridge: Cambridge University Press, 1965.

Palmer, Clare. "Stewardship: A Case Study in Environmental Ethics." In *The Earth Beneath: A Critical Guide to Green Theology,* edited by Ian Ball et al., 67–86. London: SPCK, 1992.

Pannenberg, Wolfhart. *Systematic Theology.* Vol. 2. Translated by Geoffrey W. Bromiley. Edinburgh: T. & T. Clark, 1994.

Passakos, Demetrios. "Clean and Unclean in the New Testament: Implications for Contemporary Liturgical Practices." *Greek Orthodox Theological Review* 47 (2002) 277–94.

Paquette, Sébastien Rioux. "Importance of the 'Crocodile Hunter' Phenomenon." *Conservation Biology* 21 (2007) 6.

Paul VI. *Pastoral Constitution on the Church in the Modern World: Guadium et Spes.* Washington, DC: National Catholic Welfare Conference, 1965.

Peterson, Dale. *The Moral Lives of Animals.* New York: Bloomsbury, 2011.

Pew Commission on Industrial Farm Animal Production. *Putting Meat on the Table: Industrial Farm Animal Production in America.* Online: http://www.ncifap.org/_images/PCIFAPFin.pdf.

Phelps, Norm. *The Dominion of Love: Animal Rights according to the Bible.* New York: Lantern, 2002.

Philo of Alexandria. *On the Creation of the Cosmos according to Moses.* Edited by David T. Runia. Leiden: Brill, 2001.

———. *Philo Suppl. I.* Translated by F. H. Colson and G. H. Whitaker. Loeb Classical Library. London: Heinemann, 1929.

Picone, Christopher, and David van Tassel. "Agriculture and Biodiversity Loss: Industrial Agriculture." In *Life on Earth: An Encyclopedia of Biodiversity, Ecology, and Evolution*, edited by Niles Eldredge, 99–105. Santa Barbara, CA: ABC-CLIO, 2002.

Pilley, J. W., and A. K. Reid. "Border Collie Comprehends Object Names as Verbal Referents." *Behavioural Processes* 86 (2011) 184–95.

Pitre, Brant. *Jesus and the Jewish Roots of the Eucharist*. New York: Doubleday, 2011.

Plato. *Republic*. Translated by G. M. A. Grube. Revised by C. D. C. Reeve. Indianapolis: Hackett, 1992.

Pohl, Christine. *Making Room: Recovering Hospitality as a Christian Tradition*. Grand Rapids: Eerdmans, 1999.

———. "Responding to Strangers: Insights from the Christian Tradition." *Studies in Christian Ethics* 19 (2006) 81–101.

Pritchard, Rusty. "A Different Shade of Green: Evangelicals and Animal Stewardship." *Prism Magazine*, May/June 2011, 9.

Project Nim. Directed by James Marsh. New York: HBO Documentary Films/BBC Films, 2011.

Pseudo-Athanasius. *The Life of Blessed Syncletica*. Translated by Elizabeth Bryson Bongie. Toronto: Peregrina, 1999.

Purdue University. "Fish May Actually Feel Pain and React to It Much Like Humans Do." *ScienceDaily*, April 30, 2009. Online: http://www.sciencedaily.com/releases/2009/04/090430161242.htm.

Rad, Gerhard von. *Genesis: A Commentary*. Philadelphia: Westminster, 1972.

Rainey, Anson, Aaron Rothkoff, and Joseph Dan. "Sacrifice." In *Encyclopaedia Judaica*, edited by Michael Berenbaum and Fred Skolnik, 14:639–49. Detroit: Macmillan, 2007.

Ratzinger, Joseph Cardinal. *God and the World: A Conversation with Peter Seewald*. San Francisco: Ignatius, 2002.

Rogerson, J. W. "What Was the Meaning of Animal Sacrifice?" In *Animals on the Agenda: Questions about Animals for Theology and Ethics*, edited by Andrew Linzey and Dorothy Yamamoto, 8–17. Urbana: University of Illinois Press, 1998.

Rolston III, Holmes. *Environmental Ethics: Duties to and Values in the Natural World*. Philadelphia: Temple University Press, 1988.

Russell, Bertrand. "Why I Am Not a Christian." In *The Basic Writings of Bertrand Russell*, 566–78. London: Routledge, 2009.

Russell, Letty. *Just Hospitality: God's Welcome in a World of Difference*. Edited by J. Shannon Clarkson and Kate Ott. Louisville: Westminster John Knox, 2009.

Safrai, Ze'ev. *The Economy of Roman Palestine*. New York: Routledge, 1994.

The Sayings of the Desert Fathers: The Alphabetical Collection. Translated by Benedicta Ward, SLG. Kalamazoo, MI: Cistercian, 1975.

Schäfer, Alexander, OFM. "The Position and Function of Man in the Created World, Part I." *Franciscan Studies* 20 (1960) 261–316.

Schottroff, Luise. "Om att avstå herravälde och om försoningens tjänst.'" In *De nedtystades Gud: Diakoni för livets skull*, edited by Sigurd Bergmann, 54–70. Stockholm: Proprius, 1992.

Schüssler Fiorenza, Elisabeth. *In Memory of Her: A Feminist Theological Reconstruction of Christian Origins*. New York: Crossroad, 1994.

Schwartz, Richard. *Judaism and Vegetarianism*. New York: Lantern, 2001.

Schwöbel, Christoph. "God, Creation and the Christian Community." In *The Doctrine of Creation: Essays in Dogmatics, History and Philosophy*, edited by Colin Gunton, 149–76. London: T. & T. Clark, 2004.

Shumaker, Robert, Kristina Walkup, and Benjamin Beck. *Animal Tool Behavior: The Use and Manufacture of Tools by Animals*. Rev. ed. Baltimore: Johns Hopkins University Press, 2011.

Simonetti, Manlio, editor. *Matthew 1–13*. Ancient Christian Commentary on Scripture 1a. Downers Grove, IL: InterVarsity, 2001.

Singer, Peter. *Animal Liberation*. New York: Avon, 1990.

Skinner, John. *A Critical and Exegetical Commentary on Genesis*. Edinburgh: T. & T. Clark, 1910.

Sorabji, Richard. *Animal Minds and Human Morals: The Origins of the Western Debate*. Ithaca: Cornell University Press, 1993.

Southgate, Christopher. "The New Days of Noah? Assisted Migration as an Ethical Imperative in an Era of Climate Change." In *Creaturely Theology: On God, Humans and Other Animals*, edited by Celia Deane-Drummond and David Clough, 249–65. London: SCM, 2009.

Spanner, Huw. "Tyrants, Stewards—or Just Kings?" In *Animals on the Agenda*, edited by Andrew Linzey and Dorothy Yamamoto, 216–24. London: SCM, 1998.

Stewart, Columba, OSB. *Prayer and Community: The Benedictine Tradition*. Maryknoll, NY: Orbis, 1998.

Stieglitz, Robert. "A Late Byzantine Reservoir and Piscina at Tel Tanninim." *Israel Exploration Journal* 48 (1998) 54–65.

Ström, Ingmar. *Glädjebudet enligt Markus*. Älvsjö: Verbum, 1983.

Tertullian. *On Fasting*. In vol. 4 of *The Ante-Nicene Fathers*, edited by Alexander Roberts and James Donaldson. Grand Rapids: Eerdmans, 1968.

Thomas, Keith. *Man and the Natural World: Changing Attitudes in England, 1500–1800*. New York: Penguin, 1984.

Thomas of Celano. *St. Francis of Assisi*. Translated by Placid Hermann. Chicago: Franciscan Herald, 1988.

Ticciati, Susannah. *Job and the Disruption of Identity: Reading Beyond Barth*. London: T. & T. Clark, 2005.

Tietz, Jeff. "Boss Hog: The Rise of Industrial Swine." In *The CAFO Reader*, edited by Daniel Imhoff, 109–24. Berkeley: University of California Press, 2010.

Toulmin, George Hoggart. *The Antiquity and Duration of the World*. Boston: J. P. Mendum, 1854.

Vaclavik, Charles. *The Vegetarianism of Jesus Christ*. Platteville, WI: Kaweah, 1986.

Waal, F. B. M. de. *The Age of Empathy: Nature's Lessons for a Kinder Society*. New York: Harmony, 2009.

Waddell, Helen. *Beasts and Saints*. Grand Rapids: Eerdmans, 1934.

———. "St. Jerome and the Lion and the Donkey." In *Beasts and Saints*, 27–28. Grand Rapids: Eerdmans, 1934.

Ward, Benedicta. *The Lives of the Desert Fathers*. London: Oxford University Press, 1981.

Webb, Stephen H. *Good Eating*. Grand Rapids: Brazos, 2001.

———. *On God and Dogs: A Christian Theology of Compassion for Animals*. New York: Oxford University Press, 1998.

———. "Whatever Happened to the Sin of Gluttony? Or: Why Christians Do Not Serve Meat with the Eucharist." *Encounter* 58 (1997) 243–50.

Welker, Michael. *What Happens in Communion?* Grand Rapids: Eerdmans, 2000.

The World of the Desert Fathers. Translated by Columba Stewart, OSB. Kalamazoo, MI: Cistercian, 1986.

Wright, David P. "The Study of Ritual in the Hebrew Bible." In *The Hebrew Bible: New Insights and Scholarship*, edited by Frederick E. Greenspahn, 130–33. New York: New York University Press, 2008.

Yang, Yong-Eui. *Jesus and the Sabbath in Matthew's Gospel.* Sheffield: Sheffield Academic, 1997.

Yardley, William. "Knot of Worry Tightens for Fishermen." *New York Times*, October 20, 2011, A16.

Yoder, Perry. *Shalom: The Bible's Word for Salvation, Justice, and Peace.* Nappanee, IN: Evangel, 1987.

York, Tripp. "Crocodile Lover: Learning from Steve Irwin." *The Christian Century*, October 3, 2006, 9–10.

———. *Third Way Allegiance: Christian Witness in the Shadow of Religious Empire.* Telford, PA: Cascadia, 2011.

Young, Richard Alan. *Is God a Vegetarian? Christianity, Vegetarianism, and Animal Rights.* Chicago: Open Court, 1999.